'This is the story of how successful retailers have moved towards solving problems for people and enhancing their lives. How they think about their stores will never be the same again. If you want to understand the dramatic acceleration of change brought about by COVID-19 then read Mark Pilkington's excellent book – and be optimistic about a highly innovative and entrepreneurial future'.

Lord Hague of Richmond, Former UK Secretary of State for Foreign and Commonwealth Affairs

'I always learn something from Mark's books. This one is full of brilliant insights. A must read for any retailer'.

Mary Portas, Retail Expert, Chief Creative Officer at Portas

'*Retail Recovery* is a fascinating book explaining why we should be excited about the future of shopping, even as we wring our hands over the fate of high streets and shopping malls. Forget the retail "apocalypse". This is the inside story of its rebirth.'

Henry Tricks, Schumpeter Columnist, The Economist

'What's incredible about Mark's book is it's a full survey of nearly everything going on: an ambitious undertaking and one that lights the way on the future of retail in a post-COVID world. If you want to know where we're headed next in the world of brands and retailers, you've got to read Mark's audacious book'.

Andy Dunn, Co-Founder Bonobos, Red Swan Ventures, Monica & Andy, Stealth Company; former EVP Digital Consumer Brands, Walmart

'Mark hits the nail on the head. For too long we have been stuck in the "push" mindset of physical retail and selling, rather than as Mark states the pull mindset of radical thought, building our retail offers so that customers actively would want to come and visit them as a part of an omnichannel relationship with retailers and brands'.

Fraser Brown, Retail & Property Director, Heathrow Airport

'The pandemic has accelerated the pace of change in retail. But the future cannot lie only in the "endless aisle" of online. Consumers want the emotional connection and excitement of physical stores. This book gives you hope that there are retailers who can provide this – creating jobs as part of the adventure'.

Anne Ashcroft, Property and Finance Writer and Commentator; former Editor of The Times Bricks & Mortar

'Some excellent insights into how retailers can take advantage of the chaos caused by the Coronavirus outbreak – an indispensable guide to those looking to understand the post-apocalyptic world.'

Hannah Middleton, Knowledge Exchange Lead at London College of Fashion and Fashion Business Consultant

Mark Pilkington

Retail Recovery

How creative retailers are winning
in their post-apocalyptic world

BLOOMSBURY BUSINESS
LONDON • OXFORD • NEW YORK • NEW DELHI • SYDNEY

BLOOMSBURY BUSINESS
Bloomsbury Publishing Plc
50 Bedford Square, London, WC1B 3DP, UK
29 Earlsfort Terrace, Dublin 2, Ireland

BLOOMSBURY, BLOOMSBURY BUSINESS and the Diana logo are trademarks of
Bloomsbury Publishing Plc

First published in Great Britain 2021

A catalogue record for this book is available from the British Library

Library of Congress Cataloguing-in-Publication data has been applied for

ISBN: HB: 978-1-4729-8717-4; TPB: 978-1-4729-9282-6;
eBook: 978-1-4729-8720-4

2 4 6 8 10 9 7 5 3 1

Typeset by Deanta Global Publishing Services, Chennai, India
Printed and bound in Great Britain by CPI Group (UK) Ltd, Croydon CR0 4YY

To find out more about our authors and books visit www.bloomsbury.com
and sign up for our newsletters

I would like to thank my agent, Andrew Hayward, for his tireless enthusiasm in promoting my ideas, and my publisher, Ian Hallsworth at Bloomsbury Business, for believing in the potential of my work. I would also like to thank my family for their love and support in writing this book.

Contents

Introduction

On 23 March 2020, the British government announced the shutdown of all non-essential retailing in response to the threat from the Coronavirus – the new pandemic, which had been sweeping around the world since the beginning of the year. The United States did not order a federal lockdown, but nevertheless, from mid-March, many key states, such as New York, New Jersey and California, started to do so. The news was not entirely unexpected: new cases and deaths from the COVID-19 virus had been rising sharply in the preceding weeks and people had watched as countries such as China, Italy and Spain had started to close down their economies.

These announcements caused great consternation in the boardrooms of the major retail groups in both the UK and the US. Those retailers lucky enough to have food businesses, such as Marks & Spencer, John Lewis & Partners, Walmart and Target, would be somewhat protected, but those in non-essential categories faced the prospect of a catastrophic loss of sales.

The virus also separated the leaders from the laggards in terms of internet-readiness. For those retailers that had had the foresight to create substantial online businesses, e-commerce would potentially provide some mitigation. For example, UK fashion retailer Next had spent the previous 20 years building up its e-commerce sales to 50 per cent of its business and after a brief shutdown to virus-proof its warehouse, it was able to keep trading[1]. However, those that had rejected the internet, such as fast fashion group Primark, faced the grim prospect of zero sales as they shuttered their stores[2].

As the worried people of Britain and America hunkered down in their homes, their chief immediate concern was for their food supply. Panic buying had stripped the stores of essentials like toilet paper, bleach and toothpaste and durable foodstuffs such as flour, rice and pasta, and although there appeared to be fresh foods still available, no one had any idea how long this would continue. In the event, the food retailers and their suppliers were to do a great (and largely unsung) job of keeping the lifeline going. However, as the number of daily deaths exploded over the next few weeks into the thousands, large numbers of people became anxious about going to the stores at all. Many turned to buying online, and vulnerable people had to be helped out by their neighbours or by local shops, which created special times for them to visit.

The rise of online

Into the gap left by the retailers sailed the online companies. After an initial stutter, as their websites were briefly overwhelmed by the high volume of transactions, they managed to increase their capacity rapidly and more and more households learned to rely on the delivery services offered by Amazon Fresh, Instacart, Tesco and Ocado.

The grocery sector had traditionally lagged the rest of the market in moving online. Prior to the crisis, in 2018, UK online sales of grocery represented only 7 per cent of the market, according to Mintel, versus e-commerce's overall share of retail, which was at 18 per cent[3]. The prime obstacle was the cost of delivery – grocery is a low-margin business and shipping costs are high. However, in the crisis, customers were willing to pay and by June 2020, online sales accounted for 13 per cent of all UK grocery sales, up from 7.4 per cent in March. The same was true of the US, where a survey by RBC Capital Markets showed that, by 7 April 2020, 42 per cent of people were buying groceries online at least once a week, up from 22 per cent in 2018[4].

In the non-grocery area, the switch to online was even more marked. For example, in fashion, e-commerce increased its market share by almost three times, as most of its retail rivals were forced to shut down completely[5]. Overall, UK online sales increased 56 per cent in the quarter ending June 2020 versus the previous year, boosting its share to nearly a third of the market versus 18 per cent in April 2019[6]. Many consumers became used to the convenience of home delivery, forming new habits that would be difficult to break.

As people sweltered in their homes amid the unseasonably hot weather of the summer of 2020 ('Typical!' said the Brits), figures started to emerge that showed the true extent of the devastation that had been created in the high streets and the malls.

The damage to retail

UK retail sales dropped 4 per cent versus the previous year in March 2020 and then a record 18 per cent in April at the height of the initial lockdown[7]. In the US, sales similarly plunged 4 per cent in March 2020 and 20 per cent in April[8]. The situation for clothing was even more bleak, with UK sales down 35 per cent in March and 69 per cent in April[9].

One by one, the news came in of a series of disastrous bankruptcies in the UK retail sector – Debenhams, Oasis, Warehouse, L.K. Bennett, Laura Ashley and Cath Kidston, to name but a few[10]. And in the US, major groups, such as Neiman Marcus, J. Crew, Lord & Taylor and JC Penney went into Chapter 11 bankruptcy protection[11].

Other major players, such as the UK's Arcadia Group Limited (parent company of High Street stalwarts such as Topshop, Dorothy Perkins and Burton, which was owned by Sir Phillip Green), appeared to be wavering on the brink (by the end of November 2020, it too would join the ranks of businesses going into administration). Even previously strong retailers were coming under pressure. For example, L Brands' sale of Victoria's Secret to Sycamore Investments fell through and John Lewis announced that they would probably not reopen all their stores after the initial lockdown ended[12]. A study by Alvarez & Marsal predicted that non-food retailers could see a decline in sales of 17 per cent over the whole of 2020 – equating to over £37 billion of lost revenue[13].

The impact on brands and landlords

And it was not just the retailers who were suffering. There were many other businesses that depended on retailing, such as branded suppliers, manufacturers and marketing agencies, many of which were severely affected.

Behind this in the supply chain stretched the vast commercial property sector – the companies that owned the malls and shopping centres – a huge industry with trillions of dollars of assets. As retailers closed down, it meant unpaid rents; without those rents, the retail property groups lay like so many landed fish, gasping for water. For example, intu – the owner of the Trafford Centre and Lakeside malls in the UK – declared bankruptcy in June 2020, while the big players in the US, such as Simon Property Group and Seritage Growth Properties, lost 80 per cent of their market value when measured against their peak levels[14].

This crisis hit a retail industry already badly weakened by years of decline. A lethal combination of factors had eaten into the sector over the preceding 10 years, including the rise of e-commerce, the communications revolution, generational change, growing cost pressures, unfair tax systems, protectionist trade policies and private equity ownership. These factors are more fully covered in Chapter 1 of this book (pages 9–16), but suffice it to say this unholy combination of threats had already wiped out large sections of the industry and left the survivors in an increasingly fragile state as they faced the COVID-19 crisis. Many of them would not reopen their doors when lockdown was over.

A fragile recovery

Even when the economy started to open up, it did not mean that the retail sector would be able to bounce back immediately. Firstly, the reopening would be partial and then there was the issue of further outbreaks and lockdowns, as occurred in the UK, parts of Europe and the United States from the autumn of 2020 into 2021.

Despite the promising news in November 2020, that a number of vaccines had been developed, it did not resolve the uncertainty hanging over the retail industry and other businesses such as restaurants and hotels. Questions remained as to how quickly the vaccines could be distributed, whether everyone would be prepared to participate and whether the vaccines would provide immunity against new variants of the disease.

Secondly, consumer confidence and spending power was predicted to remain subdued. Despite the generous government aid, UK unemployment rose by over 25 per cent, reaching nearly 5 per cent of the workforce in the quarter ending September 2020. In addition, 9.6 million workers remained on furlough in November of that year[15]. In the US, the rise in unemployment was even sharper – from 4.4 per cent in March 2020 to nearly 7.0 per cent in November, the fastest increase since records began[16].

Lastly, even prior to the COVID-19 outbreak, the global economy was already precariously balanced at the top of a 10-year cycle, sustained by lax money and near-zero interest rates, with many forecasters predicting that any shock could set off a long-term downturn[17]. Coronavirus was probably the biggest such shock ever administered and therefore the risk of a global downturn remained elevated.

The retail crisis was spectacularly bad news for both the economy and for society. In 2019, retail was the largest private sector employer in both the UK and the United States. In Britain, it accounted for around a quarter of the total private sector workforce, if one included the businesses that depended on it – suppliers, brands, service providers and retail property companies[18].

In the US, it was even more important, employing, either directly or indirectly, 42 million people, or around a third of all private sector employees. Therefore, it is not an understatement to say that the Coronavirus crisis represented a very serious blow to a vital industry[19].

An opportunity for a reset

While COVID-19 has certainly been a huge negative for retailing and the economy in general, there is a sense in which it has also created a 'burning platform', which has forced brands, retailers and landlords to re-examine all of their policies. By throwing the key strategic imperatives facing the business into stark relief, it has blown away whatever was left of the complacency that used to blind its collective leadership, creating a kind of 'reset' moment for the entire industry. And, as we shall see, the changes that have been set in motion during this painful period amount to nothing less than the greatest shift seen in the business since it originally came into being at the time of the Industrial Revolution.

As it went through these difficult changes, the groundwork was being laid for a potential, yet very substantial, Retail Revival. Wherever we look, in the aftermath of Covid, we can see new shoots of recovery emerging from the wreckage of the old order – new brands, new ways of providing value and new methods of creating excitement to draw in consumers and re-start the economy.

How to use this book

This book will examine the nature of this long hoped-for Retail Revival and is broken down into three parts.

- Part One covers the crisis and its causes, and shows how its very severity has acted as a spur for real change.
- Part Two looks at the new trends which are rapidly re-shaping the retail industry and picks out the winning strategies that are driving long-term success.
- Part Three includes in-depth interviews and case studies covering some of the most innovative players in the industry, in the hope of drawing out key learnings for the rest of the business.

It is important, even in the most challenging of times, to keep focused on the bright rays of hope which can guide us onwards. The aim of this book is to draw together these positive trends and provide practical aid to brands, retailers and property owners who want to understand more fully the changes that are sweeping through the industry.

PART ONE

The Apocalypse and its Causes

CHAPTER ONE

The Crisis Brews Up – The Long-term Causes

The Coronavirus crisis of 2020 hit a retail industry already weakened by years of decline. From 2015 onwards, this previously reliable business was hit by large numbers of bankruptcies, store closures and redundancies.

In Britain, major retailers like Debenhams, House of Fraser, Mothercare and BHS had already fallen into insolvency, while the United States had lost brands like Sears, Kmart, Toys "R" Us, Barneys, Claire's and Aeropostale[1]. Large numbers of stores had been closed, leaving shopping malls and high streets half-empty. The situation was so severe, many commentators were already describing it as a 'Retail Apocalypse'.

In order to understand why this happened, it is helpful to look at the long-term changes that were affecting the industry at this time. These causes can be divided into three main areas: the supply chain changes wrought by the technology revolution; the demand-side changes brought about by growing generational inequality and other factors affecting retail, including cost pressures, unfair tax policies and ownership issues. Let us consider each, in turn.

Supply chain changes

The traditional supply chain, with which we are all familiar, has existed since the Industrial Revolution. This revolution, which occurred from the mid-eighteenth century onwards, involved the switch from manual to machine production and enabled a huge increase in output. However, it also meant that there had to be a mass distribution system to get products to consumers. This system, which is collectively known as the 'supply chain', consisted of four different stages and looked like this:

Factory   →   Brand   →   Store   →   Consumer

The factories produced large quantities of goods at low cost; the brands stamped their names on them and spent heavily on marketing to create consumer demand, using their salesforces to sell-in the products to retailers. The retailers created product-collection points (stores) near to where the consumers lived and used their staff to sell the product on to the final user. The consumers played their part in the chain by visiting the stores and carrying the product home. Goods flowed down this chain, picking up costs as they went. Although the manufacturing expense might have been quite low, by the time it had been marked up by all the players in the chain, the product ended up costing the consumer seven to eight times more.

The other thing that flowed down the chain was information. Around 90 per cent of the knowledge that consumers had about products came from the brands and retailers themselves, via their advertising, PR and shop sales teams. The whole chain was driven by economies of scale. Factories, brand advertising, sales forces and stores were expensive items, which could only be afforded by large companies. They acted as barriers to entry to the brand/retail business, which ended up being a kind of oligopoly, with a few players dominating each vertical.

Consumers played a relatively passive role in the process, meekly ingesting the advertising messages and obediently showing up in store, like so many Pavlovian dogs. Any buying choice was effectively limited to a few stores near to where the customers lived. This supply chain remained in place for nearly 200 years, until the late 1990s. Then, two shock waves came along and disrupted the cosy world of brands and retailers: the e-commerce revolution and the communications revolution.

The growth of online commerce provided an alternative to retailing in bypassing the shops stage of the supply chain and massively increasing consumer access to products. At the same time, the communications revolution (incorporating the development of online search, social media, peer reviews and influencer blogs) dramatically weakened the traditional brands' monopoly over information, providing almost perfect knowledge to consumers.

Once consumers could buy products directly from factories, with only a 'brand-lite' internet site in between, and obtain independent information about those products from the net, it dramatically changed the economics of the supply chain, which now potentially looked like this:

Factory   →   Internet brand   →   Consumer

Instead of paying seven to eight times factory cost, it became possible to obtain things at far lower mark-ups. It is estimated that the potential consumer savings achievable through a systematic adoption of this shorter supply chain could be as much as $15 trillion on a worldwide basis.

This cost reduction was not limited to the obvious expense of mass media marketing budgets, wholesale salesforces, store-build costs, rents, rates and staff costs. There was also the question of inventory. The long pipeline – from factory to brand warehouse, from brand warehouse to retail distribution centre, and then on to multiple stores – also entailed very heavy amounts of inventory, which was extremely costly. By contrast, a centralized e-commerce distribution warehouse could operate on lower levels of stock.

On top of these cost advantages, there were also gains in efficiency to be had through the new way of doing business. For example, when brands ran advertising in traditional media, it was difficult to measure the precise effects on sales. As one pundit famously put it: 'I know that half my advertising budget is wasted, the only problem is that I don't know which half.'

Modern Web marketing is far more personalized and accurate. One can buy highly targeted audiences on social media like Facebook and Instagram, and, in the case of Google Ads, the consumer pre-qualifies themselves through the very act of searching for a specific product. In addition, performance marketers can track how specific advertisements are performing with individual consumers, analysing their level of engagement, click-through rates and sales conversion. The whole sales and marketing funnel is visible in real time so that advertisements can be introduced, rotated and withdrawn, depending on how they are performing.

Once the consumer reaches the website or store, there are also key differences. Going into a retail store, the consumer is often unclear as to where to find a product. Websites, on the other hand, are equipped with search engines that can take the user directly to the product. On top of this, there is the ease of check-out. Many websites now have 'one-click' checkouts, which are fast and user-friendly. Trying to pay in stores is often a lengthy process, with difficult-to-find staff and long queues.

Finally, there is the question of delivery. Getting to the store can be challenging, with crowded roads and public transport, parking restrictions and the issue of having to carry heavy goods home with you. Compare this to the ease of making a few clicks and then having the product show up at your door. In summary, if one evaluates the two channels (stores versus online) purely as 'goods-purchase' mechanisms, it would appear that online trumps physical stores on a number of levels.

In addition to the process points mentioned above, there were two further areas where online had an advantage over retail: product choice and customer relationship management. Although large retail stores are capable of offering considerable levels of choice, they have always been constrained by their 'four walls', whereas websites can offer what is known as the 'endless aisle', because it is very cheap to add additional products online. For example, Amazon offers over 350 million product options, whereas Macy's – the world's largest department store group in 1999 – only had 4.2 million products in its stores at that time[2].

Finally, online stores are typically much more sophisticated at collecting and using customer data than their physical equivalents. Most retail store groups do not really know very much about their customers as individuals. Websites, by contrast, know almost everything about their clients – critically, whether they are new or existing, their demographics, what products they like and much more. They then use this information to market more effectively to these consumers using advanced relationship-management techniques.

Armed with these advantages, the online companies had been steadily gaining market share from the retailers in the two decades leading up to the Coronavirus crisis. Although the latter had forewarning of the impending threat, they were somewhat complacent about meeting it. As a result, by 2017, they had allowed Amazon to grab over 43 per cent of the online market in the US, whereas the top six retailers – the Walmarts, the Best Buys and the Macys, who had dominated retailing in the 1990s – had only managed 12 per cent between them[3].

Demand-side changes

Adding to these supply chain changes, there was also a major demand-side shift which gradually undermined the retail industry – that of growing generational inequality. Historically, at least since the 1950s, it was the younger generation who had driven the growth in retail. While in their teens and twenties, they set the trends in areas like fashion, beauty, music and consumer electronics. When, slightly later, they married and had children, they bought properties and filled them with furniture, decorations, children's clothes, toys and the like. However, since the mid-1990s, younger people have increasingly been squeezed, economically speaking, such that they have not been able to afford to marry, start families and buy property as easily as before. This is linked to a number of factors.

Firstly, real wages have not kept up with asset prices, which have exploded over the last 20 years, driven by the 'cheap money' policies of the Fed and other central banks. For example, the median price paid for a home in England and Wales rose by 380 per cent between 1997 and 2017, whereas earnings only rose by 68 per cent[4]. Secondly, employment has become increasingly insecure, with the gig economy, low job security and miserly pensions. Thirdly, education has grown more and more expensive, with many young people struggling under the burden of student debt. As a consequence, we have now arrived at a situation of huge generational inequality: in 2018, people over 45 years old owned 86 per cent of all the wealth in the UK, while those under 45 owned only 14 per cent. The numbers in the US are 89 per cent and 11 per cent, respectively[5].

The cash-strapped Millennial generation is delaying marriage, children and house buying. More British people in their twenties are living with their parents than at any time since 1940[6]. Now, older people are not as useful to retail because they spend less on products like fashion and beauty, already own their own furniture and tend to spend their money in other areas, such as travel and healthcare[7].

When the young do open their increasingly slim wallets, they are not inclined to buy expensive retail brands; rather they turn to the new generation of online brands, which are, as we have seen, offering better value for money. So, a demand-side problem and a supply-side solution have neatly dovetailed to create a perfect storm for the traditional, high-cost brand/retail industry, with devastating consequences.

Other factors

Apart from these main points, there have been two other factors that undermined retailing in the five years before the Coronavirus crisis.

The first was rising cost pressures, directly or indirectly imposed by government policy. In the UK, government measures such as the National Living Wage, the Apprenticeship Levy and the upward revisions to the Business Rates, all hit retailing hard. In addition, the decline in Sterling following the Brexit referendum of June 2016 raised product sourcing costs[8].

In the US, the restrictions on immigration led to an increase in real wages and the tariffs on Chinese products had the effect of increasing purchasing costs. On top of that, retailers shouldered the full burden of state and local taxes, while many of their internet competitors were able to avoid paying them on out-of-state deliveries[9].

The second thing that really hurt the industry was the fact that, during the 10 years preceding the crisis, large parts of it were taken over by private equity (PE) companies. The venture capitalists had been attracted to retailing initially because of its historically steady cash flows and had invested heavily, taking on large amounts of debt with a view to rapid expansion. Unfortunately, PE's extreme focus on short-term results meshed badly with the needs of an industry that turned out to be going through rapid change *and* in need of a lot of investment. At the very moment when long-term vision was needed, the industry ended up being run by people who did not really understand it.

It is no coincidence that 10 of the 14 largest American retailers which went bankrupt between 2012 and 2019 were owned by PE companies, including Toys "R" Us (Bain Capital, LP, Kohlberg Kravis Roberts (KKR) and Vornado Realty Trust), Claire's (Apollo) and Sears (ESL Investments)[10].

Summary

In summary, all these forces were acting together to create a crisis in retailing, even before Coronavirus came onto the scene. Online's share of the market grew steadily during the period 2015–19, reaching 19 per cent in the UK by November 2019. In the US, it was estimated to be around 14 per cent[11]. This gradual loss of share to the online players ate into the retailers' revenues just at the moment when rising costs put a powerful squeeze on their profits.

Unfortunately, retail is a difficult business in which to downsize effectively. Store closures mean heavy write-offs, inventory loses its value easily and there are substantial redundancy and pension obligations. In addition, the risk of damage to the retailer's brand reputation is high.

This then was the state of the retail industry at the point where it was hit by the Coronavirus. Weakened by five years of losses and reversals, it was in poor condition to face the oncoming onslaught.

CHAPTER TWO

The Spectre Haunting the Land – The Coronavirus Pandemic

On 27 December 2019, most Western retail executives were in the middle of their post-Christmas sales and were not paying much attention to events in faraway China. Nevertheless, like the shots that occurred in Sarajevo on 28 June 1914, a message from an obscure doctor in a small town in central China was to have repercussions around the world.

On that day, Dr Zhang Jixian, head of the respiratory department at Hubei Provincial Hospital of Integrated Chinese and Western Medicine in Wuhan province, reported to health officials in China that he was treating dozens of cases of a new type of pneumonia with an unknown cause. The epicentre of the outbreak was the Huanan Seafood Wholesale Market, a live animal and seafood market[1].

Days later, researchers in China identified a new virus from the Corona family. They gave it the name COVID-19, standing for Corona (CO) Virus (VI) Disease (D) 2019.

On 11 January 2020, Chinese state media confirmed the first death – that of a 61-year-old man – a regular customer of the market[2]. This report unfortunately came just before the start of the Chinese New Year holiday, when hundreds of millions of Chinese would travel across the country and internationally.

At first, all this seemed very far away for people in other parts of the world, but unbeknown to them, viruses do not recognize borders and cases were soon being identified in other countries. The disease is believed to have reached Britain on 29 January, when two people fell ill at a hotel in York[3].

Initially, the UK government's response was muted. They advised voluntary social distancing and self-quarantine in the case of any symptoms, but did not follow the Chinese or Italian models of lockdown until 23 March, nearly two months later[4]. Senior politicians continued to gather for briefings and, in an ironic twist of fate, the Prime Minister himself – Boris Johnson – was admitted to hospital on 5 April 2020 after testing positive[5].

In America, the response was even more patchy. Despite the early arrival of the disease on 19 January 2020, when a man, recently arrived from Wuhan, tested positive in Washington State, the Federal Government did not order a nationwide lockdown, preferring to leave the decision to individual states[6]. Starting with California in mid-March, the vast majority of states eventually implemented 'shelter-in-place' orders[7].

Nevertheless, in both countries, the relatively late lockdowns meant that the disease became established in the population and would take a correspondingly longer time to bring under control.

The effect on retail

In the initial stages of the outbreak, retailers remained relatively optimistic. At the end of February, the American National Retail Federation said that it was maintaining its prediction of annual sales growth at 3.5 to 4.1 per cent, while Macy's CEO Jeff Gennette said on 25 February: 'At this time, we have not factored in any potential negative impact from Coronavirus into our 2020 guidance'[8]. Most of the concern was about the supply chain in China and how it might be disrupted. In the same call, Gennette said: 'We expect a slowdown. Nothing concerning yet, but we are watching this one very carefully'[9].

In the event, the supply chain actually held up quite well and by the end of March it was the least of the retailers' concerns. As the lockdowns came into operation, the majority of retail was forced to close down across Europe and North America.

Essential retail, including food stores, pharmacies and household goods stores, were permitted to continue trading, but all the other stores had to bring down the shutters. At the time, the measure was only planned to last three weeks. However, as it turned out, it was to persist until 15 June in the UK and around the same time (depending on which state) in the US[10].

Three whole months with virtually no trading: this was a disaster of unprecedented proportions for the retail trade. Even during wartime, with the Luftwaffe bombing London, the stores managed to stay open. The sight of all those high streets and malls boarded up was, for many people, akin to something out of a horror movie.

The consequences for the non-essential half of the industry were immediate and devastating. Those retailers that had reasonable e-commerce channels were able to salvage something from the disaster, but those that had failed to invest in online faced an immediate loss of up to 100 per cent of their sales. The same was true of restaurants and cafés, which were forced to shut down at the same time.

Government support

Some cushioning of the blow was provided in the form of government measures. In the UK, the Chancellor of the Exchequer, Rishi Sunak, announced a 'Furlough Scheme', whereby the government would meet 80 per cent of workers' wages up to a limit of £2,500[11]. The measure was intended to last until October 2020, with government support tapering off towards the end of the period. By June, around nine million workers had been included in the scheme, or nearly 25 per cent of the working population[12].

The UK government also announced the suspension of business rates for a 12-month 'holiday' from April 2020 to April 2021 and the deferral of £30 billion worth of VAT payments from the period March to June 2020, until 31 March 2021. Finally, they announced £330 billion of government-backed loans for small businesses, to be administered via the banks[13].

Similarly, in the US, the Federal Government passed the Cares (Coronavirus Aid, Relief and Economic Security) Act, which included a number of measures to help small businesses such as retailers[14]. The Paycheck Protection Program provided $669 billion in loans that might be forgiven if the firms used them to keep workers on payroll until the end of June 2020. The loans could be used to cover two months' worth of wages, rents, mortgage interest and utilities[15]. The US government also allowed employers to defer payment of the employers' share of social security tax for up to two years and gave tax credits of $1,200 per person to those earning up to $75,000 per year[16].

While helpful in mitigating the short-term impact of the initial lockdown, the measures did not prevent retailing from suffering a grievous blow. Matthew Shay, President of the National Retail Federation in the US, described the Cares Act as a 'Crucial bridge for retailers', but added, 'With no cash coming in the door, we can't get it flowing quickly enough'[17].

Mark Cohen, Director of Retail Studies at Columbia University and a former chief executive of Sears Canada, doubted federal loans could resuscitate heavily indebted companies: 'A business that was struggling going into this crisis and is already leveraged up is unlikely to recover by taking on additional loans even on favourable terms,' he said[18].

Helen Dickinson, Chief Executive Officer of the British Retail Consortium, spoke for many when she said: 'The scale of this crisis is unrecognizable to us all'[19].

Retail versus online

Grocery and other essential retail were less severely affected as food purchasing continued, but other areas, such as fashion, saw an almost total loss of sales. For example, Primark sold nothing from the first lockdown date of 23 March until the reopening on 15 June – the loss of nearly three months of sales[20].

Online companies, on the other hand, saw a huge growth in their businesses. In the UK, e-commerce's market share rose from 19 per cent in November 2019 to nearly 33 per cent in May 2020, an increase that had previously taken 10 years to achieve[21]. As former Sainsbury's boss Mike Coupe put it in June 2020: 'Online groceries have taken 25 years to get to 8 per cent of our business and eight weeks to get to 15 per cent, and it's still growing like there's no tomorrow'[22].

In the US, online sales jumped by 44 per cent in the second quarter of 2020, even as overall retail sales fell by more than 4 per cent – boosting online's adjusted share to nearly 20 per cent, from around 14 per cent a year earlier[23]. Even as retailers laid off millions of workers, Amazon announced that it was taking on 75,000 staff to meet increased demand[24].

It was not just retailers who suffered: restaurants faced ruin as they were forced to close their doors. The British Beer and Pub Association Chief Executive, Emma McClarkin, said the industry was facing an 'Existential crisis as a direct result of the guidance issued by the government'. She added: 'Thousands of pubs and hundreds of thousands of jobs will be lost in the very short term unless a proactive package creating cash and liquidity is provided immediately to the industry'[25].

Many retailers were forced to cancel major orders with their suppliers, thus passing the problem up the supply chain. For example, more than a million Bangladeshi garment workers were sent home without pay, or lost their jobs, after Western clothing brands cancelled or suspended tens of billions of dollars-worth of existing orders, according to data from the Bangladeshi Garment Manufacturers Exporters Association (BGMEA)[26].

Primark, Matalan and the Edinburgh Woollen Mill were among retailers that collectively cancelled £1.4 billion of orders and suspended an additional £1 billion, as they scrambled to minimize losses, according to the BGMEA. This included nearly £1.3 billion of orders that were already in production or had been completed[27].

Brands and landlords also suffer

Brands also suffered as their retail customers shut down. For example, athletic apparel maker Under Armour reported a 23 per cent fall in revenue in the first quarter of 2020. The company also laid off about 600 staff at its US-based distribution centres, extended store closures and withdrew its forecast for the year, as it reported a net loss of $590 million compared with a profit of $23 million a year earlier[28].

Revlon reported sales down 18 per cent in the first three months of the year, along with operating losses of $182 million, up from a loss of $23 million during the prior-year period. The higher operating loss was driven primarily by $124 million of non-cash intangible impairment charges reflecting the financial impacts of COVID-19[29].

Many retailers were also forced to re-negotiate their rental payments with landlords. For example, brands as diverse as Debenhams, New Look, Arcadia, Primark, JD Sports and Burger King refused to pay their landlords the rent they were due. New Look threatened its landlords with a pre-pack administration if they did not reduce the rents[30].

The problem thus passed down the line to the retail property owners. Hammerson – owner of the Bullring in Birmingham and Brent Cross in London – said that it had only received 37 per cent of the rent due in the second quarter of 2020[31]. Intu – the owner of The Trafford Centre in Manchester and Lakeside near London – fell into administration in June 2020[32].

In the US, a leading commercial real estate broker in New York said there was widespread refusal from retailers to pay rent from the beginning of April 2020. Tenants including Mattress Firm and The Cheesecake Factory said they would not be meeting their obligations[33].

Simon Property Group, the largest shopping centre owner in America, furloughed almost a third of its 4,500-strong workforce[34]. CBL – a major American retail real estate investment trust (REIT) – started skipping its interest payments from 1 June 2020 (it was later to declare Chapter 11 bankruptcy in November 2020)[35]. Washington Prime and Pennsylvania Real Estate Investment Trust were also rumoured to be in financial trouble[36].

Ongoing uncertainty

Even as the bruised economies of the United States and the UK started to open up from the middle of 2020 onwards, a second wave of the virus was already brewing. Cases started to surge from September 2020 onwards, reaching record highs by the end of the year and the beginning of 2021.

Reluctant politicians in the UK were forced to impose a second lockdown in November 2020[37]. In the US, the question of whether to impose fresh restrictions was hotly debated in the Presidential Elections of November of the same year. In the midst of the debate came the news that President Trump himself had contracted the virus, as had First Lady Melania Trump[38].

With the retail industry facing disaster during its busiest holiday season, the Director of the Confederation of British Industry (CBI), Carolyn Fairbairn, predicted a 'bleak midwinter' for UK firms[39]. Even the announcement, in November 2020, that various vaccines had been successfully developed, did not provide an immediate solution for retailers. The timescale for the deployment of the vaccines remained uncertain, as did the questions of their effectiveness against new variants and whether everyone would be willing to be vaccinated[40].

In summary, we can see that the COVID-19 outbreak, accompanying lockdowns and ongoing uncertainty as to when things could get back to normal, had a devastating effect on a retail sector already traumatized by years of structural decline.

CHAPTER THREE

We're Gonna Party Like It's 1929

Many people in the financial sector believed that the recovery from COVID-19 would be 'V-shaped': in other words, that the global economy would bounce back quickly once lockdowns ended – in particular, because of the huge stimulus administered by governments and central banks.

The state of the stock market at the time of writing certainly indicated the validity of this point of view. As of February 2021, the Dow Jones Industrial Average stood at over 31,000 – above where it was on 26 February 2020 and 69 per cent above its COVID-19 nadir on 23 March 2020[1]. Politicians on both sides of the Atlantic were quick to claim success in piloting their economies through the crisis. However, there were reasons to be extremely cautious about the likelihood of a quick recovery.

Reasons to be cautious

Firstly, the economy was still anaesthetized by the huge quantities of financial painkillers swirling around in its system. As described, many countries had introduced incentives for companies to maintain their labour forces, but as soon as these ran out, firms would be quick to lay people off. Likewise for the moratoria put in place on rent payments, tax liabilities and other debts. At some point, all these obligations would have to be met.

Secondly, it was unlikely that all consumers were going to rush out and travel, shop, eat in restaurants and socialize in the same way as before, even when the lockdowns were lifted. Many would remain wary so long as there was a perceived risk of contracting the virus. In practice, this was likely to continue until effective vaccines were fully distributed, which could take a substantial amount of time. In addition, the continued spread of the disease in poorer parts of the world, and the appearance of multiple variants presented ongoing challenges for the global economy. There were concerns as to whether the new strains of COVID-19 might be resistant to the available vaccines.

Thirdly, it was likely that the recovery would be uneven. Some sectors, which had been badly hit might take years to return to normal, and see heavy unemployment. Others, where productive capacity had been reduced by the pandemic, might see supply shortages, which, in turn, could lead to price rises. This combination of high unemployment and inflation – known as stagflation – might pose a dilemma for policy makers. They might be forced to tighten monetary and fiscal policy, damaging the recovery and threatening asset values.

Fourthly, we must consider the effect of the lockdowns on people's financial status. Households had lost income due to people being furloughed and firms had lost profit due to a lack of business. People were unlikely to be able to travel in the same way as they used to, as long as there was a threat from the virus, which would be devastating for the airline and tourist industries[2]. And unemployment was high – for example, in the US, it was over 6 per cent in January 2021 – which was bound to limit consumer spending[3].

Fifthly, the level of government borrowing needed to support the rescue packages had been colossal. According to the Office for Budget Responsibility, the total cost of the UK government's program would be in the region of £123 billion[4]. In addition, tax receipts had plunged, due to the 'holidays' granted on business rates, the loss of income tax and National Insurance and the drop in VAT receipts[5].

As a consequence, UK borrowing surged to £62 billion in April 2020, versus £11 billion in April 2019, and government debt stood at 98 per cent of GDP[6]. To give this some context, the equivalent level of national debt at the same point of the 2008 crisis was 50 per cent[7].

In the US, the numbers were even more scary. The cost of the Cares Act was projected at over $2 trillion and many economists believed that it and other initiatives might cost as much as $4 trillion before the crisis was over[8]. Tax receipts, both at federal and state/local level, took a massive hit, with New York City alone facing a $7.4 billion tax loss[9]. As a result, US government debt reached $27 trillion by October 2020, which was over 100 per cent of GDP – the highest ever[10]. Repaying all this debt was going to take years of higher taxes and lower government spending. It was likely to mean that a whole generation would languish under the burden of austerity for the foreseeable future, much as occurred in the UK after the Second World War.

The economic cycle

Lastly, as we saw in the Introduction, we need to consider where the world was, in terms of the economic cycle, just prior to the outbreak. In January 2020, the global economy was poised at the top of a remarkably long boom, having enjoyed over 10 years of growth, fuelled by the cheap money handed out by nervous central banks in the aftermath of the Great Recession of 2008[11]. The normal length of the cycle is around seven years, so many commentators were expecting a recession in the near future. All it required, they believed, was some kind of trigger[12].

The Coronavirus probably qualifies as the most damaging 'trigger' ever experienced, since it has affected the whole world simultaneously. Therefore it was likely to lead to a period of considerable economic uncertainty. Already the predictions from leading experts were worrying. The President of the World Bank Group, David Malpass, has described Coronavirus as 'a devastating blow' for the global economy[13]. In January 2021, the International Monetary Fund (IMF) forecast that global economic growth would be negative 3.5 per cent in 2020, which would be far worse than the flat GDP recorded in 2008, at the height of the Great Recession[14].

In the UK, GDP dropped 9.9 per cent in 2020, according to the Office of National Statistics, while in the US the decrease was 3.5 per cent according to The Bureau of Economic Analysis[15]. All of which indicates a painful period of economic uncertainty – a far cry from the rosy prospect of a 'V-shaped' recovery, so beloved of the financial markets. If this is indeed the case, then business leaders need to adjust their thinking in new and radical ways if they are to survive what looks like being the worst global economic crisis since the Great Depression.

CHAPTER FOUR

Last Man Standing – The Impact on Retail

For traditional retailers, this economic scenario was nothing short of a disaster. As previously seen, the industry had already been weakened by years of decline since around 2015, and, for many shop owners, the Coronavirus and its accompanying slump was to be the coup-de-grâce. Already, we have seen substantial damage all round the world. We will look at each area in turn.

The UK

Retail

The UK witnessed a rash of bankruptcies, closures and lay-offs in 2020. Many famous retailers fell into insolvency or shut down, including Debenhams, Arcadia, Warehouse, Oasis, Clarks, Jigsaw, L.K. Bennett, Laura Ashley, Cath Kidston, Edinburgh Woollen Mill Group (owner of Bonmarché, Jaeger and Peacocks), Monsoon, Accessorize, Virgin Media stores and Victoria's Secret UK. Other brands suffering the same fate included Antler UK (luggage), Quiz (fashion), Aldo UK (shoes), Beales (department stores), Johnson's Shoes, Dawsons Music, Autonomy (clothing), Lombok (furniture), BrightHouse (household goods), TJ Hughes Outlet Division (discount), Poundstretcher (discount), Oddbins (off licence), Hearing & Mobility, Hawkin's Bazaar (toys and games), GO Outdoors, Long Tall Sally (outsize fashion), Oak Furnitureland and Oliver Sweeney (handcrafted shoes)[1].

Apart from the above-mentioned casualties, other companies also suffered. Primark lost sales of £650 million per month during the first lockdown and Next had a sales hit of £1 billion in total[2]. Dixons Carphone's profits fell to £166 million from £339 million in 2019–20, while Office (shoes) was put up for sale after announcing the closure of half its stores[3]. Ted Baker announced a sales drop of 46 per cent in the half year-ending August 2020, along with pre-tax losses of £39 million and 950 job cuts[4].

Debenhams announced on 1 December 2020 that it was going into liquidation, and the brand was sold to Boohoo for £55 million on 26 January 2021, as an online-only operation with the loss of its 118 stores and 10,000 employees[5].

Arcadia Group Limited – owner of Topshop and Dorothy Perkins – went into administration on 30 November 2020, marking the end of owner, Philip Green's long and chequered career as 'King of the High Street'. The Topshop and Miss Selfridge brands were acquired by ASOS for £330 million; Burton, Dorothy Perkins and Wallis were likewise acquired by Boohoo for £23 million and Evans by City Chic for £23 million. In each case the brands were to go forward without retail arms, meaning the loss of most of Arcadia's 444 stores and its 13,000 employees. Sir Philip Green left Arcadia with a £350 million hole in its pension scheme[6].

John Lewis announced job losses of 2,800 and the closure of eight stores, as it fell to a pre-tax loss of £635 million in the half-year ending July 2020 (compared with a profit of £192 million the year before). It also said that it was downsizing its Oxford Street flagship store and suspending bonus payments[7]. Sainsbury's announced in November 2020 that it was closing 420 Argos stand-alone stores and laying off 3,500 employees[8].

Many of the surviving groups were in negotiation with their landlords and other creditors, as at the time of writing, regarding reduced rents and debts, in order to determine whether they could continue trading. Linked to this, the industry was hit by a record number of store closures as 14,000 shops shut down in the nine months to September 2020. Overall, it was estimated that 20,000 stores would be closed in 2020 in the UK, versus 4,500 in 2019 (including major brands and small independent stores)[9].

Amongst those announcing closures or threats of store closures were Carphone Warehouse (531 stores), Arcadia (444), Argos (420), Poundstretcher (250), BrightHome (240), Boots (200), Travis Perkins – including Toolstation and Wickes (165), Debenhams (124), Marks & Spencer (100), Arcadia (100), Oasis/Warehouse (90), GO Outdoors (67), TM Lewin (66), Halfords (60), Cath Kidston (60); Oddbins (56), Virgin Media (53), Clarks (50), Harveys (50), Jack Wills (50), Laura Ashley (50), Edinburgh Woollen Mills (50), Office (50), M &Co. (47), Monsoon-Accessorize (35), Victoria's Secrets (25), DW Sports (25), Beales (22), Shoe Zone (20), Antler (18), Jigsaw (13) and John Lewis (8 stores)[10].

At the same time, the industry has seen a record number of jobs lost or under threat, including Arcadia (13,000), Debenhams (12,000), Marks & Spencer (7,000), Boots (4,000), Argos 3,500, Carphone Warehouse (2,900), GO Outdoors (2,400), Poundstretcher (2,000), Edinburgh Woollen Mills (860) and Oddbins (550). In total, it is estimated that over 175,000 retail jobs were lost across the year 2020, up from 93,000 in 2019, which was itself the worst year for retail for a quarter of a century[11].

Even the luxury goods market has been badly affected, both by the UK downturn and by issues in areas such as the Middle East. For example, Burberry saw sales drop in Europe and the Middle East by 75 per cent in the quarter ending June 2020 and announced that it was cutting 500 jobs. Harrods announced the loss of 680 jobs due to what it called 'the devastation in international travel', while Aspinal of London (leather goods) and DVF Studio (Diane von Furstenberg fashion) launched Company Voluntary Arrangements[12].

Cafés and restaurants

Cafés and restaurants have been among the hardest hit and it is estimated that a quarter will not reopen after the lockdowns end. The devastation has been particularly acute in major city centres as most people have been working from home. Among those which have fallen into insolvency or closed down are Carluccio's Ltd, Bella Italia, Le Pain Quotidien, Café Rouge, Las Iguanas, Frankie & Benny's, Garfunkel's, Chiquito, Byron Burgers, Pizza Express, Bistrot Pierre, Vapiano and Gourmet Burger Kitchen[13].

Companies which were very dependent on commuters suffered especially badly during the lockdowns. For example, SSP Group plc – owner of Upper Crust – reported in July 2020 that up to 5,000 jobs would be cut across its UK outlets and head office as it struggled with global sales which were 95 per cent below the previous year. Even by December 2020, it said that only a third of its 2,800 outlets were open[14].

Pret A Manger was in a similar position, announcing in August 2020 that it was closing 30 outlets and laying off 3,000 employees on the back of sales, which were down by 68 per cent[15].

Pub and bar groups have also been very badly affected. In November 2020, the British Beer & Pub Association (BBPA) warned that 12,000 pubs and bars (nearly a third of the UK's total) would have to close down permanently after the second lockdown[16].

Revolution bars fell into insolvency, while Tokyo Industries – owner of 45 leading club venues – announced in September 2020 that it was 'hibernating' the business, with the loss of 1,800 jobs. A number of major pub groups announced job losses or jobs-at-risk, such as Whitbread – consisting of Brewers Fayre, Premier Inn and Beefeater – Marston's, Greene King and JD Wetherspoon[17].

Cinemas, estate agents, banks

Cinemas have also suffered very badly. In January 2021, the largest cinema group in the world – AMC – came close to bankruptcy, and had to be rescued by an equity injection from shareholders. In October 2020, Cineworld announced the closure of all its 127 venues in the UK and its 536 Regal theatres in the US, with the potential loss of 45,000 jobs. Vue said that it would put 25 per cent of its cinemas on three-day-per-week working[18].

Even estate agents have not escaped the damage. Countrywide, owner of Hamptons International, Bairstow Eves and Gascoigne-Pees, was already suffering before COVID-19, and was said to have closed 23 per cent of its branches on the back of poor 2020 revenues. It lost £44 million in the first half of 2020 and its share price was down 99 per cent from its peak value. It was subsequently acquired by Connells in December 2020, at a fire-sale price of £130 million. Foxtons also saw revenues decline 10 per cent in the third quarter of 2020 and its share price was 91 per cent down on its peak[19].

Finally, retail banking was not immune. Banks had been closing branches for many years, with an estimated 3,303 closing down from 2015 to 2019, but the advent of COVID-19 made things far worse. NatWest announced in August 2020 that it was cutting 550 jobs in branches, while other major banks announced branch closures, such as TSB, Barclays, Lloyds Bank, HSBC UK and Virgin Money/Clydesdale Bank[20].

North America

Retail

In the US, the situation was, if anything, even worse. UBS, a bank, reported that more than triple the number of retailers would close their doors over the following five years than shut during the last recession. That was upwards of 100,000 retail shops to be shuttered and the total number of stores was predicted to decline from 883,000 in 2019 to 782,000 by 2025. The commercial real estate data firm CoStar, estimated that 2020 alone would see a record number of closures – around 12,200 major chain stores (not including small independent stores). This was far higher than the 9,000 closed in 2019, which was, itself, the worst year on record[21].

Store groups that have gone bankrupt or closed down include Neiman Marcus, JCPenney, Lord & Taylor, Brooks Brothers, J. Crew, Pier 1 Imports, Inc., Ascena Retail, Tailored Brands, Century 21, Gold's Gym, Payless, GNC, Papyrus, Lucky's, Art Van Furniture, Earth Fare, Stein Mart, Modell's Sporting Goods, Guitar Centre, Tuesday Morning, Goody's, Palais Royal, Bealls, Peebles, and Gordmans, Muji USA, The Paper Store, True Religion, Lucky Brand Jeans and G-Star RAW. Some of these are iconic names in the history of American retailing[22].

Other retailers reported results that were sharply down. Dick's Sporting Goods saw same-store sales for the first quarter of 2020 decrease 29 per cent. Barnes & Noble announced lay-offs and the closure of its New York flagship store. Nordstrom's second quarter 2020 results showed sales $2 billion down on the previous year and net losses of $255 million. Meanwhile Macy's suffered a loss of up to $431 million for the second quarter of 2020. American Eagle Outfitters, Inc., suffered a $257 million loss for the quarter ending 2 May. According to a SEC filing: 'Store closures and aggressive inventory liquidation had a significant impact on our first-quarter financials,' Chief Executive Officer Jay Schottenstein said in a statement[23].

Employment was also badly affected, with the US Bureau of Labor Statistics reporting 1.9 million store-based employees out-of-work in June 2020[24]. Even the luxury sector has not been spared. Ralph Lauren cut 3,700 staff, or 15 per cent of its workforce, while the French luxury group LVMH tried unsuccessfully to pull out of its proposed takeover of Tiffany[25].

Within retail, COVID-19 produced a huge shift in the profitability of different sectors. As Greg Buzek, Founder and President of IHL Group, put it: 'The pandemic has produced one of the greatest wealth transfers' in the history of retail. In North America, some $125 billion in retail sales have shifted from general merchandise retailers (e.g. department stores and apparel retailers) and hard goods retailers (e.g. furniture, appliances, jewellery, sporting goods retailers) to grocery, mass merchants, warehouse clubs and online (e.g. Amazon), according to IHL. This was because the latter were permitted to stay open (as they were deemed to offer 'essential goods'), whereas the former were forced to close[26].

Meanwhile, S&P downgraded its ratings on Victoria's Secret and Gap. As we saw in the Introduction, Victoria's Secret's future was looking shaky after private equity firm Sycamore Investments pulled out of a deal to buy the brand. There were serious concerns as to whether its owner, L Brands, Inc., could survive with its heavy debt load and painful losses[27].

This analysis has tended to concentrate on larger 'name' brands, but there is also a much more pernicious trend affecting small retailers. According to IHL, there was a huge transfer of wealth from small retailers (50 or fewer locations) to big retailers. The company estimated that some $250 billion in sales moved out of small businesses' cash drawers to large corporations over the period of the lockdown.

'Walmart, Costco, Target, and others were allowed to be open and sell clothing, sporting goods, crafts, education materials, and every other product in most regions while the small business was forced to shut down. Sadly, many are not going to survive,' says Buzek. He estimated that this cash drain will force 285,000 small businesses to close, including retailers, hospitality, theatres and restaurants[28].

Restaurants and gyms

As in the UK, the restaurant sector has been badly hit, with bankruptcies declared by companies as diverse as Chuck E. Cheese, Le Pain Quotidien, Dean & DeLuca and California Pizza Kitchen. Starbucks announced in June 2020 that it was planning to close 400 stores, after predicting their revenue loss attributable to COVID-19, could be up to $3.2 billion. The company suffered a net loss of $678 million in the quarter ending June 2020[29].

Gyms were also very badly affected due to long periods of lockdown. For example, 24 Hour Fitness announced in June 2020 it had filed for Chapter 11 bankruptcy protection and that it was closing more than 130 gyms[30].

Canada

In Canada, 2020 saw the following retailers announce bankruptcy and/or store closures: Aldo (1500), Carlton Cards (78), Addition Elle (77), Thyme Maternity (54), Lowe's and Rona (34), Ronson's (18), Ten Thousand Villages (10), Army & Navy (5), Links of London (5), Sail Outdoors (outdoor wear), Reitmans (clothing), Henry's (photographic), Bootlegger (jeans), Cleo (womenswear) and Ricki's (apparel)[31].

CHAPTER FIVE

Rocking all Over the World

The main focus of this book is on the UK and American markets, but it is worth noting that the retail crisis brought on by COVID-19 is a global phenomenon, affecting all areas of the world. This is unusual, because previous economic crises have normally flared up in particular sectors or regions – for example, the Asian 'Tiger Economy' crisis of 1997, the Dot-Com crash of 2001 or the American Sub-Prime collapse of 2008.

Europe

Starting with continental Europe, we can see that there has been widespread damage to retail, wherever the virus outbreak has been sufficiently severe. Holland's largest retailer – Hema – went bankrupt in August 2020, while Hudson's Bay Netherlands, which took over 15 of the old Vroom & Dreesmann department stores, also became insolvent[1].

In Sweden, MQ (fashion) and Holland & Barrett Sweden (health food) have been declared bankrupt, while leading fashion retailer, H&M, saw sales down 18 per cent in the year ending November 2020, and announced 50 net store closures in that year, and 250 in 2021. Meanwhile, in June 2020, Ikea – the world's leading furniture retailer – announced the permanent closure of a number of stores, including one in the UK[2].

Germany's Galeria Karstadt Kaufhof, an ailing department-store chain, filed for bankruptcy in April 2020, and agreed a rescue plan in September to close nearly 50 stores and lay off 5,000 workers. Vapiano, an Italian restaurant chain, headquartered in Germany, Poggenpohl (upscale kitchenware) and Esprit (fashion) also declared bankruptcy. Up to 50,000 German retailers — or one in every six retail shops in Germany — could go bankrupt due to the Coronavirus crisis, according to the head of the German Retail Association, Stefan Genth, in a statement made in January 2021[3].

In France, the Coronavirus was the second major shock to hit the retail industry after 2019's 'Gilets Jaunes' (yellow vests) protest over rising fuel prices, which shut down a lot of town centres. The damage has been considerably worse: CPME, France's small-business federation, said in April 2020 that 55 per cent of small firms (many of them shops and restaurants) were concerned about bankruptcy[4].

Orchestra Prémaman, a troubled clothing retailer, filed for receivership in April 2020. Camaïeu, a fashion company with 3,900 employees and 634 shops in France also sought bankruptcy protection, as did Naf Naf (a fashion group with 1,170 employees), La Halle (a fashion company with €847 million in revenue and 5,400 employees), André (a shoe retailer) and Alinéa (a furniture retailer with 2,000 staff). Conforama (a furniture retailer with 9,000 employees) was rumoured to be on the verge of bankruptcy and had to be rescued by a €300 million bail-out from the French government[5].

Galeries Lafayette, arguably France's most famous high-end department store with 61 large outlets across the country, was facing a $1 billion loss as it struggled in the wake of the Coronavirus lockdown: 'It is very hard. We reopened the Champs-Élysées store on May 11, but we have to face the fact that a lot of customers are missing,' said Chief Executive Nicolas Houze, sharing that footfall was down 20 per cent compared to 'normal' times[6].

In Italy, the La Rinascente department store group forecast in June 2020, that its sales would drop by up to 25 per cent over the full year, while footwear retailer Geox experienced a 39 per cent sales drop over the first half[7].

In Spain, Inditex, one of the world's largest clothing retailers and owner of Zara, was hit hard during the pandemic, with sales down

44 per cent to €3.3 billion in the quarter ending 30 April 2020. The company reported a net loss of €409 million during the quarter and has announced plans to close 1,200 stores[8].

El Corte Inglés – Spain's biggest department store group, lost €510 million between March and May 2020 as it laid off its 22,000 workers during lockdown, and ratings agency, Fitch, put the group on a negative rating watch[9].

Much of Southern Europe – France, Spain, Italy and Greece, for example – is heavily dependent on tourism, so the travel shutdown had a particularly bad effect on the shops and restaurants in the region.

The losses were dramatic. The European Commission estimated in May 2020 that the EU's hotels and restaurants would lose half their income. Tourism revenues fell by 95 per cent in Italy and 77 per cent in Spain in March alone, according to the banking group UBS. Across southern Europe, where recovery from the 2008 crisis relied to a significant extent on tourism, the sector is vital to national economies. It accounts for 20 per cent of GDP in Greece, 18 per cent in Portugal, 15 per cent in Spain and 13 per cent in Italy, according to the World Bank. At the time of writing, in January 2021, with much of Europe under a second lockdown, increasingly desperate business owners were demanding action. The EU's internal market commissioner, Thierry Breton, called for a 'Marshall Plan' using funds from Europe's vast economic stimulus packages to pull hotels, restaurants and tour operators back from collapse[10].

Asia

In Asia, the Japanese retail industry was hit by its internal lockdown and also the collapse in the number of foreign tourists, especially from China. The Japan Department Stores Association said that the apparel sales among its 205 member stores fell 40 per cent in the first half of 2020 – the largest drop on record – as Japanese citizens opted to stay home and the number of overseas visitors plummeted by more than 90 per cent[11].

From March to May 2020, operating losses across the top four department store groups – J. Front Retailing Co. Ltd. (Daimaru and Matsuzakaya stores), Takashimaya Co. Ltd., Sogo & Seibu Co. Ltd. and Matsuya Co. Ltd. added up to nearly ¥37 billion[12].

In Hong Kong, the virus also hit retailers hard, coming on top of the losses they suffered during the political protests of 2019. The first ten months of the year saw a slide in sales of 27 per cent[13].

An estimated 10,400 retail workers were thought to have been laid off and 5,200 shops closed down by the end of June 2020, according to the Hong Kong Retail Management Association, which also said that 96 per cent of the 152 companies it surveyed had suffered losses since the health crisis had broken out. Folli Follie and Links of London announced that they were pulling out of Hong Kong, with 12 stores due to close[14].

Singapore's retail industry was already suffering with a year of consecutive monthly sales declines before the Coronavirus hit. With the advent of the virus, the economy was thought to have shrunk by between 6 and 6.5 per cent in 2020 as a whole, according to the government's forecast. Sales in the spring of 2020 were down as much as 50 per cent, according to Trading Economics. The famous Robinson department store group was forced to close down in October 2020, along with the local operations for Topshop, Esprit, Sportslink and Universal Traveller. Even in September 2020, retail sales were still nearly 13 per cent down on the previous year[15].

South Korean retail sales through physical stores dropped by 8 per cent in March 2020, due to the lockdown and a drop in foreign visitor numbers, particularly from China. Unemployment rose to a 10-year high in May 2020. Leading local retailer Shinsegae Inc. saw its sales drop by 28 per cent in the first two quarters of 2020, while the Lotte and Shilla duty-free stores in Jeju City were shut down in May 2020[16].

Australia and South Africa

Australian retail declined by as much as 18 per cent in the spring of 2020 and a large number of retailers suffered as a consequence. Among those going under or closing down were Designworks/Jets Swimwear, Jeanswest, G-Star Australia, Harris Scarfe department stores and Jigsaw Australia. Other groups which were struggling included leading department store group David Jones, which announced the closure of 10 stores, fashion retailer, Colette, which is closing 100 stores and Wesfarmers, which is closing 75 Target stores. Meanwhile, fashion retailer Mosaic Brands – owner of marques like Noni B, Rivers, Millers and Katie – announced the closure of 250 stores[17].

The South African economy was already in recession in 2019 before the Coronavirus hit. Unfortunately, the impact of the pandemic was very severe in the country, due to the challenges in social distancing in overcrowded townships and the overstretching of the medical facilities.

Retail sales dropped by up to 50 per cent in the spring of 2020 and were still 2 per cent down in October, indicating a slow recovery. The unemployment rate rose to over 30 per cent in the third quarter of 2020. It was forecast that GDP would drop back to below 2010 levels over the course of the year[18].

A number of big retailers took substantial hits from the lockdown. Edcon, owner of Edgars Department Stores and budget retailer Jet, filed for bankruptcy, putting 39,000 workers at risk. Woolworths – owner of Woolworths department stores and David Jones in Australia – was downgraded by S&P in September 2020 after net profits after tax plunged more than 20 per cent in the year ended in June 2020. Truworths was also badly affected, with profits diving by 28 per cent in the year-ending June 2020, while Walmart-owned Massmart (Makro and Game supermarkets) saw losses of $65 million on a drop in sales of 10 per cent during the first half of the year. Scandal-hit home retailer Steinhoff's first-half losses more than doubled to $1.7 billion in 2020[19].

The BRICs (Brazil, Russia, India, China)

Brazil has been very hard hit by COVID-19, with over 8 million cases reported by mid-January 2021 (the third highest number in the world) and many problems with social distancing and a lack of medical facilities in poorer areas. Brazil's Economy Ministry forecast in September 2020 that GDP would shrink by nearly 5 per cent over the full year, which would have a devastating effect on the retail sector[20].

Lojas Renner (apparel) was said to be grappling with dramatically lower sales and profits, while Magazine Luiza (electronics) reported substantially lower revenues. Fashion retailer Restoque announced in June 2020 that it had reached a deal with its creditors to restructure its debt[21].

Russia was also badly affected by the virus and recorded nearly 3.5 million cases by the middle of January 2021. Despite the bad numbers, the country reopened in the autumn of 2020, leading to a second wave of the disease. Its economy also received a major blow from the collapse in oil prices, which accompanied the pandemic[22].

Russia's retail sales crashed by as much as 23 per cent in the spring of 2020 and were still 3 per cent down in November as unemployment soared by 39 per cent. Losses in Russian non-food retail in 2020 were forecast at 6.08 trillion roubles ($80 billion) according to the Russian Association of Retail Companies (AKORT). Roughly a third of smaller companies, including many retailers, indicated they were frightened that they would go bankrupt during the crisis[23].

Like Brazil and Russia, India suffered very badly from the virus, with nearly 10.5 million cases confirmed by mid-January 2021. Again, conditions in India's tightly packed sprawling mega-cities did not create ideal circumstances for social distancing, nor could the country's poor afford to be in lockdown for substantial periods. In addition, the disease was likely to overstrain the already fragile hospital system[24].

The World Bank predicted that the Indian economy would shrink by 9.6 per cent in 2020 and according to the Confederation of All India Traders (CAIT) in May of that year, up to 20 per cent of retailers were likely to wind up their businesses over the course of the year. For example, Aditya Birla Fashion Retail Limited – owner of the famous Pantaloons brand, as well as a slew of western franchised brands, such as Ralph Lauren, Ted Baker and American Eagle – saw its income decline 50 per cent in the quarter-ending September 2020. Other large retailers also suffered: Reliance Retail saw a halving of its profitability in the quarter ending June 2020, while Future Retail made losses of nearly $700 million in the second quarter and Avenue Supermarts took a hit to profits of 38 per cent in the quarter ending September 2020[25]. Future Retail was subsequently acquired by Reliance in August 2020.

By contrast, China has emerged from the Coronavirus relatively unscathed. By locking down the country very promptly in mid-January, the government managed to all but eliminate cases by mid-March 2020 and to reopen its economy from the end of that month. However, while it did not see a major re-occurrence of the disease, retail sales were slow to recover, going from being 21 per cent down in January and February to 16 per cent down in March, to 7.5 per cent down in April. It did not reach positive territory until August – a far cry from the growth of 8 per cent that it was experiencing in December 2019, prior to the start of the outbreak[26].

China's economy has also been hit by a reduction in manufacturing demand from the rest of the world – exports fell by 39 per cent in January and February 2020 versus December 2019 – and did not get back into positive territory until September 2020. The Chinese government tried to stimulate local demand to take the place of lost exports by handing out $1.7 billion's-worth of vouchers for consumers to spend[27].

China was already home to some of the most sophisticated e-commerce players in the world, such as Alibaba and JD.com. The COVID-19 crisis gave them a huge opportunity to win market share and they took full advantage of it. Online sales grew 12 per cent in the first five months of 2020, and e-commerce's share of physical goods sales went up to 26 per cent by May 2020. JD.com's '618 Grand

Promotion' – an annual sales event held in June – saw its sales grow by 74 per cent versus the previous year[28].

The Middle East

The Arabian Gulf, known for its extravagant retail scene, has had to draw in its horns due to the outbreak of COVID-19. The companies of the region had been slow to move online, with the prevailing attitude being that the consumers of the region 'liked to shop' and therefore it was not necessary to invest much in e-commerce. As a result, the share of online sales was less than 5 per cent in 2018 versus around 20 per cent in the UK. The advent of the Coronavirus has exposed the flaw in this logic and as a result, the damage has been extreme. With malls closed, e-commerce grew to an estimated $24 billion in sales in 2020, reaching over 9 per cent of the market. Conversely, store sales dropped sharply, and EFG Hermes predicted a sales drop of at least 20 per cent across 2020. 50 per cent of Dubai restaurant and hotel business owners surveyed by the Dubai Chamber of Commerce predicted that they would go out of business due to COVID-19[29].

Kuwait's Alshaya Group, the Gulf's largest franchise operator, with brands including Starbucks, Pottery Barn and The Cheesecake Factory, provided a grim outlook in April 2020 in an internal staff video reported by Arabian Business: 'Today, less than 5 per cent of our stores are open … Our revenues have shrunk by 95 per cent, whilst our cost base has stayed the same,' said acting Chief Executive John Hadden. 'This is not sustainable for any business anywhere in the world'[30].

Dubai Mall owner, Emaar Properties, halted construction on two projects – a mall near the site of the Expo 2020 world fair and a 185,000 square-metre mall in the Dubai Hills residential area. Majid Al Futtaim (MAF), the Middle East's biggest mall-operator, told Reuters it had delayed the launch of its fifth and largest centre in Oman, the 145,000 square-metre Mall of Oman, because retailers did not have the cash at hand to fit out stores[31].

The region was also hit by a significant decline in the price of oil from $50 a barrel down to less than zero at its lowest point. The governments of the Gulf Cooperation Council (GCC) countries are heavily dependent on oil revenue and were compelled to cut back on spending, meaning long-term austerity in the region. Under these circumstances it is difficult to see retailing bouncing back very fast.

'If I tell you some of the sales of my units, they are an absolute joke,' said Sami Daud, managing director of Daud Group and founder of Gourmet Gulf, which together are responsible for brands like Hamleys, House of Fraser, YO! Sushi and Hummingbird Bakery, among many others.

'I mean AED100, AED300, AED700, where we used to do AED20,000, AED50,000 or AED100,000. What I've noticed is people are now going to malls not to hang out and walk around; it's become very transactional ... In the retail side, you really see that, and in the F&B [Food and Beverage] side, nobody's going. Fear is a major factor and that is here to stay for a good while'[32].

There has been a wave of closures and mergers as retailers have sought to consolidate their cost bases. For example, Gulf Greetings General Trading LLC, owner of Toy Store and Hallmark was placed in liquidation in January 2021. Gulf Marketing Group, which owns the Sun & Sand sports chain, acquired Royal Sporting House from Al Futtaim in December 2020[33].

International travel retail

Finally, a word about the international travel and duty-free retail market – a huge business in its own right, with nearly $80 billion of revenues in 2019 and previously expected to grow to over $150 billion by 2025. COVID-19 has been a catastrophe for airport retail as international travel has been all but eliminated[34].

Heathrow airport announced losses of $1.5 billion in the first 9 months of 2020, while Sidney airport in Australia saw a 98 per cent reduction in flights in the month to mid-May 2020: 'It's a ghost town, all the high-end stores are closed out there,' Brenda, a shop assistant at the airport, told the *Guardian* in June 2020[35].

With future restrictions on leisure travel, including quarantine periods, and businesses switching to meeting via Zoom calls, it seems that this key part of the global retail economy is going to be depressed for some time.

So, in summary, things are looking bleak for traditional retailers all round the world. Rarely has there been a time when so much of the global retail economy has been hit all at the same time. Normally, crises blow up in particular sectors, markets or regions, but to have the whole world involved simultaneously is something new and truly shocking.

CHAPTER SIX

Where Has All the Business Gone? The Effect on Brands

Sitting behind the retailers and restaurants in the supply chain are the brands and manufacturers who create and market the products distributed in the stores and eateries. These businesses depend on retailers and restaurants to purchase their products and millions of jobs depend on this trade. As retail has been thrown into lockdown, so these brands have seen their businesses dry up. The situation has been exacerbated by retail buyers' practice of de-stocking at the start of the Coronavirus crisis, which saw many orders cancelled.

Clothing

Hanesbrands Inc. (underwear) saw a drop in revenue of $181 million in the first quarter of 2020, leading to a net loss of $8 million versus a profit of $81 million in 2019[1]. Wolford AG (hosiery) saw its share price down 82 per cent from its peak as it experienced a drop in sales of 50 per cent in the first two weeks of March 2020[2]. VF Corporation (owner of the Wrangler, Lee and Vans brands) suffered a net loss of $484 million in the first quarter of 2020 (versus a profit of $129 million the previous year) on sales down 11 per cent[3].

Under Armour – the famous sportswear brand – suffered a net loss of $590 million in quarter one, wiping out a huge proportion of its net assets of only $1,550 million[4]. PVH, previously known as Phillips-Van Heusen (owner of Tommy Hilfiger and Calvin Klein) saw its stock drop 50 per cent as revenue decreased 43 per cent in the first quarter, causing a net loss of $1,097 million on net assets of only $4,500 million[5].

Toys

Mattel (the owner of Barbie) saw sales drop by nearly $100 million in quarter one and net losses increase to $211 million from $176 million in the equivalent period for 2019, causing its share price to drop to below 20 per cent of its peak value[6]. Hasbro (owner of Monopoly and Play-Doh) saw net losses of $70 million[7].

Beauty

The beauty industry was growing fast prior to the Coronavirus outbreak. However, it has taken a substantial hit as people have stayed at home, obviating the need for products like cosmetics. The only exception to this is skincare, which has grown during the lockdowns.

Long-troubled brand Revlon saw revenues down 26 per cent in the first three quarters of 2020 and a net loss of $385 million. The company had very heavy debts and had lost 98 per cent of its peak share value by January 2021, leading to substantial doubts as to its long-term future. In November 2020, the company was forced to restructure its debt in order to remain afloat[8].

Coty (owner of Max Factor, Cover Girl and Calvin Klein) has been forced to sell its Wella division to KKR Venture Capital in order to shore up its liquidity in the light of a 25 per cent drop in revenues in the year-ending June 2020, leading to net losses of $364 million. It was carrying over $8 billion of debt, which looked unsustainable under the circumstances, despite the sale, and Moody's gave the stock a high credit risk rating[9].

Even L'Oréal, the French beauty giant, reported sales down 7 per cent in the first three quarters of 2020. The results would have been even worse, had it not been for the fact that the company had invested in developing its digital sales to be 25 per cent of the business, and seen this channel grow over 60 per cent in the period[10].

Estee Lauder – also a very strong company – reported sales down 4 per cent in the year-ending June 2020, with a 60 per cent drop in net earnings from the year before. They announced in August 2020 that they would lay off up to 2,000 employees, and close 10–15 per cent of freestanding stores[11].

FMCG

In general, Fast-moving Consumer Goods (FMCG) (or Consumer Packaged Goods (CPG) in the US) fared reasonably well during the outbreak as they manufactured essentials like food, drink and household products. Items like cleaning agents, tinned foods, cleaning wipes and toilet paper actually experienced an increase in demand, and in some cases, price rises, due to panic buying and stockpiling, especially in the first few weeks of the lockdown. There were, however, some products that fared less well.

Unilever saw its sales drop 2 per cent in the first three quarters of 2020 as gains in areas like household soaps were offset by lower ice cream sales due to the drop in tourist numbers and lower food shipments to the restaurant and café trade[12].

The Kraft Heinz Company has struggled since the 2015 mega-merger between Kraft General Foods and Heinz, and its share price in January 2021 was only a third of its peak in 2017. It had already seen its 2019 fourth-quarter net sales decrease 5.1 per cent as it disclosed impairment charges of $666 million, including writing down the value of its flagship Maxwell House coffee brand by $213 million and being hit by lower demand in the US for cheese, coffee, cold cuts and bacon. The company experienced net losses of $676 million in the first three quarters of 2020, mainly due to charges related to the sale of its cheese businesses[13].

Coca-Cola's share price lost 14 per cent of its value versus its peak by mid-January 2021. Part of that was due to a longer-term loss of sales due to increased concerns about the health impact of carbonated drinks. On top of this, the Coronavirus hit hard, with its second quarter 2020 sales down by 28 per cent due to loss of business in the out-of-home segment – sales in places like pubs and restaurants – which usually make up almost half of Coca-Cola's turnover. It also offered severance terms to 4,000 employees, in the US, Canada and Puerto Rico alone[14].

There was also the threat of the virus to supply chains. Tyson Foods, one of America's largest meat producers, warned that 'the food supply chain is breaking' amid the Coronavirus crisis. The company was hit by a scandal as over 11,000 cases of Coronavirus were reported linked to its factories. It was forced to close, or reduce production at, several facilities throughout the US, including a pork-processing plant in Iowa, where several workers tested positive for the virus[15].

British American Tobacco (BAT) – owner of cigarette brands Lucky Strike and Rothmans – had, by mid-January 2020, lost nearly half of its peak share value due to longer-term health concerns and Covid-related tobacco bans in markets like South Africa, Mexico and Argentina. At the same time, Philip Morris International – owner of Marlboro and Benson & Hedges – lost a third of its peak share value by mid-January 2021. It had been affected by the virus, which led to 20 per cent of its global manufacturing capacity being shut down, and second-quarter 2020 sales being down by 10 per cent[16].

Danone – the French-based owner of dairy products like Danone and Actimel – was also negatively affected by the outbreak, with its share price down 35 per cent from its 2019 peak in mid-January 2021. Sales were 5.4 per cent down in the first three quarters of 2020, driven mainly by a 21 per cent reduction in its bottled water (Evian and other brands) business, which was negatively affected by the shutdown in travel and restaurants[17].

AB InBev – owner of beer brands Budweiser and Stella Artois – saw its share price drop by half in January 2021 versus its peak. During the first three months of 2020 total volumes decreased by 9.3 per cent, with China dropping a massive 46 per cent[18].

All in all, Coronavirus has proved to be a very challenging time for brands – reliant as they are on their retail, bar and restaurant customers to get their products to market.

Direct-to-consumer

For many brands, the global situation also underlined the importance of developing a direct-to-consumer online channel. For brands that had made the investment in doing so, the Coronavirus pandemic was much less painful. For example, Nike's share price was at record levels in January 2021, because it had developed a strong digital business channel, representing more than 20 per cent of sales in 2019. In the quarter-ending November 2020, the company reported revenues up 9 per cent, supported by an explosive 84 per cent growth in brand digital sales. The company also said that it expected rising consumer concerns about health and fitness to have a long-term positive impact on its future. We will look further at Nike's digital vision later in Chapter 48 (pages 262–7)[19].

Unfortunately, Nike is something of a lone star among brands in terms of having a consistent direct-to-consumer strategy. Most brands seem to have preferred to continue to rely on their retail and restaurant customers despite the clear evidence that this distribution channel is in long-term decline. Many of them have very low sales going through their own websites. For example, Hanesbrands Inc. made 12 per cent of its 2019 sales in the US through what it describes as 'consumer-directed' channels, but this includes sales through Amazon and other pure-play online retailers, as well as those through its outlet stores and through the e-commerce sites of its bricks-and-mortar retail customers. It is likely that its 'real' direct-to-consumer business via its own website is in the region of 5 per cent or less[20].

Under Armour has stated that 12 per cent of its sales in 2018 were through e-commerce channels, which would include its own website and third-party websites. Thus, stripping out perhaps 50 per cent of this as being third-party e-commerce, we are left with a figure of around 6 per cent for its own website. As we have seen above, that has not been enough to carry it through the Covid-related closure of its retail outlets[21].

Revlon's e-commerce business represented 9.5 per cent of the company's total net sales in 2019. However, this includes sales through third-party websites like Amazon, so it is safe to say that sales through its own website are probably in a similar range to the above two companies[22].

PVH, Mattel and Hasbro do not even mention the percentage of revenues going through their e-commerce channels in their annual reports, which may say something about how much emphasis they give to this key metric. Coty's e-commerce sales were 10 per cent of the total in the quarter-ending June 2020, but again, this includes third-party e-commerce, so it is likely that its own website sales are around 5 per cent[23].

Prior to the pandemic, PepsiCo had less than 2 per cent of its sales online and this was mainly through third-party websites. Most of its major brand websites, like Pepsi.com and Gatorade.com, did not, as of November 2020, offer the opportunity to buy products directly and instead routed the consumer to partner websites or stores[24].

Coca-Cola did not even mention e-commerce in its 2019 annual report, and it was impossible to buy the product on its website. As mentioned earlier, the COVID-19 crisis hit the company hard and there is some evidence that it may finally be waking up to the need to offer its consumers the opportunity to buy its product directly. As Chief Executive Officer James Quincy said in April 2020: 'We're going to embrace some seismic consumer behavior shifts, especially in e-commerce'[25].

Unilever's 2019 annual report logs e-commerce sales at 6 per cent of the total, but this includes sales through third parties like Amazon and its retail customers' websites, so its own website sales would be lower than this[26].

Nestlé has made more efforts than many and has achieved 8.5 per cent of its revenues from e-commerce in 2019. However, that figure also includes sales through third-party websites[27].

Other FMCG companies have zero or very low direct e-commerce sales: Mondelez's e-commerce sales percentage was reported as being in mid-single digits in their 2019 accounts; prior to the COVID-19 outbreak, The Kraft Heinz Company did not sell its products directly on its own websites. Danone had only 4 per cent of its sales online in 2018 and virtually all of this was via third-party websites[28].

AB InBev mentioned some internet initiatives but did not break out the percentage of sales that was done through e-commerce. BAT and Philip Morris International did not even mention e-commerce sales in their annual reports[29].

Channel conflict

At first sight, it is difficult to understand why brands have not leapt onto the direct-to-consumer opportunity with enthusiasm, as it potentially allows them to free themselves of those annoying middlemen (otherwise known as retailers), who swallow so much of their margin and obstruct them from connecting with their end-consumers. In doing so, they would have potentially gained an advantage in two huge areas – cost and personalized customer relationships.

We have seen in Chapter 1 (pages 9–16) how digitally native direct-to-consumer brands have cut out the costs of retailing and thus have been able to offer high-quality products at better prices. They have also been able to form one-to-one relationships with their customers, with far greater understanding of their behaviour. Finally, they have been able to control the presentation of their brands far more than any traditional brand can do working through third-party retail. These advantages could accrue to major incumbent brands if they would only invest in building their own direct-to-consumer businesses. However, if one looks more deeply into the issue, one sees that, prior to COVID-19, they were too frightened of offending their incumbent retailers. They were also put off by the apparently high cost of building direct businesses. This latter point was often exacerbated by their relative lack of skills in navigating the maze of social media brand-building and personalized marketing, which is so well understood by the digitally native, direct-to-consumer brands.

As we have seen, in the absence of having large-scale e-commerce operations of their own, major brands were caught flat-footed by the closure of so much of their retail and restaurant distribution during Coronavirus and therefore suffered heavily in terms of lost sales.

CHAPTER SEVEN

Mall Cried Out

As we have seen in Chapter 1 (pages 9–16), the retail crisis was brewing up over a long period from 2015 to 2020, well before the Coronavirus hit the world. As retailer after retailer went bankrupt and hundreds of stores closed down, the impact on the malls and shopping centres which depended on them was correspondingly severe.

The loss of 'anchor tenants' such as department stores has been particularly catastrophic for these shopping centres. For example, the monthly sales of department stores in the US have fallen from their height of $20 billion in 2002 to $9.3 billion in 2020, causing widespread closures. As these key tenants have disappeared, it has dragged down the malls as well, as 30 per cent of mall space was historically taken up by department stores.

In the US, around a third of all the enclosed malls (or around 400 of them) have either been closed down or are in terminal decline. There is even a website – deadmalls.com – that is dedicated to this phenomenon. For example, malls like Metro North Mall in Kansas City, Randall Park Mall in Cleveland, Northridge Mall in Milwaukee and Jamestown Mall in Florissant, Missouri – once flourishing centres of their communities – all now lie empty and in ruins, as brilliantly captured by photographer Seph Lawless in his book, *Autopsy of America: The Death of a Nation*[1].

With the advent of COVID-19, the pressure on malls increased considerably. Even highly prestigious new developments, such as the American Dream mall and Hudson's Yard have run into trouble.

American nightmare

The American Dream megamall project in the New Jersey Meadowlands was supposed to be the development that proved all the doubters wrong. A massive luxury mall with 3 million square foot of space – one of the largest in North America – it featured a theme park, ice rink, water play-area and indoor ski centre in addition to over 450 shops. However, even before the pandemic shut down retail, there were troubling signs that it was not getting the hoped-for support from retailers. When it launched, in October 2019, American Dream had only one retail store open, and it announced in January 2020 that it had only drawn 790,000 visitors during its first three months – or 9,000 visitors a day – well below the 109,000 daily visitors that had been promised.

Then COVID-19 hit, forcing American Dream to close on 16 March 2020 as New Jersey and much of the US issued stay-at-home orders. The results were predictably disastrous. American Dream immediately confirmed that it was eliminating approximately 100 jobs – 7 per cent of its property management and operations team at the complex – as part of a restructuring triggered by the pandemic.

By the time the mall reopened on 1 October 2020, it still had only 33 shops open and Triple Five – its owner – defaulted on $1.4 billion of debt such that it had to hand over a 49 per cent interest in the net income of its flagship properties (Mall of America and West Edmonton Mall) which it had used as collateral.

Bond market news site The Bond Buyer reported that investors were fleeing Triple Five bonds, driving their value down to junk status. 'The American Dream is a nightmare,' said one analyst quoted in the story[2].

The horror on the Hudson

Another key development is the Hudson Yards Mall in New York. On 15 March 2019, the new $25 billion neighbourhood of tall glass towers on Manhattan's West Side celebrated its grand opening. Featuring a seven-storey retail mall, as well as stylish restaurants, it had a park, a hotel, a huge climbing structure and two towers of expensive condominiums. It had 18 million square feet of commercial and residential space and was supposed to feature over 100 luxury stores, with 125,000 people planned to live, work or shop there every day. Unfortunately, the onset of COVID-19 turned it into a wasteland. Condominium sales slowed down and the shops and restaurants shut down following the shelter-in-place guidelines triggered by the pandemic. The lack of tourists also removed a large slice of planned demand.

The biggest blow came from Neiman Marcus Group, the anchor tenant in the mall, which had taken a three-level, 188,000-square foot mega-space in the new development. It had opened in 2019 to much fanfare, being the Texas-based luxury retailer's first store in New York City. Unfortunately, Neimans went bankrupt in May 2020 and subsequently decided to close down the store. This was terrible news for the mall because many of the retailers in Hudson Yards had co-tenancy clauses in their lease contracts, which enabled them to renegotiate rents or even exit the mall in the event of an anchor store closing.

When Hudson Yards reopened in September 2020, only 50 of its stores were open and its event space – Hudson Mercantile – had gone bankrupt. Its owner – The Related Companies – only managed to collect 26 per cent of its retail rents in April 2020 and was still at only 50 per cent in August.

With only 10 per cent of the normal number of workers still commuting into Manhattan, law firm Boies Schiller Flexner LLP – a prominent Hudson Yards tenant – announced in October 2020 that it would be quitting its Tri-Level offices in the development.

Although many commentators took the view that Hudson Yards was too big to fail, as it had received $5.6 billion in public subsidies, the ultimate cost of what has come to be called the 'Horror on the Hudson' (as the *Guardian* described it) may be much higher. As Bridget Fisher of the New School for Social Research, who has made an in-depth study of the funding for Hudson Yards, puts it: 'The main point here is that the city took on enormous risks in how they decided to structure their Hudson Yards investment, with taxpayers ultimately footing the bill if and when anything goes wrong'[3].

If these two mega malls are struggling, one can only imagine the plight of lesser shopping centres all across the United States. Apart from the immediate financial impact of the shutdowns on the malls and their retailers, there is also the ongoing Covid-related safety problem implicit in spending long periods in enclosed spaces. Many malls have had to cut capacity in order to provide social distancing and also to mandate the wearing of masks, which seems hardly likely to promote all-day visits.

Can't pay, won't pay

With retailers unable to pay their rents, the income of the mall groups has dwindled substantially. Nearly half of US commercial rents went unpaid in April and May 2020 and even by September, this had only increased to 86 per cent. In addition, many tenants sought to convert their leases to more flexible terms, such as percentage rents. For example, in June 2020, Nordstrom announced to its landlords that it would only pay half of its rent for the balance of 2020. Brands as varied as Gap, Barnes & Noble, H&M and Foot Locker have delayed or cancelled rental payments. In June 2020, Simon Property Group filed a $66 million lawsuit against Gap for failing to pay rent at its stores[4].

The UK

In Britain too, the loss of key stores has had a devastating effect on its high streets. Less wealthy areas, like Shields Road in Newcastle, Walton Road in Liverpool or Tonypandy in Wales, have seen up to a third of their shops closing. Britain does not have as many malls as the United

States, but they are equally in difficulties. Shopping centres such as Broadmarsh in Nottingham, Nicholsons in Maidenhead and Callendar Square in Falkirk, Scotland, have either closed down or lost substantial numbers of stores[5].

There were some indications that enclosed malls were being disproportionately hit even during the brief reopening period in summer 2020. For example, in the UK, shopping centre footfall was over 40 per cent lower annually in July 2020 and was the 'most negatively affected location', according to the British Retail Consortium. Retail parks, by contrast, experienced only a 20 per cent decline, helped by their 'wider open spaces'[6].

China

And, lest one should think that this is purely a problem in the West, large numbers of Chinese malls are also at risk of collapse. China enjoyed a huge property boom from 2005 to 2015, and as many as 4,600 malls were built during this period (over half the new malls in the world). However, the startling rise of e-commerce in the country, led by Alibaba and JD.com, caught the retailers and property developers by surprise, with the result that many areas of China effectively 'missed out' on the organized retail stage of development, going straight from street markets to an internet-dominated society. In consequence, many of the new malls never opened properly: the New South China Mall in Dongguan, for example, lay empty for years, before finally filling up; the Bainaohui Mall in Shanghai was half-empty in 2020, while the e-World Mall in Beijing was forced to close completely[7].

We can see that the COVID-19 crisis has ratcheted up the pressure on mall-owners and high-street landlords already feeling the long-term effect of the decline in retailing. In the next chapter, we will examine the impact of this on the broader financial markets.

CHAPTER EIGHT

Dislocation, Dislocation, Dislocation

As we have seen, the steady decline of the retail sector, in the five years preceding COVID-19, had already had severe consequences for the Real Estate Investment Trusts (REITs) that owned the commercial property in the malls, shopping centres and high streets. Their traditional business model had been to borrow money long-term to finance the building of these edifices, secured against the leases they had signed with their retailers. In many parts of the world, these leases were very long-term (for example, typically five to 10 years in the UK) and thus provided what was seen as a reliable source of future income.

This model worked well for many years until the retailers started to go bankrupt at an alarming rate and used bankruptcy protection measures such as Company Voluntary Arrangements (CVAs) in the UK and Chapter 11 in the US to negotiate exits from their onerous leases. At this point, the REITs started to run into trouble and many of them saw their share prices decline steadily through the period running up to the Coronavirus crisis. In addition, their debt – typically bundled into bonds known as Commercial Mortgage-Backed Securities (CMBS) – also faced steep declines in value. The collective worth of these assets was very considerable. In 2017, the *Economist* suggested that the total amount of capital supporting US retail and retail property, including both equity and debt, was around $ 2.5 trillion[1].

Two wrongs don't make a REIT

The advent of the Coronavirus crisis acted as a second blow to this heavily leveraged and declining commercial property giant. The lockdowns shut down malls and shopping centres for months on end, causing immediate and terrible damage to the incomes of these property groups.

The Dow Jones U.S. Retail REIT Index fell by 33 per cent between February 2020 and January 2021, putting the survival of some of these REITs into question. Indeed, two of the biggest US players went into bankruptcy within 24 hours of each other in early November 2020 – CBL & Associates and Pennsylvania Real Estate Investment Trust (PREIT)[2].

CBL owned a portfolio of B- and C-grade malls and shopping centres like Arbor Place in Douglasville, Georgia, CherryVale Mall in Rockford, Illinois, and CoolSprings Galleria in Franklin, Tennessee, which had suffered disproportionately over the previous few years. The additional strain of Coronavirus delivered the final blow to CBL's survival. For example, traffic at its Ashville Mall in North Carolina had been 30 per cent down year-on-year in September 2020 and it had only been able to collect 27 per cent of its overall rents during the lockdown period[3].

Pennsylvania Real Estate Investment Trust also owned low-grade properties like Magnolia Mall in Florence, South Carolina, Valley View Mall in LaCrosse, Wisconsin, and Viewmont Mall in Scranton, Pennsylvania, all of which were hit hard by the COVID-19 disaster. At their peak, the two groups' shares had been collectively valued at nearly $15 billion, which was all wiped out by the crisis. In addition, their bonds saw sharp falls in value[4].

Other big groups, while not at immediate risk of failure, were nevertheless suffering in 2020. Washington Prime saw its share price drop from around $180.00 at its peak to around $9.00 in January 2021. It owned a similar portfolio of second-grade mall properties like Clay Terrace in Carmel, Indiana, Whitehall Mall in Whitehall, Pennsylvania, and North Ridge Shopping Centre in Raleigh, North Carolina. Its credit rating was cut to junk status by Standard & Poors and a small uptick in the share price in June 2020 evoked the jolly headline 'How High Can a Dead Cat Bounce?' from seekingalpha.com[5].

Simon Property Group – America's largest REIT, with $100 billion of assets and more than 22 million square metres of gross leasable area (GLA) – had also suffered badly from the retail crisis over a number of years. Unfortunately, it decided to double down on its exposure to the troubled sector just before the COVID-19 pandemic hit, by signing a deal to buy its competitor, Taubman Centers, in February 2020, for $52.50 per share in cash – a 50 per cent premium to Taubman's share price[6].

Now, Taubman owned some good-quality malls, like New Jersey's Mall at Short Hills, Florida's Mall at Millenia and California's Beverly Center, but the ink was barely dry on the deal when the lockdown shut down all of Simon's new assets, leaving it on the hook for the $3.6 billion it owed Taubman.

Not surprisingly, it tried to back out of the deal and the case ended up in court in the second half of 2020. As the lawyers of both sides prepared, the atmosphere was not helped by the news that Taubman's net operating income had dropped 31 per cent in its most recent quarter. In the end, the matter was resolved through an 18 per cent cut in the purchase valuation, with the deal finally going through at the end of December. A torrid 2020 left Simon's stock down at 39 per cent of its peak by January 2021[7].

CMBS-over

It was not just the share prices of the REITs that were at risk. As we have seen, the mortgages that they had taken out on their properties were wrapped into commercial mortgage-backed securities (CMBS). The delinquency rate for CMBS spiked from 2 per cent in April 2020 to over 10 per cent in June – the biggest increase since records began. Within this, Retail CMBS delinquencies increased from 4 to 18 per cent[8].

In 2020, there was about $4.6 trillion's worth of commercial mortgages in the US, half of which were housed on the balance sheets of big banks. According to a senior Wall Street banker, reported in *Vanity Fair* in April 2020, about 2,600 CMBS borrowers had contacted banks looking for relief on nearly $500 billion's worth, or 12 per cent, of the total; 30 per cent were retailers.

'That was just in March,' he said. 'This thing is not staying at 12 per cent default, which was higher than we ever saw in the 2008 crisis on commercial mortgage-backed securities. This is going to spike.'

Some of the big Wall Street banks were in worse shape than others: in April 2020 Wells Fargo had around $125 billion of real estate mortgages on its balance sheet, Bank of America had $85 billion and JPMorgan Chase & Co. $65 billion. This is reminiscent of the sub-prime crisis of 2008, when toxic residential mortgages were wrapped into collateralized debt obligations (CDOs) with disastrous consequences. The results this time risk to be the same over the next few years[9].

The UK

The situation was very similar in the UK, where the collapse of hundreds of retailers left property groups very exposed. For example, as we have seen, Britain's largest retail property group intu, which owned 17 shopping centres across the UK, including Lakeside and The Trafford Centre, went bankrupt in June 2020. After the lockdown had taken effect, intu had received only 29 per cent of the rent it was due[10].

Hammerson, which owned the Bullring shopping centre in Birmingham and Brent Cross in London, as well as Bicester Village – the famous factory store centre in Oxfordshire – saw its share price go down to 3 per cent of its peak by January 2021. Ratings agency Fitch downgraded it to negative, indicating a substantial long-term risk of failure. It completed an emergency rights issue for £552 million in September 2020 to keep itself afloat[11].

Unibail-Rodamco-Westfield (URW), owner of Britain's number one mall, Westfield, and a slew of other top-end malls in Europe and the United States, saw the value of its shares drop by over 70 per cent from its peak by mid-January 2021, and its credit rating cut by Moody's. Meanwhile, British Land, owner of Meadowhall and Canada Water, saw its share value drop by 65 per cent from its peak by mid-January 2021, and reported a £1 billion drop in the value of its property portfolio. This collapse in the valuations of the 'big four' retail property groups in the UK speaks volumes about the damage wrought by the retail crisis and Coronavirus on this important part of the commercial property market[12].

Hospitality and office REITs

And was not just the retail REITs that were suffering. With the shutdown of the travel and tourism industry, the hospitality sector was also in severe difficulties.

Park Hotels and Resorts (owner of many Hilton hotels) saw its share price decline 44 per cent from its peak by January 2021. Pebblebrook Hotel Trust, which owned prestigious properties like the Mondrian and Viceroy in Los Angeles and the W Hotel in Boston, similarly saw its share value drop by nearly 60 per cent by the same date. Diamond Rock, owner of L'Auberge in Sedona, The Gwen in Chicago and The Landing Resort and Spa in Lake Tahoe, likewise lost 55 per cent of its value[13].

Another huge part of the commercial property market is in the office space business. One of the side consequences of the lockdown was that most people started working from home and had their business meetings via Zoom or Microsoft Teams. Even once the COVID-19 pandemic ends, it remains questionable whether companies will go back to having large office spaces. According to investment community Seeking Alpha, more than half of American companies are planning to shrink their offices in the wake of COVID-19. For example, Facebook and Google initially told their employees to plan to work from home until 2021, before joining Twitter in going one step further and allowing the majority of its staff to work remotely indefinitely[14].

WeWork, the alternative office space company owned by Soft Bank, was particularly hard hit. Its leasing model was to take spaces long-term and then re-rent them out at higher prices in smaller, more flexible lots to start-ups and early-stage companies. Unfortunately, when the COVID-19 crisis hit, this meant that many of its clients were able to pull out of their leases.

In 2020, WeWork was forced to restructure its operations, reducing employee numbers drastically and pulling out of space obligations where it could – for example, it exited a fifth of its space in Hong Kong. Despite these remedies, rating agency DBRS Morningstar downgraded the company, saying its survival was 'questionable' in light of it having $47 billion in lease obligations. Its valuation dropped from over $47 billion, prior to its aborted IPO in September 2019, to under $3 billion in May 2020. Softbank – the owner of most of WeWork – tried to extract itself from a $3 billion share buyout agreed in late 2019 and was immediately sued by some of the WeWork directors[15].

Some of the largest conventional office REITs in the US have also been badly affected: Boston Properties – the largest, with a 17 per cent share of the office market – saw its stock price drop by over a third from its peak by mid-January 2021; Vornado Realty Trust saw an even bigger drop – about 60 per cent by the same date; and Equity Commonwealth, which has more exposure to smaller cities, has seen its stock more than halve. Troubled Empire State Realty Trust, owner of the Empire State Building, fired its President in June 2020 as its stock slid from a peak of nearly $22.00 (September 2016) to $9.00 (January 2021), amid news that a third of its tenants were demanding rent relief. In addition, there was a lot of extra supply due to come on the office market in 2020. The value of office space under construction in the US in 2018/19 was over $130 billion, far higher than any time in the previous ten years, and all this hit the market just as COVID-19 struck[16].

When we consider the impact of the Coronavirus on these major property markets – retail, hospitality and office – we can see that there is potentially a huge crisis brewing in the whole commercial property sector. This crisis is going to affect many people, through their pension investments. Pension funds have invested heavily in this asset class, due to its apparently safe nature and relatively healthy returns, such that it now forms 10 per cent of the average portfolio, up from 5 per cent in 2000. With the delinquency rate on American commercial mortgage-backed securities (CMBS) rising from 2 per cent in January 2020 to over 10 per cent in August in the same year, commercial property may turn out to be less safe than expected[17].

CHAPTER NINE

To the Victor the Spoils – The Triumph of the Dot-coms

The main beneficiaries of the retail crisis and the COVID-19 lockdowns have been the online companies. Online had been growing its share of the global retail market for many years, driven by the advantages described in Chapter 1 (pages 9–16). As we have seen, the impact of COVID-19 was to increase this share dramatically. To give a feeling of the extent of this shift, consider the change in penetration between 2019 and the early months of 2020.

In February 2020, the UK had 19 per cent of retail sales through e-commerce, but by March 2020, this had risen to 22 per cent; by April, it was 30 per cent and by May, 33 per cent. This kind of increase had previously taken 10 years to achieve![1]

In the US, e-commerce represented about 14 per cent of all US transactions in 2019. After COVID-19 hit, online sales jumped by 49 per cent in April 2020, even as overall retail sales fell by 15 per cent – boosting e-commerce's share to nearly 20 per cent in the second quarter. But even these huge shifts understate the move to e-commerce in specific sectors. For example, in the UK clothing sector, e-commerce grew enormously, representing nearly 50 per cent in May 2020[2].

Marketplaces

The most obvious winner among the internet companies was Amazon, which saw its revenues grow 39 per cent in 2020. It announced that it was hiring 100,000 additional workers and its market capitalization reached nearly $1.59 trillion in January 2021[3].

In the Far East, the giant Alibaba grew revenues by 32 per cent in the six months ending September 2020, while rival JD.com grew net sales of general merchandise by 34 per cent in the second quarter of 2020 and 29 per cent in the third[4].

In the UK, fashion online marketplaces also did very well. Boohoo grew sales by 36 per cent during 2020, on the back of having acquired the online rights to the retail brands Karen Millen, Coast, Oasis, Warehouse, Debenhams, Dorothy Perkins, Wallis and Burton (but not their UK physical stores, all of which were closed down)[5].

ASOS saw sales increase 19 per cent in the financial year ending August 2020, and 23 per cent in the four months-ending December 2020, and acquired the brand rights to Topshop, while prominent German e-tailer Zalando saw an increase in sales of 25 per cent in 2020[6].

Grocery

Even the grocery sector, long a hold-out in e-commerce terms, saw online increase its share of the UK market from 5 per cent in December 2019 to over 11 per cent in May 2020. After a rocky start, where websites crashed due to excessive demand, the huge increase in available delivery slots across the sector meant nearly one in five British households bought over the internet in the month to mid-June, totalling 5.7 million shoppers[7].

Ocado – the online grocer, now part-owned by Marks & Spencer – benefited significantly from increased orders as people were required to stay inside during the lockdowns (and many vulnerable people isolated indefinitely). The retailer was inundated with orders, leading to the introduction of a queuing system on the site: 'We were experiencing four times the demand of our highest-ever peak,' said Duncan Tatton-Brown, Ocado's Chief Financial Officer. Sales grew by 42 per cent over the 12 weeks to mid-June 2020[8].

'Online grocery is experiencing an inflection point,' said Tim Steiner, Ocado's founder and chief executive. 'The current crisis is proving a catalyst for permanent and significant acceleration in channel shift globally, which we believe will redraw the landscape for the grocery industry worldwide. The significant acceleration in online grocery provides us with greater opportunities than ever before'[9].

One of the obstacles facing online grocery was the high cost of delivery in relation to the relatively low margins in the industry. This led the online grocery companies to charge for delivery, which in turn put off consumers. However, as the scale of business grew, especially in lockdown, they were able to operate with full van-loads of deliveries to specific areas, which reduced the delivery cost percentage considerably. Some players started to offer free deliveries – for example, Amazon decided to wrap Amazon Fresh into its Amazon Prime loyalty scheme, which offers free deliveries[10].

Direct-to-Consumer

Apart from the big online platforms mentioned above, there was a huge network of direct-to-consumer brands, focusing on specific product verticals, which did very well during the pandemic. For example, Huel – the meal supplement brand – saw a 43 per cent growth in sales in 2019–20 and reported positive earnings. Online CBD company Equilibria reported growth of 20 per cent month-over-month during 2020. Grounds & Hounds Coffee Co. benefited from 35 per cent growth, while BarkBox pet supplies saw its subscriptions increase by 58 per cent[11].

Turning to service businesses, Peloton, the online gym workout brand offering cycling machines and digital fitness sessions led by super-enthusiastic trainers, grew exponentially during lockdown as gyms closed. The firm's global membership base hit 3.1 million at the end of June 2020, more than double a year earlier, lifting revenue to $607 million – an increase of 172 per cent year-on-year[12].

Online meal delivery services unsurprisingly did very well during the crisis. Deliveroo's estimated sales grew from £476 million in 2018 to nearly £1 billion in 2020, leading it to start planning an Initial Public Offering (IPO) at a valuation of up to £5 billion. Just Eat saw a 46 per cent growth in sales in the third quarter of 2020, while Grubhub reported a 53 per cent increase in revenues in the same period. Additionally, many independent restaurants and cafés set up delivery services during lockdown[13].

In summary, the advent of COVID-19 and the resulting lockdowns acted as a huge windfall for the e-commerce players, effectively forcing hundreds of millions of consumers to go online to meet their daily needs. Online companies are expert at retaining customers through sophisticated relationship management systems, so it is likely much of this shift will be permanent.

CHAPTER TEN

Together Alone

One of the major things that happened during the Coronavirus crisis was the shift to Working From Home (WFH). In the pre-Covid period, there had been a lot of talk about flexible working and virtual meetings, but while most companies paid lip service to this trendy idea, the truth was that inertia kept everyone showing up at the office most days and engaging in a lot of business travel for international meetings and conferences. It was only when this possibility was forcibly cut off from March 2020, that most people were compelled to work from home and communicate at a distance. The development of technologies like video conferencing (Zoom, Google Hangouts, Microsoft Teams, etc.) and cloud-based document sharing (Google Docs, Slack) meant that they were able to do so, and after a few days, companies noticed that they were able to keep going quite well without needing to meet face-to-face.

Even after the government-imposed lockdowns ended worldwide, many companies – starting with the tech industry – opted for continuing to work from home. For example, Jack Dorsey, Chief Executive Officer of Twitter, informed his employees that they could continue to work from home 'forever'. Mark Zuckerberg, Chief Executive Officer of Facebook, followed this with his own announcement that his teams could also continue to work from home indefinitely[1].

Shopify Chief Executive Officer Tobi Lütke tweeted, 'As of today, Shopify is a digital by default company. We will keep our offices closed until 2021 so that we can rework them for this new reality. And after that, most will permanently work remotely. Office centricity is over'[2].

Google, Microsoft, Morgan Stanley, J.P. Morgan, Capital One, Zillow, Slack, Amazon, PayPal, Salesforce and other major companies also extended their work-from-home options[3].

Other companies from outside the tech and banking industries have been moving in the same direction. For example, French automaker Groupe PSA – which makes Peugeot, Citroën, DS, Opel and Vauxhall – announced a 'new era of agility', in which its non-production staff would work remotely. The company's spokesperson said: 'Given the positive experience and efficient measures already taken in the context of the COVID-19 crisis, Groupe PSA has therefore decided to strengthen teleworking and to make it the benchmark for activities not directly related to production.' The company also redesigned its offices to allow for in-person collaboration when needed, but reduced office costs by moving over 1,000 employees out of its central Paris location to a smaller one outside the city[4].

This sense of caution about returning to work seems to be supported by most employees. A May 2020 Gallup poll revealed that: 'Now that some of these employees may be able to return to their workplace, it appears only a quarter are emotionally ready. A quarter are reluctant to return specifically because of concerns about contracting COVID-19, while half have a personal preference for working remotely'[5].

Kate Lister, President of Global Workplace Analytics, said, 'Seventy-seven percent of the workforce say they want to continue to work from home, at least weekly, when the pandemic is over.' She estimates, 'Twenty-five to thirty percent of the workforce will be working-from-home multiple days a week by the end of 2021'[6].

Positives

Once one removes the need for the daily commute to work, almost everything changes. People do not need to live in big cities anymore: in the short term, they may be stuck where they are, but in the long term, they will be able to move to cheaper, leafier places. Many already choose to live in dormitory towns outside major cities and make the daily commute into town in order to have a lower cost of living. Imagine how far away they might opt to live if they were only coming into town once or twice a fortnight. This change would have side benefits in a number of areas. For example, there is the potential advantage to the environment as fewer people commute to work and travel for business meetings. This is more fully explored in Chapter 11 (pages 75–78).

We may also get a more balanced economy. Facebook co-founder Mark Zuckerberg pitched this idea when he said: 'When you limit hiring to people who live in a small number of big cities, or who are willing to move there, that cuts out a lot of people who live in different communities, have different backgrounds, have different perspectives'[6].

Negatives

On the other hand, there may be other effects that are less palatable, especially in the short term. There have already been signs of a collapse in residential rentals in city centres. New leases plunged 71 per cent in Manhattan in April 2020 and a survey indicated that nearly three quarters of New York's technology and finance employees would like to move out of the city if they could[7].

In London, average rents in March 2020 dropped by 0.5 per cent compared with a year earlier, the steepest drop since at least 2014 when the monthly data was first collected. For reference, February had seen growth of 1.5 per cent[8].

Leading UK office property companies with high exposure to London saw a collapse in their valuations. Capital & Counties Properties' share price dropped 69 per cent from its peak by January 2021, while Land Securities Group saw a decrease of nearly three quarters in its valuation and had its credit rating cut to negative by Fitch[9].

Along with the daily commute into town come a lot of other activities: buying the daily Starbucks on the way to work; having lunch in city centre restaurants; popping into a department store to pick out a new outfit or enjoying drinks in the pub and eating out after work. As these daily visits reduce, all these ancillary activities start to drop away. Instead, people are working from home, living in comfy T-shirts and jog pants, eating in, shopping locally or on the net, staying up to date with school friends from their areas rather than moving on to new friends in the big city and socializing online. The result is a steep drop in economic activity – particularly retail-related – in major cities. For example, economists at law firm Irwin Mitchell and the Centre for Economics & Business Research estimated that London businesses were losing £575 million a day at the height of the first lockdown and the total cost to London's economy from the start of the pandemic to the end of August 2020 was in the region of £66.9 billion in lost GDP. Included in these costs were £3.5 billion of lost fare revenue at Transport for London, £1.4 billion in lost Council Tax for London councils and nearly £0.5 billion lost tax revenues for the Greater London Authority[10].

In the US, cities like New York have suffered correspondingly. Unemployment in the city reached 16 per cent in September 2020, double the national average. Only a third of the city's hotel rooms were occupied. Shootings were on the rise; New Yorkers were fleeing for the suburbs; businesses were pulling out of office spaces – all symptoms reminiscent of those which preceded the city's previous fiscal collapse in 1975.

'We're on the verge of a tragedy,' said Richard Ravitch, the former state official who helped put together the rescue of New York City's finances in the 1970s, in September 2020. He believes that this time will be worse, saying, 'I don't know what's going to happen to the city'[11].

Thus, as we can see, the shift in people's habits caused by COVID-19 and working from home would seem remorselessly to point towards a secular drop in consumption in city centres. Without being compelled to walk past all the panoply of temptation that is the modern city – frappuccinos, organic burgers, happy hours, new movies and special fashion offers – people may not find themselves buying these things as often.

As people move out of town, it has profound implications for the balance of the economy. Residential property prices drop in the cities and rise in the surrounding areas. Shops, cafés, bars and restaurants in the centres find that demand has drained away, while local village stores and organic farm shops are doing well. Socializing may go back to something closer to the 1950s model, where more people went to local get-togethers at sports clubs, community centres and the like rather than the recent tendency for people to congregate in large towns and cities. Above all, people are spending less, enjoying a simpler, less stressful life: good for individuals personally, potentially terrible for the economy.

CHAPTER ELEVEN

Generation 'C'

Time Magazine describes the story of a young student named Clavey Robertson, who, in March 2020, took a study break and walked up onto the roof of his dorm at Berkeley, California. He had been writing his senior thesis on the thinning out of the social safety net since the Great Depression and needed some air. From his vantage point, Robertson could see out in San Francisco Bay the vague outline of a ship: it was the *Diamond Princess* cruise ship, carrying people infected with COVID-19 to the United States.

Two months later, the end of Robertson's degree course was cut short. He decided not to bother with logging onto his online graduation event and was back home living with his parents. Coincidentally, they had lost their jobs in the travel market and all the job leads he was pursuing had gone cold: 'No longer am I just a student writing about the Great Depression,' he said. 'Now there is a depression'[1].

This story illustrates very well the disaster facing young adults at this time. The generation that is coming of age at the time of the Coronavirus is going to be scarred and shaped by this traumatic experience, just as the previous generation (Millennials) were impacted by the Global Financial Crisis a decade earlier

As we saw earlier in Chapter 1, pages 9–16, young people had already been under pressure from changes in wealth distribution prior to the outbreak. We looked at how the credit bubble had put most types of assets, including property and financial instruments, beyond their reach, and how as a result, 85 per cent of wealth in both the UK and the US belonged to people over the age of 45, leaving only a paltry 15 per cent for the young. We also saw how they were forced to live with high student debt and the 'gig economy', making it hard for them to get onto the ladder of life and thus staying at home longer and delaying marriage and child-raising.

This generation was already disaffected. Only 8 per cent of Americans between 18 and 29 believe the US government to be working as it should be and fewer than 1 in 5 consider themselves 'very patriotic', according to the 2020 Harvard Kennedy School Institute of Politics survey of young Americans[2].

Suspended animation

All of this is going to pale by comparison with the crisis facing young people in the aftermath of Coronavirus. For one thing, as we have seen, the global economic recession is far worse than 2008 – an estimated drop of 3.5 per cent in world GDP, as opposed to being flat. For another thing, having paid exorbitant fees for their college degrees, they are not getting the same standard of education with online lectures, nor enjoying the social life they expected[3].

Many of them have not even been able to complete their educations or graduate properly. In the UK, the government shut all secondary schools and universities from 20 March 2020 and did not reopen them until September. As a result, all of the students who were due to take degrees and A-levels lost part of their education and saw their exams cancelled and replaced with calculated grades, based on a range of evidence, including non-exam coursework assessments and mock exam results[4].

It was the same situation in the US, where most states closed down high schools and colleges from around the middle of March 2020. They too have had to live with 'ersatz' passing-out qualifications. Employers are already questioning how far they will be able to have confidence in their grades[5].

Above all, young people are debauching onto a difficult job market. 'I'm not sure they've fully processed what 25 per cent unemployment, disproportionately affecting younger Americans, will actually mean,' says John Della Volpe, Director of Polling at the Harvard Kennedy School Institute of Politics. 'There almost are no opportunities in any sector. It's like suspended animation'[6].

Don't call us ...

To make things worse, young people could not even go out to look for jobs as many of them were self-isolating due to the virus. The class of 2020 was essentially frozen in place by a pandemic that trapped the nation inside their homes.

In the US, some 30 per cent of college seniors had their summer internship offers rescinded entirely, according to a survey of over 1,000 college students conducted by Handshake, a job-search site. The overall number of postings on the online jobs platform ZipRecruiter fell by nearly half from mid-February to mid-July 2020, while new postings for entry-level positions plummeted more than 75 per cent, according to ZipRecruiter labour economist Julia Pollak[7].

In the UK, it was a similar picture – youth unemployment grew from 10 per cent in early 2020 to 20 per cent in September, and might top one million once the furlough scheme ended, according to a report from the Resolution Foundation[8].

Justine Tanomjit, a commercial law student at Aberystwyth University, was looking forward to trying out for a job as an insurance broker that would have begun in June 2020. Two weeks later, she got a call saying the interview was cancelled. 'I feel so sad and frustrated,' she said. 'I'd been nervous about leaving uni and getting an interview was really exciting'[9].

Lia Campbell, a 22-year-old film and television student from Newtownards, Northern Ireland, had job opportunities lined up on productions in Dublin and Belfast for when she graduated, but all of them postponed filming due to COVID-19. 'This was the right place, the right time,' she lamented, and now a month away from being able to go out and avail of those opportunities, it's suddenly all been taken away'[10].

Elise Lauriot-Prévost, from Lyon, France, finished her master's degree in June 2020. After sending 50 job applications, she received little encouragement. 'You are getting the responses, "Thanks for applying, however, because of Coronavirus, we are suspending our job hunting and we will let you know when things have moved on", but none of us know when that will be,' she said. 'At this point I [wonder] what field I can even work in. I do not even have anything to do to hold me over until a job in my field, which is very competitive, opens up again. I cannot do babysitting, I cannot do all the jobs that I usually do, which I have done during school, to be able to earn money'[11].

Businesses such as retail, restaurants and hotels have always been big employers of young people and as we have seen, they have all been very badly affected. In April 2020 alone, the American leisure and hospitality industry lost 47 per cent of its total workforce, with 7.7 million workers newly unemployed, according to the Bureau of Labor Statistics[12].

Implications for retailers and brands

What are the implications of this situation for brands and retailers? At a superficial level, it is not good news. As we have seen, historically, young people have been the most important demographic for many parts of the brand/retail industry, particularly in areas like clothing, beauty and home products. The fact that their spending power has been depressed by the COVID-19 outbreak, and is likely to remain so in the medium term due to the resultant recession, points to uneven levels of consumption over the next few years. However, while this might not be good news for brands and retailers at the macro level, this generation has specific needs and concerns that make it a unique group, and companies who can address these requirements with skill and sensitivity have the opportunity to succeed, despite the overall situation. We will explore how they can do this in Part 2 of this book.

CHAPTER TWELVE

Fish Swimming in the Venice Canals

As the lockdown spread across the world, one of the biggest changes was to the environment. As the factories shut down, flights were cancelled and commuting stopped, the earth seemed to take a breath.

In China, the world's biggest source of carbon, emissions were down about 18 per cent between early February and mid-March 2020 – a cut of 250 million tonnes. Europe saw a reduction of around 390 million tonnes. Significant falls were also experienced in the US, where passenger vehicle traffic – its major source of CO_2 – fell by nearly 40 per cent. Compared with the same period in 2019, levels of nitrogen dioxide also fell by 40 per cent[1].

Fish were observed swimming in the Venice canals; coyotes were seen on the Golden Gate Bridge in California; deer grazed in the gardens of Washington homes a few miles from the White House. In April 2020, 6,000 fewer children in Europe developed asthma compared with a year earlier, according to the Centre for Research on Energy and Clean Air. There was something quite beautiful and life-affirming about how quickly nature bounced back as soon as the human race took its foot off the accelerator[2].

For the French philosopher Bruno Latour, the experience of COVID-19 taught us a valuable lesson – that it is possible, in a short period, to apply the brakes to the global economy, which would have been seen previously as impossible: 'The incredible discovery is that there was in fact in the world economic system, hidden from all eyes, a bright red alarm signal, next to a large steel lever that each head of state could pull at once to stop "the progress train" with a shrill screech of the brakes,' he said in the *Guardian* in April 2020[3].

It is likely that this experience of the world's leaders being actually prepared to pause the world economy to stop a short-term virus will lead people (particularly young people) to demand a similar effort to stop a long-term environmental threat.

During the Coronavirus crisis, there was a marked increase in consumer demand for sustainable products and a higher level of interest in the idea of the circular economy. Recycling of clothing through second-hand stores and websites increased dramatically, and there was a growing distaste for the fast fashion industry, with its wasteful approach to clothing production and consumption[4].

Fashion recycling websites saw a huge increase in demand. Leading second-hand clothing company, thredUP, saw a 31 per cent increase in shoppers in May 2020 and launched an Initial Public Offering in March 2021. London-based rival Depop saw a 300 per cent increase in items sold during lockdown. StockX, which sells second-hand sneakers online, saw very strong sales during the same period. Excluding promotions and holidays, it recorded 18 of its top 20 sales days in the second quarter of 2020[5].

Dying of consumption

The rampant individualism and consumerism that dominated the 1990s and early 2000s was already coming under pressure in the period leading up to the outbreak of the Coronavirus. Younger people (younger Millennials and Gen Z) were questioning these values for reasons we have already discussed – the rampant inequality of society, the crash of 2008 and the growing environmental concerns. COVID-19 may have put the final nail in the coffin of the go-go consumerist economy of the last 20 years. Given that millions of people have died around the world and bankruptcy and mass unemployment are daily news stories, who wants to be seen consuming frivolous luxury products sold at excessive prices?

'The supply chain is broken, the fashion calendar is no longer in place, and who wants to be out buying designer brands with all the social questions we're asking ourselves right now?' said Thomai Serdari, who teaches luxury branding and marketing at New York University's Stern School of Business. 'There's too much happening at the same time. We have to rethink this industry'[6].

There is a feeling that we may have reached a limiting point for materialism. Many people feel that the earth is literally dying from the consequences of excess consumption. As Steve Howard, Chief Sustainability Officer at Ikea, put it: 'If we look on a global basis, in the West we have probably hit peak stuff. We talk about peak oil. I'd say we've hit peak red meat, peak sugar, peak stuff … peak home furnishings'[7].

As we shall see in Part Two, this shift in priorities will have profound implications for the brand and retail industries going forward.

CHAPTER THIRTEEN

Summary – A 'Reset' Moment for Retail

When one puts together all of the above impacts and trends, one can see that retailers and brands face very significant challenges:

- Firstly, we have the short-term impact of the virus and related lockdowns. Never before, even during wartime, has the global economy been simultaneously shut down. This alone has delivered a severe (and, for many retailers, mortal) blow.
- Then we have the likely nature of the medium-term recovery – the stuttering process of opening up, followed by further waves affecting key regions or whole countries. Given that the virus was still spreading on a global level, and reaching desperate stages in the poorer parts of the world at the time of writing, it seems unlikely that international travel or trade will be able to operate anywhere near normally during this period.
- And finally, even after the worst of Coronavirus, we will still have the long-term effects of COVID-19 – the heavy unemployment and depressed spending power in some sectors, and the shortages and inflation in others. To say nothing of the sky-high levels of government debt and years of austerity and potential tax hikes needed to pay it off. For some affected by the virus their health will never be the same again.

It does not take much imagination to see what all this might mean for retailers, brands and commercial property owners, especially as the global economy was already vulnerable at the point the virus struck. A huge chunk of the incumbent retail industry is simply going to disappear. We will see a stream of bankruptcies, wave after wave of store closures and some shotgun mergers as former rivals are forced to consolidate their costs. Restaurants and hotels will face even bigger problems as it is difficult to see them getting back to anywhere near normal until after the Coronavirus threat has receded. And as retail 'doors' close for ever, it is going to put increased pressure on brands as they see their routes to market narrowing sharply. Again, we will see some closures and mergers as brand owners seek to consolidate their cost bases.

Commercial property, long seen as a safe haven for funds, is going to become very risky for a period. As retailers play hardball over rent, using the threat of bankruptcy to escape burdensome leases, then the heavily indebted REITs will struggle. As they, in turn, pass the parcel of insolvency onto the banks, we may even see some financial institutions getting into trouble, and needing to be bailed out by governments, as occurred in 2008. All in all, it would be difficult to imagine a more perfect storm for the key players in the consumer markets.

Necessity is the mother of invention

And yet the very scale of the crisis is spurring new creativity. From the wreckage of the old order, we are already seeing some phoenixes arising. There are new business models appearing from innovative start-ups and there are even signs of some established companies turning to radical new solutions.

The positive from this crisis, if there is one, is that it has finally blown away the cobwebs from the old order. The brand, retail and commercial property industries have been under notice of change since Jeff Bezos put up the handwritten 'Amazon.com' sign on the wall of his garage in 1997. Yet the industry was guilty of terrible complacency and stuck to its cherished beliefs, cultures and ways of doing things, even as the ground started to move underneath it from 2015 onwards. An older generation of merchant princes, who thought they had the formula, dug their heels in and closed their minds to change. And those who sought to warn against the incoming changes were often derided as Cassandras – false prophets of doom – and self-publicists, who sought to exaggerate the 'Retail Apocalypse' for their own ends.

The good thing about the post-Covid world is that no one can say that anymore: the apocalypse has actually happened and it was real. But at least the ground is cleared and the green shoots of radical new thinking can finally push their way into the light of a new dawn. The scale of the disaster has created a 'reset' moment for the industry. In doing so, it has set the stage for the coming Retail Recovery, which will enable the new brand and retail industries to thrive in the long term.

In the next section, Part Two, we will look at the key themes which will drive this recovery, and then in Part Three we will turn to review some in-depth case studies to see how the pioneers among retailers, brands and shopping centres are creating a bright new future out of the ashes of the past.

PART TWO

Retail Recovery

CHAPTER FOURTEEN

Embracing the Omniverse

We will start this section by taking an overview of how the COVID-19 crisis has finally shifted the way in which retailers and brands see the world. As stated at the end of the previous section, if there is one good thing to come out of the disaster it is that it has finally forced a complete shift in the industry's thinking. To understand the degree of this change, one needs to understand that the leadership of the retail industry grew up in a supply chain that was dominated by producers – manufacturers, brands and retailers – who collectively pushed product at relatively passive consumers. Consumers needed stores in order to get access to products.

When the internet came along in the late 1990s, it created an alternative route for consumers to buy products, posing a threat to the retailers' dominance. They responded by opening their own websites, but failed to understand the potential of the new channel and continued to focus on their stores as the primary way of transacting. As e-commerce grew – driven by the advantages discussed in Chapter 1 (pages 9–16) – and remained dominated by pure-play digital companies, it began to inflict severe damage on the retail industry. At this point, one might have thought that the writing would have been on the wall and that the major retailers would have shifted their attitudes. However, it took the COVID-19 crisis to really shake the industry out of its deep-set complacency. The government-mandated closure of their stores – something that had not occurred even during wars, revolutions and other upheavals – finally turned off this distribution route completely. And, in the echoing silence of their empty stores, there finally came a kind of epiphany: the realization that the world no longer needed stores to survive and that, in future, they would have to make people actually 'want' to visit them.

The key thing to understand about this reset is that it is not just a change in thinking about e-commerce, it is much more fundamental than that. After all, the retailers had had websites for 20 years and it failed to change much about their fundamental mind-set.

Six key themes

The real reset has gone much deeper and encompasses six key themes, all of which are linked:

1) The shift from a push system, based on producer dominance, oligopolistic competition, limited supply and restricted access, to a pull system driven by consumer dominance, near-perfect competition, perfect knowledge and ubiquitous access to goods.

2) The change from mass marketing, based on a few research and segmentation studies, to personalized marketing, based on individual customer data.

3) The realization that the e-commerce revolution and the communications revolution (social media, user reviews, influencers, etc.) has broken the traditional supply chain, with its multiple players – manufacturers, branded wholesalers and retailers – all supping from the margin cup and adding their mark-ups to prices, and replaced it with a shorter and more direct route to market.

4) The realization that the stores channel was not the only, or even best, way of moving goods from factories to consumers. Indeed, that it was inferior to the e-commerce channel in many respects as a pure goods-transmission mechanism.

5) That putting the consumer at the heart of the business model required seeing the different channels as the consumer saw them – not competing, but complementary to each other.

6) That based on this, the traditional model of the store, as a 'warehouse' piled high with stock and with just a narrow fringe of branding and customer service on top, was obsolete and that only a ruthless attention to the remaining added value of physical stores could ensure their continued relevance and survival.

In the rest of Part Two, we will explore these themes, as we attempt to describe the Retail Recovery in detail and to create a road map for the future.

CHAPTER FIFTEEN

Push Me, Pull You

As we have seen in Chapter 1 (pages 9–16), the last 20 years have witnessed a profound revolution in the relationship between producers and consumers. I would like to illustrate this change by means of a personal story.

When I started my job as a marketing manager in the headquarters of a branded manufacturer in 1988, the first thing that the senior managers in the business impressed on me was the need not to mess up the smooth working of the factories. The factories liked to keep things simple. They wanted to set up their production and run it for as long as possible before making any changes. This minimized their costs and enabled the company to make money. The senior executives warned against what they called 'marketing madness', which they defined as launching a lot of new products that did not really add much to sales, but would definitely complicate the work of the factories.

One of my mentors was a great admirer of Procter & Gamble. Although it was known as a marketing company, he told me, its logic was actually driven by production. To minimize production costs, it needed mass manufacturing. For mass manufacturing, it needed mass consumption. And to drive mass consumption, it needed mass advertising.

I soon realized that I would have to be pretty sure of two things: firstly, that any new product I launched would have to appeal to new consumers that we did not already cover through our existing range; and, secondly, that there would have to be a substantial number of said consumers, such that it added materially to sales rather than cannibalizing our existing products. So, I did what many brands did: I conducted consumer research to try to find out if there were different groups of customers with different needs – a practice known as 'segmentation'. The logic was that if I could divide the market into segments, I could figure out an area that we did not serve and launch a new product into that gap.

I seem to recall that we identified three segments in the market and proceeded to develop products for each. The key point was that the logic of this whole process was driven by the factories. At no point would it have been considered desirable to try to understand customers at a personal level. Nor would there have been any point – our factories were not flexible enough to make shorter runs of products, anyway.

In those days, we had very little knowledge of our individual customers. We had a salesforce, which sold to department stores and other retailers. We never really had any direct contact with customers, apart from a few bits of research. Funnily enough, neither did our customers, the retailers. Despite the fact that their staff were meeting clients every day, they did not collect very much personal information about them, except in so far as they were able to enrol them in store card schemes. For us, the name of the game was to 'sell in' as much product as we could to the retailers and then rely on mass advertising to 'sell it through'.

As I moved on to creating the advertising, the same logic applied to that as to the development of the products themselves. What I was aiming to do was to find out what emotional buttons I had to press with the particular segment we were targeting and then get a clever advertising agency to push them as hard as possible.

From producer control ...

The key point is that we – the producers – were in control of the process. We learned only the minimum amount necessary about our consumers to manipulate them into buying. The brand image was constructed very carefully to reflect the desires and aspirations of those consumers. We tried to create as perfect an image as possible of what we thought these people wanted to be like. It was a tightly controlled process and woe betide any junior brand manager who departed from the carefully prepared script. And, on the whole, it worked pretty well. We ran the advertising, people showed up in store and walked away with the product. The stores were happy with the uptake and placed repeat orders.

The atmosphere in the industry was quite cosy. There were around six big brands and probably 10 major retailers. We all knew each other and used to socialize together at exhibitions and industry charity events.

The market seemed competitive at the time, but it was a race between a few runners. The high cost of setting up factories, brands and shops kept out new players and the roster of brands and retailers had remained relatively unchanged for the previous 20 or 30 years.

The other thing that struck me, when I first arrived in the job, was the way that costs built up in the supply chain. I recall trying to upgrade some minor component in one of our products and was told fairly sharply that it would involve an unacceptable loss of margin. It only cost 50p more, but by the time we added our 300 per cent mark-up, it would add £1.50 onto the wholesale price; and by the time the retailers had put *their* 300 per cent mark-up on that, it would be an extra £4.50 on the price in the store. The sales director told me in no uncertain terms what I could do with my component.

What impressed me at the time was that it was not the item itself that was expensive, but all the people and related costs that were needed to get the product from the factory gate to the consumer's hands. Nobody seemed to worry that it cost so much. The consumers did not know how little it cost to manufacture and we were not about to tell them. The high barriers to entry kept out intruders who might disrupt the pricing or margins in the industry and the reality was that for most consumers, their choice of products was limited to a few stores near where they lived.

Most of the information that they got on the product came from us – the producers – through our advertising, PR or packaging, or from the retail staff. Consumers were nervous about departing from tried and tested brands and new players had to get past the hurdle of the retailers, who tended to be risk-averse in their brand selections.

… To consumer power

Contrast that situation with what we see all around us now. As I sit here, I have just put the name of my category into the search box of Google and it has come back with 506,000,000 listings. I search for my old brand, which used to be number one in the UK. I cannot find it and give up after the first 10 pages.

That cosy little world I have described has been blown away by a fundamental shift in the relationship between supply and demand, between producers and consumers. Mobile e-commerce has literally put a whole world of products into people's hands. I go on AliExpress – the consumer arm of Alibaba – and they are offering over 4,000,000 options of my old product, straight from the Chinese factories to my door. And obviously no one told them about the cost of that 50p component, because they are offering whole products for less than $4.00. But will this product be any good? I ask myself. A quick check at the bottom of the page indicates that it has received a score of 4.6 out of 5 from over 8,000 reviewers. I check the brand name on Facebook and it has hundreds of thousands of followers so, it seems like it is probably alright …

I go to another website, which leads with a questionnaire: if I fill it in, it offers to make customized products, individually tailored to my needs. What about the factories, I ask, won't this mess up their nice clean schedules? Nobody seems to worry about that anymore – the factories are all computerized now so they can switch products at the drop of a hat.

I visit a news site. Already word seems to have got around that I am in the market for this product category and I am immediately served up scores of relevant adverts.

I buy another product online and it arrives broken. I complain, but get no change from the website, so I post my complaint on their Instagram feed in rather trenchant language. Within hours, someone is on the phone offering me a refund and a free gift.

I feel powerful ...

And that is because, as a consumer, I *am* powerful. The boot has moved from my producer foot to my consumer foot.

The three revolutions

When I re-read this story, I am struck by how radically things have changed. We are not talking about one revolution, but in reality, three:

1) The e-commerce revolution, which has usurped retail's role as the most efficient system for distributing goods.
2) The communications revolution, which has replaced brand reputations created through advertising, with ones based on peer review and influencer opinion, and also handed the consumer perfect knowledge about products.
3) A manufacturing revolution, which has massively increased the flexibility of production. Together, they have upended the entire brand/retail supply chain and changed all the rules. And COVID-19 has just accelerated that whole process by 10 years.

It is clearly not enough for retailers to see the solution to their problems as being about investing more in their websites. It is much more profound than that: it has to do with accepting the consumer's awesome power and putting them at the heart of the business.

CHAPTER SIXTEEN

Beyond the Transaction

The key philosophical reset that is needed is to see the world through the customer's eyes. Today's customers understand instinctively the power that they now enjoy over producers. They know that they have an endless choice of goods and that it is usually possible to find these goods at a cheaper price if they look for them online. So why would they continue to buy from established brands or retailers?

The answer is that although most retailers think in terms of selling 'goods', customers look at their needs in terms of an end-result which may go well beyond just the 'goods' themselves.

Goods and services

It is interesting to note that in most retail sectors, there are 'goods' businesses and then there are equivalent 'service' businesses. For example:

- In the beauty sector, we have beauty stores and then we have beauty salons;
- In toys, we have toyshops and then play centres;
- In consumer electronics, we have electrical stores and then electrical handymen;
- In the medical sector, we have pharmacies and then we have medical clinics;
- In clothing and accessories, there are fashion stores and then there are styling consultants;

- In home goods, we have furniture stores and then we have interior designers;
- In gardening, we have garden stores and then we have gardeners/ landscape architects;
- In active wear, we have sports shops and then we have sports centres, gyms and personal trainers;
- In the book sector, we have bookstores and then we have book clubs and libraries;
- In the food industry, we have grocery stores and then we have cafés, restaurants and food delivery services;
- In the auto sector, we have auto parts stores and then car repair services;
- In the drinks sector, we have off-licences and then bars or pubs.

In most cases, the service providers charge higher prices than the goods providers. The fact that they are able to do this indicates that consumers are prepared to pay more for the services than for the goods alone.

Consumers' real needs

Why is this? Well, the answer is that the consumer's real need is not 'goods' as such, but the solution of a problem or the enhancement of a positive factor in their lives. Thus, when we go to the sports store, we are actually seeking 'fitness'; when we visit the pharmacy, we are actually searching for 'health'; when we go to the toy store, we are actually craving 'happiness-for-our-children' (and possibly some peace and quiet for ourselves). Similarly, when we go to the beauty store, we are really searching for 'attractiveness'; when we buy beer from the supermarket, we are actually seeking 'relaxation' or 'conviviality'; when we buy a cable for our television, we are looking for 'entertainment' or 'distraction'.

In addition, the process of buying from a brand can create benefits beyond meeting even these broader need states. How does the way in which this brand interacts with us make us feel? Does it treat us as individuals? Does it give us the courtesy of time? Does it seem to 'care' about us? Does it listen to our feedback?

I recently moved to a new house and installed a new broadband and television service. My previous provider had been a real problem to deal with and had frustrated me enormously, to the extent that I was driven to post some sharply worded comments on their social media feed. I warned potential customers against using them and was gratified to see that lots of other people had said the same thing.

So, I decided to change provider. When I called them, they amazed me by actually answering the telephone. I was further impressed that they spent around 45 minutes sorting out my problem. They apologized for the length of time, explaining that their systems were not working very well (it was during lockdown and they were working from home). The woman told me: 'I am not going to let you go until I am certain that your order has gone through, because you really don't want to have to do all this again, do you?'

Although I was busy, I was very grateful for this approach. I actually felt like she cared about me. In fact, the company's technology was not quite as good as the previous people's, but I was so impressed with their attitude that I posted glowing reviews about them on my social media.

The key thing is that the interaction made me feel, for a brief moment, that the universe might not be so unfeeling after all. The way they interacted with me created added value, over and above the product.

A higher purpose

Another area which affects how people feel about a brand is whether its values appear to match theirs and whether they feel that it is a force for good in the world. As we have said, the traditional focus of the brand/ retail industry was typically all about transacting – in other words, moving volumes of goods through the supply chain. There was a sense that a brand should provide decent quality, fair prices and reasonable service, but not a lot of time was spent on airy concepts like 'higher purpose'. This was fine, so long as we were dealing in a situation where there was a shortage of available goods and consumers were glad to be able to own them in decent quantities. However, it is not adequate for a situation of oversupply and massive availability.

As we have seen, if retailers and brands want to fight it out on the basis of the goods transaction alone, they will be fighting a losing battle. Where goods are a commodity, it is critical to have a brand story to tell, which is about more than just selling things. This is particularly true for younger consumers, who are growing up with higher levels of education and idealism than ever before.

Many of the most successful 'disruptor' brands that have sprung up in the last 10 years – like Warby Parker in eyewear, Allbirds in footwear and SF Bay Coffee in beverages – have been clear about placing a higher purpose at the heart of what they are doing. These brands have been adopted with enthusiasm by younger consumers and have been propelled to success through their active endorsement, especially on social media. We will deal with this subject in more depth in Chapter 20, but for now, suffice it to say that having a higher purpose can be an effective way to distinguish brands from the mass of competitors fighting it out on the basis of price[1].

Summary

So, in summary, if retailers and brands can lift their eyes for a moment from their obsession with the goods transaction, they will see three things:

1) That their customers have need states which go well beyond the pure goods that they are selling.
2) That the way in which they interact with their customers can elicit emotional responses ranging from powerful dislike to affection and loyalty.

3) That having a higher purpose can create a compelling reason for consumers to buy from them and spread the good news about them.

If brands and retailers can see the world through their customers' eyes and meet their broader needs, while at the same time creating a warm relationship with them, then they can lift their offer out of the morass of pure 'goods' competition, which, as we have seen, is not a battleground that is favourable to them. Over the next few chapters, we will look at how creative retailers and brands are doing this and how it is powering them through the current crisis.

CHAPTER SEVENTEEN

'Servicizing' a Goods Business

In the last chapter, we looked at how customers' need states can stretch well beyond the actual goods that they are buying. Some of the most successful retailers today have already made the breakthrough of understanding this point and have turned what were basic 'goods' businesses into service-providers which meet customers' broader needs.

An innovative example of a large business doing this comes from CVS Health – the leading American drugstore group. They have understood the key point that when their customers walk in through the door to buy medicines and medical equipment, they are actually looking to improve their health. And they have also understood that healthcare in the US is very complex and costly for many families. This breakthrough has led them to create a new format called 'HealthHUB', which aims to offer an end-to-end solution to customers' basic health needs. This includes offering blood tests, diabetes monitoring, immunization, dietary and weight loss advice, dealing with sleep apnoea and helping with mobility issues. Customers are looked after by expert 'Care Concierges', who take the time to learn the health needs of the person and their family, and also help sort out insurance issues[1].

As a result of switching their approach from selling goods to understanding customer needs, the company has substantially changed its product range, adding new durable medical equipment, supplies and various new product and service combinations. The fact that many of the services are free and the accompanying products are all available in the same place makes it much cheaper and more convenient than going to conventional clinics and then having to pick up products from a separate pharmacy.

The fact that the Care Concierge gets to know the whole family means that the initial single customer contact actually becomes a broader relationship. For example, a woman comes in to buy her diabetes medicine, but in the course of the consultation shares that her father is in need of treatment for the rheumatism in his knee. The Care Concierge invites her to bring him next time and sorts out a suitable knee-brace for him. The format takes up around 20 per cent of the store space, so, to make room, CVS has reduced the stocks of commodity items like snacks, which are now sold through iPads connected to the CVS website and shipped direct to the home. They have changed the balance of their product range in the test stores, stocking a broader selection of more serious medical accessories[2].

Alan Lotvin, MD, Chief Transformation Officer for CVS Health, said: 'Our HealthHUBs are generating a tremendously positive customer response. The opportunity to engage with a team of in-store and remote colleagues, including pharmacists, nurse practitioners, care managers and support staff, resonates with consumers. We're thrilled to be creating this seamless, long overdue experience that consumers want'[3].

The experiment has obviously been very successful. The HealthHUB stores have performed favourably against a control group of stores, with a 15 per cent increase in visits associated with chronic services. This success has led the company to announce that it is rolling the concept out to 1,500 stores by 2021. And CVS's third-quarter 2020 results showed a solid increase in revenues of 3.5 per cent, despite the pandemic[4].

Groupe Fnac Darty is another company which has long defined the consumer need as being more than just buying goods. The well-known French electronics group have been marketing what they call the 'Contrat de Confiance' for the past 40 years. This is based on three promises: guaranteed low prices, choice of equipment and, most importantly, quality service – seven days a week. Over the last few decades, the brand has built up the reputation of always being there for its customers, particularly in terms of repairing broken equipment quickly in the home. The resulting customer trust seems to have helped the company through the recent crisis: it enjoyed revenue growth of 7.3 per cent in the third quarter of 2020[5].

Another company that is 'servicizing' a former goods business in the consumer electronics space is Best Buy, which is covered in some depth in the case study in Chapter 38 (*see also* pages 219–222).

CHAPTER EIGHTEEN

Feelings

The other area discussed in the previous chapter is how the interaction with the brand makes customers feel. As we have seen, this is a combination of the following:

- Care: Whether it seems to care about them – for example, by going the extra mile to make sure they are happy or giving sufficient time to the customer;
- Individual recognition: Whether the brand makes people feel that it treats them as individuals rather than as part of the herd;
- Involvement: Whether it involves them in the life of the brand and listens to their feedback;
- Community: Whether the brand makes them feel part of a community.

Care

Most businesses would say that they care about their customers. However, making it happen across millions of transactions and thousands of team members is not easy in practice. Companies are afraid of being taken advantage of and usually create strict rules about things like returns and exchanges. IT systems are typically inflexible – witness the frustration of dealing with automated telephone systems. Retail work is tough, hours long and pay low, so it is hard for staff to show enthusiasm at all times. To truly care for customers requires a more flexible approach, more trust in team members and the use of sophisticated technology.

A great example of a business which has built its culture around providing care to its customers that is above and beyond the call of duty is the famous American department store, Nordstrom. Nordstrom's service culture predates the current crisis by several decades and stories are legion of the amazing lengths to which it goes to keep its customers happy. For example, according to one story, in 1975, Nordstrom opened a store in a new location that had formerly been a tyre shop. One day, a customer brought a set of snow tyres into the store and asked to return them. Of course, Nordstrom is a department store – it does not sell tyres. However, without a word about the mix-up, the tyres were accepted and the customer was fully refunded the purchase price[1].

In a different story, a customer tried on several pairs of shoes but failed to find the right combination of size and colour. As she was about to leave, the clerk called other Nordstrom stores but could only locate the right pair at Macy's, a nearby competitor. The clerk had Macy's ship the shoes to the customer's home at Nordstrom's expense[2].

In a third story, a customer described wandering into a Portland, Oregon, Nordstrom looking for an Armani tuxedo for his daughter's wedding. The item was not available, but the sales associate took his measurements anyway just in case one was found. The next day, the customer got a phone call, informing him that the tuxedo was available. When pressed, the sales assistant revealed that she had found one in New York and had put it on a truck destined to Chicago. Then, she had sent someone to meet the truck in Chicago at a rest stop and bring the item to Portland. The following day, she had shipped the tuxedo to the customer's address and when it arrived, he found that it had already been altered for his measurements and was ready to wear. What is even more impressive about this story is that, at the time, Nordstrom did not even sell Armani tuxedos[3].

These stories may be extreme cases, but nevertheless, they speak to a culture which goes well beyond the norm in the pursuit of customer service excellence. Key to the Nordstrom service philosophy is the latitude that it gives its team members to solve customer problems. New employees are told on their first day that there are two rules. The first rule is: 'Use your best judgement'. The second rule is: 'There are no other rules'. This is at odds with the culture of most retailers, who usually have extremely strict rules governing staff behaviour[4].

Although these are old stories, there is evidence that the service culture is alive and well at Nordstrom. For example, it accepts online returns from its rivals, like Kohl's and Macy's, because it thinks about its customer needs more than about selling its own products. Funnily enough, it finds such customers often buy other items while they are in the store doing the return. And this strong service differentiator seems to be helping the company. While the department store sector as a whole is facing disintegration, Nordstrom is faring better than most. Its revenues dropped only 2.2 per cent in 2019, as against a decline of over 8 per cent for JCPenney in the same year and a drop of 5.7 per cent for Neiman Marcus, in the nine months ending April 2019 (both of which subsequently went bankrupt). Nordstrom's third quarter 2020 results showed net earnings of $53 million, despite the ravages of COVID-19[5].

Individual recognition

One of the key things driving whether the interaction with a brand is pleasant or not is whether it treats you as an individual. Of course, there is nothing really new about this. In previous eras, when people tended to live in one place and there were more independent retailers, customers were often known individually to shopkeepers. This still exists in smaller centres, but in many places – particularly large towns and cities – it has been lost, as geographical mobility has increased and chains have replaced owner-managed shops. It was also a feature of the service provided by premium and luxury brands, where the customer's spending level was sufficient to justify the investment of time and effort. However, outside of these exceptions, the only way in which this can be delivered on a mass scale today is through a brand mastering its customers' digital data. We will treat this subject in more detail in the next chapter.

One of the key aspects of individual recognition is giving sufficient time to the customer interaction. This used to be a feature of shopping in good-quality stores, but in the modern age, with staff cuts and high labour turnover, it has largely been lost. It is clearly hard to give huge amounts of time to every transaction, especially in the mid-mass market. However, some innovative companies, particularly in the direct-to-consumer area, have developed a new way of thinking about this issue.

Direct-to-consumer brands are used to distinguishing between the process of customer recruitment and the process of servicing customer repeat business. In the digital sphere, it is expensive to win new customers but relatively cheap to remarket to them. In search of a way to recruit customers more efficiently, many direct-to-consumer brands have opened showrooms (sometimes on a pop-up basis), where they can introduce their innovative products to consumers and sign them up to their Web systems. They are typically prepared to throw more resource at this initial interaction, because they do not look at it as a single transaction, but as the start of a long-term relationship.

A good example of this is Bonobos, the premium menswear direct-to-consumer brand, which used its stores – or 'Guideshops' as it called them – to create a very pleasant first experience for potential customers. Customers would be invited to make hour-long appointments, during which sophisticated personal shoppers would serve them drinks and learn about their clothing tastes before taking them through the Bonobos range and fitting them with key items. The idea was not necessarily to 'sell' the potential customer anything. Indeed, the store did not carry any saleable stock. Instead, the intention was to create the relationship with the client, which would then lead to them buying the product on a repeat basis, online. This idea of using the store to create brand experience and the Web to transact is one to which we will return later in the book. We also cover the Bonobos story in more detail in Chapter 47 (*see also* pages 257–261)[6].

Another online brand that uses physical showrooms to create special experiences for its top customers is online brand Moda Operandi. The website's main business model is to sell high-end fashion straight off the catwalks, using shoppable videos of designer shows. However, loyal customers can pre-book appointments at its luxury townhouses in London, New York and Hong Kong. When they arrive, they have the place to themselves and all the items are in their size and to their taste. They receive the devoted attention of several personal shoppers, who also serve them drinks and snacks[7].

The whole experience is designed to reward the brand's highest-spending customers and to encourage their long-term loyalty online. Like Bonobos, Moda Operandi is leveraging the unique power of physical spaces and personal interaction to deliver stand-out 'pampering' experiences that could never be created online.

Involvement

As we saw in Chapter 15 (pages 90–95), historically, customers had little direct involvement in the life of brands. Apart from limited research to establish basic needs and segment the market, the marketing departments did not know much about individual customer needs, and saw *themselves* as the guardians of the brand. Brands were highly polished affairs and image and communications were very tightly controlled.

Today's consumers – particularly younger consumers – reject this 'cold, hard, shiny' version of brands. They want more transparency, more involvement, more of a relationship. They like feeling that they are dealing with a person – for example, the founder – rather than a corporation. Things do not have to be perfect, so long as the brand is honest about its situation and is seen to be making genuine efforts to improve. Today, brand management needs to be seen as more like a piece of open-source software; as being about curating a product category for a community of fellow enthusiasts.

Many of the disruptor brands have adopted this model and have involved their communities in the life of the brand from the very start. This is typically in areas like product development and marketing.

Womenswear direct-to-consumer brand Everlane has made a point of getting its customers to co-design new products and help with fitting and testing them. For example, when they developed their first women's trouser collection, they spent more than a year designing and refining their shapes and fits, and then invited some of their customers to try on their prototypes. These lucky individuals not only got a chance to trial the product before anyone else, but their opinions and feedback were also considered for the final release. This generated a lot of publicity for the brand, because the customers loved the sense of exclusivity and Everlane made them feel like they were actually a part of the company[8].

Another example of brands involving their communities from the start can be seen on Kickstarter. Kickstarter is a start-up funding website, which enables entrepreneurs to list their new products and attract funding from interested parties. What is fascinating is that contributors receive very little that is tangible in return – apart from a few samples or invitations to launch parties. Yet large amounts of money are regularly raised, which indicates that the mere act of involving people is enough motivation for them to give money to the cause. Indeed, Kickstarter has become so powerful that new brands now frequently go on the site just to raise awareness and start building their communities, even if they actually have the necessary funds and do not need outside investment[9].

Marketing communications is also evolving away from traditional brand messaging. As we have seen, the younger generations – Millennials and Gen Z – have grown up sceptical of corporate marketing messages. They would rather believe the evidence of more objective sources – their peers, whether it be in the form of user reviews, influencer evaluations or tweets from people they know. More brands are featuring customer pictures and videos of themselves using the product (what is known as User Generated Content [UGC]) and marketing executives are learning to adopt a looser, more relaxed attitude to how their brand is presented than in the old days, where rigid, centralized rules guided every piece of communication.

A great example of a retailer using UGC to drive its marketing is the underwear brand Aerie, which is part of American Eagle. Aerie has connected at a deep level with its followers by allowing them to define the look of the brand, rather than imposing a perfect image of beauty, like its main rival, Victoria's Secret. Whereas Victoria's Secret's advertising has been full of impossibly beautiful supermodels, Aerie's depicts happy, relaxed, real customers, comfortable with their bodies. Aerie's body-positive campaign, '#AerieREAL', has gone viral on customers' own social media feeds, meaning they themselves are promoting Aerie for free[10].

Even during the pandemic, Aerie's results have remained sparkling. Sales grew by 34 per cent in the third quarter of 2020, driven by an 83 per cent growth in its e-commerce revenues. Analysts predict that Aerie will become a $3 billion business in the next five years. By contrast, Victoria's Secret would appear to be in terminal decline: its sales dropped a whopping 14 per cent in the same quarter and, as we have seen, its proposed sale to Sycamore Partners fell through in May 2020, after the latter pulled out[11] (please see Chapter 39 for a full case study on Aerie, pages 223–5).

The key thing is to move away from a centrally driven brand communications strategy, based on traditional paid advertising, to a decentralized strategy based on natural customer enthusiasm – and to shift the focus from superficial things like brand image on to simple but deep things, like actually sitting down with customers and asking how they want the brand to evolve in terms of products, stores and messaging.

Community

The remaining area which really influences the quality of the customer interaction with a brand is whether there is a sense of community among its followers. Successful modern brands recognize that people need to feel part of a community which shares its interests and values. Many people are lonely and derive emotional value from this sense of belonging. This is particularly true in the aftermath of COVID-19.

There are many examples of successful brands that have led by emphasizing brand community over product transactions. One of the most famous is Lululemon – an upmarket activewear brand which celebrates women's health and body positivity. The brand offers many community-based activities, both online and offline. For example, it sponsors an annual 'SeaWheeze' half-marathon in Seattle, Washington State, which (in pre-Covid times) was attended by over 20,000 loyal followers. In 2020, Lululemon took SeaWheeze virtual, with nine days of online programming. The brand also normally offers free yoga classes in its stores, given by leading local teachers. It has a very active social media feed, where brand followers share stories of their workouts and pictures of themselves using the product. All this community-building activity seems to be paying off, with Lululemon reporting third quarter 2020 sales up 22 per cent[12].

Another well-known example is Rapha – the British cycling brand – which uses its stores as 'Clubhouses', where brand enthusiasts can meet and plan shared trips. For a small membership fee, it offers free coffee and buns, special equipment deals and arranged rides for which people can sign up. There is a more detailed case study on Rapha in Chapter 45 (*see also* pages 247–251)[13].

A third example is Gymshark – the wildly successful British workout-wear brand – which has created an enormous community of 18–25-year-old gym fanatics. It works with around 20 influencers such as Lex Griffin and Nikki Blackketter, who have a collective social media following of 20 million. Key to building its community have been its regular Gymshark meet-ups and 'expos' – events where fans were able to meet their favourite fitness influencers. During the pandemic, the brand has kept up the momentum through regular online events. In a market dominated by Nike and Adidas, Gymshark has built sales very rapidly and received investment in 2020, which valued it at £1.3 billion. We will discuss the Gymshark case study in more depth in Chapter 40 (*see also* pages 226–229)[14].

Thus, we can see that the really successful modern brands are those that focus on creating the right kind of interaction with their followers – interactions which go well beyond the sales transaction to make them feel good by meeting their deeper needs for recognition, involvement and community.

CHAPTER NINETEEN

'Congratulations on your happy news!'

Key to individual customer involvement and recognition is the ability to personalize marketing messages to individual customers. Thanks to new technologies such as Web analytics, big data and artificial intelligence, it is now possible to talk to consumers on a one-to-one basis. The following story illustrates this phenomenon.

One day, an angry man walked into his local Target store in the US and complained that they had been sending coupons for baby products to his daughter, along with a letter entitled 'Congratulations on your happy news!' The young woman was still in high school. Were they trying to encourage her to get pregnant?

The store manager did not know what the man was talking about, but apologized just in case. He was so concerned that he followed up with a phone call a few weeks later to apologize again. The man rather sheepishly admitted that he had talked to his daughter and she was, in fact, expecting a baby.

What had happened was that Target had been analysing the purchases of all its customers and had figured out that when a certain combination of products was ordered – cotton wool, unscented body oil, vitamins and the like – it indicated a high probability of pregnancy. Their marketing department had picked up on this possibility and therefore had sent the leaflet to the daughter before her family had figured out what was happening! Leaving aside the rather uneasy feeling that this story invokes, it does show the power of modern digital analytics and personalization[1].

As we have seen, in the traditional marketing model, mass advertising was thrown at the 'wall' of TV, outdoor and press media in the hope that some consumers would respond by going in store and buying. Little attempt was made to understand individual consumers and they remained largely anonymous to the brands and retailers who took their money.

From mass to individual

E-commerce has changed all that. The traceability of individual transactions, the necessity of collecting personal details for shipment purposes, the visibility of movements around online advertising media and brand websites, and the fact that both the marketing and the sale took place in the same medium – all of these factors meant that brands had almost perfect visibility of their individual consumers and thus could use that data to predict their behaviour and to influence their decisions.

For the most part, retailers failed to pick this up and continued to stick with old techniques. What online advertising they did do tended to be focused on general brand-building rather than the highly targeted performance marketing practised by the digitally native players.

The sophistication of some of these personalized marketing campaigns is pretty impressive. Expert performance marketers are able to track every move of consumers online. For example, they can look at individual customer journeys as they work through their social media feeds, seeing how many of them click on advertisements, how many engage with content (e.g. watch videos), how many visit the brand website and how many actually buy.

Social media like Facebook know a lot about their members from all the things that they post. They know about their interests, hobbies, likes and dislikes. They then sell brands advertising packages that are targeted against these specific demographics. So, for example, if you want to sell dog whistles, you can target dog enthusiasts.

Performance marketing

They also know where the people who are going to see the advertising are in their relationship with the brand. Direct marketing theory looks at the relationship between consumers and brands in terms of a journey: a gradual escalation of commitment, which looks like this:

Ignorance → Awareness → Engagement → Trial → Repeat → Loyalty

Performance marketers are able to track every step of an individual consumer on this journey. For example, they can obtain real time data on whether a consumer has seen an advertisement from their brand before or if it is the first time. They know whether the consumer has ever engaged with it before and whether they have previously clicked through to the brand's website. This tells the brand how individual consumers are reacting to their advertising messages. Performance marketers are thus able to divide customers into three groups depending on the degree of their relationship with the brand.

'Top of funnel' consumers are people who are encountering the brand for the first time. 'Middle of funnel' consumers are those who have interacted with the brand (for example, opened an advertisement on Facebook), or have clicked through to the brand website, but not yet bought anything. 'Bottom of funnel' consumers are those who have bought the brand before and are potential repeat customers.

The performance marketers can see how these three groups are interacting with the brand's advertising in real time. They typically have a stable of around 20 or so creative advertisements which they cycle through, looking for ones that perform well at different points on the customers' journey. For example, for new clients, they may use a very factual, scientific advertisement. However, for already-loyal clients, they may use more emotional spots – like the founder's story. By continuously analysing this data, they can optimize the effect of a given marketing budget. If a certain advertisement is not producing enough click-throughs and conversions, they can put in another one which has better metrics.

The precision of this performance marketing system does not stop with the advertising side. It continues when the customer clicks through to the brand's website. At this point, the website itself picks up the trail. It records where they came from, where they go on the site, what products they view, whether they add to basket and finally, whether they buy anything. The brand team also know if the customer is a repeat client and where they came from (for example, if they clicked through from one of the brand's marketing emails), how many times they have visited and everything that they have bought over time. And based on average figures derived from all their past customers, they can calculate the customer's potential lifetime value.

Key metrics

The key metrics in this process are:

- Advertising spend divided by Cost per advertising impression = Number of impressions;
- Number of impressions x Click-through rate = Number of outbound clicks onto brand website;
- Clicks onto brand website x Conversion rate = Number of sales;
- Number of sales x Average basket size = Sales Value;
- Sales Value x Gross Margin percentage = Gross Margin;
- Assuming this is a new customer, the brand can calculate the cost of customer acquisition (i.e. the cost of getting them to buy for the first time), which is: Ad spend x Cost per ad impression x Click-through rate x Conversion rate = Customer acquisition cost.

This can be compared to the gross margin earned on the first order, indicating whether the process was profitable or not.

As social media advertising costs have risen, many brands have been losing money on these initial customer recruitment transactions. However, they can still make money in the long term, thanks to the lifetime value of the customer. Once they have the customer's data, they can use low-cost marketing campaigns, like email or SMS, to encourage them to return and repeat purchase. The more times they repurchase, the more they know about them, and the more skilled they get at motivating them to spend more. They may also tie the customer in through subscription services (i.e. offering them a lower price to sign up to regular deliveries) or loyalty programs like Amazon Prime, whereby they get perks like free delivery and TV programming in return for an annual fee. The relationship between customer acquisition costs and lifetime value determines whether e-commerce brands make money in the long term.

The key thing about this process is that performance marketers have complete horizontal visibility of what is happening all the way along the consumer journey from awareness to loyalty. And that they are able to measure and optimize the metrics all along the path in real time.

This is a world away from the old days of mass advertising, where brands would 'Throw money at the wall and see if any of it sticks', as the old advertising saying went. Once the sophistication of this system is understood, it is not really surprising that the dot-coms were able to beat the retailers in the race to capture the online dollar.

The penny drops ...

Pushed onwards by the growing retail crisis and the COVID-19 debacle, retailers are finally coming to the personalized marketing party. Armed with individual customer data, they are belatedly starting to be able to use the types of data analytics that had long been the secret weapon of the digitally native brands, using algorithms to analyse every move the consumer makes to predict their behaviour and hopefully influence it.

Since COVID-19, there has been a huge rush by established brands and retailers through the doors of the leading digital marketing agencies, which until recently had had to depend on direct-to-consumer start-ups for their bread and butter. Agencies like Bolt Digital, Propeller and Fractyl in the UK, and Markitors, WebFX and Ignite Visibility in the US, have seen very rapid growth in enquiries from major brands and retailers[2].

According to a September 2020 survey by the Interactive Advertising Bureau (IAB), digital advertising expenditure was expected to grow by 6 per cent in the United States in 2020 despite the recession, which depressed overall advertising by 8 per cent. And, within digital advertising itself, a June 2020 McKinsey report suggested that brands and retailers were switching their spend from general brand-building to performance marketing aimed at driving online sales[3].

Companies like Walmart, Best Buy, Target and Lowe's have been hiring senior data scientists, who have been prominent in their recent revivals. For example, Paritosh Desai, who was Vice President of Business Intelligence, Analytics and Testing at Target, was an important player in the company's turnaround (which we cover in more detail in Chapter 37, *see also* pages 215–218). Not only did Desai hire a strong data team, he also created a data-driven culture company-wide. He established fluidity between the data team and managers by creating an analytics system that managers could use themselves and promoting data-driven decision-making across the board. The demand for such experts grew by 29 per cent in 2018–19 and this trend seems likely to continue in the future[4].

Thus, major brands and retailers are now investing more than ever in personalizing their marketing and creating strong one-to-one relationships with their customers.

CHAPTER TWENTY

Purpose-built

Linked to this creation of a more personalized brand/customer relationship is the notion of higher purpose. If a brand really wants to generate enthusiasm in its user community and among its team members it is really important that it stand for something more than the purely commercial.

We referred earlier to direct-to-consumer brands like Warby Parker, Allbirds and SF Bay Coffee, who put helping the world at the heart of their purpose. Warby Parker's aim is to help solve the problem of poor sight in the Third World and it donates a pair of free glasses for every pair purchased. Allbirds is committed to proving that natural materials and sustainable production methods are compatible with having a fashionable product. The founders of SF Bay Coffee personally visit the jungles of South America every year to build schools, hospitals and housing for the farmers who grow their coffee[1].

Let my people go surfing!

Another fearlessly ideological company is Patagonia. The brand has always taken a leadership position in terms of protecting the environment. Founder Yvon Chouinard set out to build an 'un-company' – one whose principal concern was taking care of employees, customers and, above all else, the planet. He set a simple goal for Patagonia: 'Do well and do good.'

The brand is all about a love of the outdoors and linked to that, a passion for protecting the natural environment. It has an irreverent, unconventional, one-of-a-kind culture. For example, its employee handbook is titled 'Let My People Go Surfing!' Patagonia understands that when the surf is up on the beaches near its headquarters at Ventura, just north of Los Angeles, or there is fresh powder at Big Bear in the nearby San Bernardino Mountains, employees will quit their desks, grab their gear and go surfing or skiing.

As Dean Carter, Vice President of Human Resources & Shared Services at Patagonia, put it: 'We hire people who love being outside, people who love the outdoors, so when the surf's up, they're going to be surfing anyway. If we didn't have a "Let My People Go Surfing" policy, we'd have a lot of performance action plans.'

Working practices are highly flexible: Patagonia has a 9/80 work schedule that gives employees a three-day weekend every other week. Employees work nine hours a day from Monday through Thursday and eight hours on alternating Fridays (making 80 hours per fortnight). They then get every second Friday off. The company also offers subsidized childcare centres for employees. The centres have bilingual programs and teachers who are trained in child development. As a result, nearly 100 per cent of female employees who have babies return to work at Patagonia afterwards.

The 'Let My People Go Surfing' culture is extremely popular among the Patagonia team – the company only has about 4 per cent staff turnover each year: 'I call us the Hotel California,' Dean Carter says. 'You check in, but you don't check out.'

The brand's care for the environment shows up in quirky ways. It runs advertisements that say, 'Don't buy this jacket,' and acknowledges that as a producer, Patagonia is part of the problem. Products come with a lifetime guarantee and Patagonia encourages customers to repair old items rather than replace them. They have the largest clothing repair facility in North America and a truck that travels the United States doing mobile repairs – whether the product was made by Patagonia or anyone else.

After an employee has been with the company for a certain period, they can take up to two months off, with pay, to volunteer with an environmental organization or project. Every year about 150 employees go all over the world to help out with supporting the environment. Carter described how he 'cleaned up sea lion poop on the Channel Islands' on his leave. The company even supports employees if their environmental campaigning lands them in jail, so long as it is peaceful: 'If they get put in jail,' Carter says, 'we throw their bail.'

In 2018, Patagonia sued the US government to block Department of Interior plans to reduce the size of two Utah national monuments. More conventionally, it has an ongoing commitment to give 1 per cent of sales to environmental groups.

Patagonia's values-based culture seems to work well for it. Listed in the '100 Best Companies to Work For' guide, it has 9,000 applicants for every job that opens up. It does roughly $1 billion in sales each year and has 3,000 employees around the world[2].

Being good is good business

Another good example of a highly successful values-led business is that of The Body Shop in the 1980s and 1990s. In those early days, it was led by its indomitable founder, the late Anita Roddick, who made no secret of the fact that what really mattered to her was her causes. She spoke out forcibly in favour of women's rights, launching the famous advertising line: 'There are 3 billion women who don't look like supermodels and only 8 who do'[3].

Roddick campaigned fiercely against animal testing, coming up with the 'cute bunny' advertisement, which helped collect four million signatures on a petition and got testing banned in the EU. She was also a great advocate for the environment and Third World workers' rights[4].

Through this approach The Body Shop built a large community of passionate followers and enthused its team members with a sense of purpose. This helped the brand win out against the huge conventional brands who dominated the beauty industry and created a worldwide business which, at its height, was worth $1.1 billion. As Roddick put it: 'Being good is good business'[5].

These are examples of brands that were founded around an idea at the start, but what about large established organizations? How can they create a sense of purpose? Fortunately, there are some great examples of major companies that have achieved this through inspired leadership.

Unilever is one such corporation. In 2011, then Chief Executive Paul Polman launched the 'Sustainable Living' plan, which involved making its supply chain and products more environmentally friendly. This vast task, carried out over 400 brands, 150,000 employees and 190 countries, involved many short-term sacrifices over a 10-year period. However, it seems this massive effort is paying off as its most sustainable brands grew 69 per cent faster than the rest of the business and delivered 75 per cent of its turnover growth in 2018. In the first half of 2020, it saw net income up 10 per cent and by January 2021 its share price had gone up by more than 200 per cent from its 2010 level[6].

Best Buy is another large corporation that has saved itself by pivoting from a transactions-based to a values-based focus. Since 2014, under the inspiring leadership of Chief Executive Hubert Joly, it has gone from decline to rapid growth by focusing on enriching people's lives through technology. This has involved services like taking care of all the electronics in people's homes, not just the ones purchased from Best Buy, and helping vulnerable and elderly people to stay in their homes longer by installing security and mobility technology. Best Buy is covered in more detail in one of our case studies in Chapter 38 (*see also* pages 219–222)[7].

Thus, in summary, we can see that an important way of lifting a brand out of the brutal transactions-based war is by creating a sense of higher purpose which motivates employees and creates a passionate and loyal customer base.

CHAPTER TWENTY ONE

Hot Data

In Chapter 19 (pages 112–118), we looked at how important it was for companies to personalize their relationships with customers. There are clearly many ways of doing this, but one of the most important is through the collection and analysis of customer data.

As we have seen, historically, retailers were just not that interested in customer data. The classical brand/retail supply chain depended on shifting the maximum volume of standardized goods to as many customers as possible. It was just not that valuable to know too much about individual customers. The manufacturing was inflexible, so it was impossible to personalize products anyway. The key piece of information as to whether the customer was new or not was ignored: the cost of the transaction was the same either way, since the fixed brand and store expenses were going to be there in either case; so it really did not make any difference.

As we have also seen, the dot-coms had a very different approach to customer data and developed extremely sophisticated methods of collecting and analysing individual client information and using it to personalize marketing messages for individual consumers. Clever performance marketers in online businesses were able to see how individual customers were reacting to the company's products, advertising messages and Web pages in real time.

Flying blind

Thus, for two decades after the launch of the internet, e-commerce businesses were able to track every movement and reaction of their customers, whereas retailers were still largely flying blind. People came into their stores, bought things and walked out, largely without retailers knowing anything about who they were or what they were doing while they were in the store.

This problem was partly a technological one. The store systems were based on Electronic Point of Sale (EPOS) software in their tills and captured only very basic information – sales, prices and stock levels. They usually did not contain individual customer information – who the customer was, whether they were new or not, or their previous sales history. The closest many retailers got to capturing customer data from their shops was through their store card and loyalty programs, but these did not cover the majority of customers. Even then, the data was often not used for much, apart from giving gifts or discounts to regular clients.

By contrast, the retailers' Web channels had much more sophisticated customer data capabilities, but these businesses were typically much smaller than the stores side of their operations and the overall culture of the organization remained focused on the traditional metrics, like sales per square foot. As a result, the retailers failed to maximize the use of this data in contrast to the dot-coms who obsessed about it, even to the extent of having chief algorithm officers on their boards.

A missed opportunity

Given that typically 90 per cent or more of the retailers' business was still coming from the stores channel, they were clearly missing a huge opportunity to capture passing customer data and feed it into their internet systems. They were paying Facebook or Google large amounts to recruit customers online, while every day, millions of them were walking through their stores for free.

Even such data that did come from the stores side of the businesses was rarely integrated with that from the Web channel. The problem was exacerbated by the retailers' organizational structure – typically, they set up their internet businesses as separate divisions from their main stores operations.

The powerful barons from the retail side (who, at that time, were making all the profits) regarded the Web upstarts as 'competitors' who wanted to steal away the store customers. The customers, in reality, alternated between buying on the website and in the stores, but the retailers were unable to get a unified picture of their individual behaviours and thus prevented from developing integrated personalized marketing campaigns to attract them.

The Toys "R" Us case

This issue is exemplified by the case of Toys "R" Us. The huge American toy brand had 19 million active customers in its 'Rewards "R" Us' loyalty scheme in 2016, which generated two-thirds of its sales (or about $7.7 billion). This means that on average each scheme member spent $405 in 2016[1].

The company's total sales were $11.5 billion, so mathematically this means that the other $3.8 billion was generated by non-loyalty scheme customers. Now, on average, loyalty scheme members spend 40 per cent more than non-members, so, if we assume that each non-member spent $405/1.4, this means they spent $289 each. If we divide the $3.8 billion by this figure, we arrive at around 13 million non-loyalty program customers. Adding the two figures together, this means that, in total, Toys "R" Us had around 32 million customers walking through its stores on a regular basis[2].

Turning to the e-commerce side of the business, we see that it was still very small in 2016 – with only 10 per cent of the brand's sales being online in the same year (or around $1.15 billion). If we pro-rate the number of Web customers from sales (using the average sales per customer across all the customers [$359]), we arrive at a figure of around 3.2 million online clients. What is startling about this figure is that it is not only a mere 10 per cent of the people walking through the stores, but only 17 per cent of the number of the people in the company's loyalty scheme[3].

How is it that the company failed to capture more of its most loyal customers into its Web data system? Digging beneath the surface, we find that the team who ran the stores saw the internet division as 'rivals', who were trying to take away their business. Thus, they jealously guarded the data in the customer loyalty scheme and refused to integrate it with the Web customer database. Toys "R" Us' organizational structure thus militated against them ever being able to get an integrated view of their individual customers' behaviour and they missed the opportunity to migrate vast amounts of free client data into their Web system.

In consequence, as the company's profits came under pressure, in the years leading up to its bankruptcy in September 2017, and its big-box stores became too expensive a channel to service its customers, it was not able to continue to reach them through its low-cost internet channel, but was forced to liquidate the whole business instead.

Ironically, once the dust had settled on the bankruptcy and 31,000 workers had lost their jobs, the owners hit on the realization that they had a huge asset in the form of all those customers in their loyalty scheme and relaunched the business as a digital-first operation, leveraging the data to drive sales. When combined with the far lower costs of their e-commerce operation, they were able to create a profitable business[4].

As the retail crisis gathered momentum in the period after 2015, retailers started to question whether this separation of the stores and online teams was sensible and belatedly started to integrate them and the data that they were generating.

A burning platform compels change

It took the 'burning platform' of COVID-19, however, to really force the retailers to address their inadequate and disintegrated data systems.

Stripped of their stores, they suddenly woke up to how far they were behind on the data front and finally took massive action to beef up their store data collection and to integrate it with the information from their online businesses to get a unified view of their individual customers.

For example, Marks & Spencer relaunched its store loyalty card 'Sparks' in July 2020 to make it a digital-first program based around an app. The scheme, which had 7 million members, was integrated with data from marksandspencer.com, M&S Bank and the newly acquired Ocado online business to create a single vision of their customers' journeys[5].

As the company put it: 'The Sparks reset is an important part of M&S becoming a data driven business, with the business seeking to unite four important data sources from across the business, including Sparks, M&S.com, M&S Bank and soon Ocado, in order to drive greater improvements and personalized experiences for all customers'[6].

Retailers are also moving away from credit card-based store loyalty programs, which were always a tough sell, due to the very high interest rates charged. For example, Macy's expanded its loyalty program to members without its store card and Nordstrom upgraded its own to allow non-card holders to participate. J. Crew launched a new loyalty scheme in August 2020 without a card requirement[7].

In addition, many retailers have launched apps, which customers can use while in the store, to provide product information, reserve sizes in fitting rooms and unlock additional benefits. Walmart and other grocery outlets offer apps which guide people around the store, speeding up their journeys, which again encourages people to download them[8].

The move towards app-based store shopping, which is covered more fully in Chapter 33 (*see also* pages 192–195), is helping retailers collect data about their customers. Another way of getting data is by offering free services – for example, Urban Outfitters started offering free WiFi and persuaded a lot of consumers to sign up that way[9].

More needs to be done in this area. Collecting data is no longer optional – it is a question of survival. Retailers need to use whatever incentive is needed – gifts, discounts and special privileges – to induce stores customers to sign up. Apart from collecting the customer data, there is also the question of integrating it, so that it is available in real time and in an easy-to-use form in both the Web and stores systems.

New software programs are helping with this. For example, Shopify – the leading website provider – has launched 'Shopify POS', which aims to bridge the gap between online and offline systems, enabling seamless communications between the two. Ksubaka Cloudshelf offers software which has also been highly successful due to its integrated approach. It seems likely in the future that all brands will run single systems recording sales and stock movements across both stores and Web[10].

What such technologies are doing is to treat all transactions as effectively Web transactions – in other words, eliminating the separate Electronic Point of Sale (EPOS) system and turning the tills into versions of the website. This is what is meant by making digital the backbone of the business.

Changing retail culture

On the cultural side, one of the key issues to overcome is the ingrained problem of retail staff seeing the company's own e-commerce operation as a 'competitor' who is going to steal their business and jobs. In order to address this issue, it is important to educate all staff to look at the business from a customer's point of view and help them understand that unless the company makes it really easy for customers to shift between channels, it likely will not be there in the future.

One way of helping to reinforce this shift in thinking is by incentivizing store staff to assist in creating online sales. For example, every customer in the company's database can be tagged according to who introduced them. Those that came in from a particular store can be identified and a percentage of all future sales from this customer across all channels can be given as commission to that store or that individual. The store can also be given the job of 'looking after' that customer – for example, personalizing emails to them, giving them the number of the store to call if they need help, or even identifying an individual sales person to call.

Thus, we can see that retailers are finally waking up to the importance of customer data and the necessity of integrating it across all channels. The impact of COVID-19 has been to accelerate this process and, as such, it could be said that it has had a beneficial effect on the long-term thinking of the industry.

CHAPTER TWENTY TWO

Digital Converter – Making Online the Backbone of the Business

Linked to this newfound interest in customer data is a shift in thinking about the relative importance of the physical and digital channels. As we have seen, traditional retailers often viewed their Web businesses as secondary to their store businesses. Although they started online operations, they did not pursue them with the passion and dedication displayed by the dot-coms. They had 20 years to build good-size online businesses, but by the time of the arrival of COVID-19, most had not succeeded in getting more than 10–15 per cent of their businesses online.

This prejudice against the internet side was not helped by the fact that the retailers were not very 'good' at e-commerce. They did not really understand how personalized performance marketing worked and as a consequence they found that building a customer base online tended to be extremely high cost, relative to the level of business it brought in. The backbone of the business was still the stores, with the Web a rather expensive problem child on the side. Despite the fact that they were suffering, they never had a moment of discontinuity sufficient to jolt them into a new mind-set. The enforced closure of their shops during lockdown provided just such a jolt. It made them painfully aware of how vulnerable their stores were to interruption and the subsequent period of social distancing and further waves of infection showed them that this might not be an isolated event. And, beyond that, there was the risk of new viruses in the future.

As we have noted, those brands which had already built substantial e-commerce businesses weathered the storm better than those who had not, and this lesson was not lost on retail leaders around the world. As a result, they went through a kind of 'Road to Damascus' conversion during the course of 2020, and came to see that they needed to treat the digital channel as the transactional backbone of their business, with the stores selectively adding value in ways that the internet cannot. This led to an enormous acceleration in retail investment in digital, which was visible across many sectors.

Fashion

As already noted, the fashion retail sector was among the worst affected by the crisis. Many clothing retailers suffered a catastrophic decline during lockdown itself and a muted reopening, due to distancing measures, which stripped away much of the pleasure from browsing for new clothes. As a result, we saw a new level of seriousness about e-commerce from the leading players.

For example, in June 2020, Inditex – the world's largest fashion retail group, and owner of Zara – announced the objective of building online sales to more than 25 per cent of the total by 2022, compared with 14 per cent in its 2019 financial year. Its founder, Amancio Ortega, said that it was to spend €1 billion on its online offering by 2022 and a further €1.7 billion in stores to allow them to integrate better with its websites for faster deliveries and real-time tracking of products[1].

H&M was set to accelerate the development of its digital capabilities following a substantial loss in sales in the first half of 2020 as a result of lockdowns. It was able to grow e-commerce revenues in the second quarter of 2020 by 36 per cent and outlined its intention to expand its online business and speed up store closures, with a net loss of around 300 shops planned in 2020–21[2].

H&M Chief Executive Officer Helena Helmersson said: 'During the pandemic it became clear how important it is that the digital and physical channels interact to meet customers' needs. We are accelerating our digital development, optimising the store portfolio and further integrating the channels'[3].

In October 2020, Gap announced its intention to close 350 mall stores and generate 80 per cent of its revenue from off-mall stores and e-commerce by 2023. This was on the back of its achievement in gaining 3.5 million new customers online and boosting its digital sales by 95 per cent in the second quarter of 2020[4].

Prior to the COVID-19 outbreak, Nordstrom had already been successful in building up its e-commerce channel to 33 per cent of its business, and it announced in June 2020 that it was investing further to accelerate this trend. Chief Executive Officer Erik Nordstrom said the company would support a 'Continued shift from what was predominantly a mall-based business toward a more diversified model that includes digital and off-price'[5].

JD Sports said in July 2020 that its e-commerce business delivered a 'very resilient performance' during the COVID-19 lockdown and that it was 'inevitable' that there would be 'some level of permanent transfer from physical retail to online' as a result of the pandemic, leading it to prioritize this channel and scale back plans for future store openings[6].

One of the leading retailers in fashion e-commerce is Next, which has invested steadily over the years, such that nearly 50 per cent of its business was online in 2019. It saw a great benefit from this strategy during COVID-19, as its third quarter 2020 results showed a growth of 23 per cent in online sales, offsetting an 18 per cent drop in store sales and leading to overall growth of nearly 3 per cent[7].

Other retail

Bed Bath & Beyond saw online sales growth of 89 per cent in the second quarter of 2020. The company announced in October 2020 that it was planning to invest somewhere between $1 billion and $1.5 billion over the next three years, a large part of which would go on creating 'a revolutionary, digital and integrated shopping experience for customers', according to Chief Executive Mark Tritton[8].

Kingfisher Group, parent company of B&Q and Screwfix, announced that its online sales grew by 164 per cent during the first half of 2020 (going from 7 per cent of the total to 19 per cent), while overall sales dipped slightly. Chief Executive Thierry Garnier said: 'We are fundamentally reorganizing our commercial operating model to serve our customers better. We have accelerated our plans around e-commerce, with a focus on fulfilment from stores'[9].

Dixons Carphone saw a huge growth in e-commerce during the COVID-19 period. As Chief Executive Alex Baldock put it in September 2020: 'Online has continued to power ahead. In the UK & Ireland alone, we grew online sales by more than £500 million in four months, growth that stayed strong even as stores reopened.' The company said it would invest further in growing its online business[10].

Luxury

Similar trends can be seen in the luxury market. Ralph Lauren announced that it had shifted its emphasis to digital, cutting its retail workforce and investing in online. As President and Chief Executive Officer Patrice Louvet said: 'The changes happening in the world around us have accelerated the shifts we saw pre-Covid and we are fast-tracking some of our plans to match them – including advancing our digital transformation and simplifying our team structures'[11].

Giorgio Armani announced in July 2020 that it was relaunching its omni-channel business, pulling together its online and offline stores in a deal with Yoox Net-A-Porter Group to create what it says would be 'a revolutionary, digital and integrated shopping experience for customers'[12].

Hugo Boss announced in July 2020 that it was embarking on a new strategy, which would help it grow online sales to more than €400 million by 2022, up from €151 million in 2019. This included launching Hugoboss.com in 24 new markets and creating a fulfilment partnership with Tmall and JD in Asia[13].

Grocery

As we have seen, grocery was less badly affected by the Coronavirus than other sectors. However, the lion's share of the gain went to those that had invested over the years in their digital businesses. These gains immediately led the top firms in the sector to ramp up investments still further.

Walmart had already embarked on a huge investment to build its digital business from 2014 onwards, under the visionary leadership of Chief Executive Doug McMillon. This involved expanding its marketplace offering to 52 million product options, acquiring Jet.com, a highly innovative e-commerce company led by digital genius Marc Lore, and sinking hundreds of billions into growing its online sales. Its stated intention was to take on Amazon head-to-head. We explore this transformation in more depth in Chapter 42 (*see also* pages 234–236)[14].

When the COVID-19 crisis hit, all this investment was rewarded by a 79 per cent jump in its digital sales in the third quarter of 2020. On the back of this success, Walmart announced that it was hiring an additional 20,000 workers into its digital business. It also revealed plans to increase its investment in its Web channel, as well as a $20 billion joint venture between its Flipkart e-commerce business in India and Tata.com in Asia Pacific[15].

In the UK, market leader Tesco saw an 80 per cent growth in its online sales in the third quarter of 2020 and announced that it was adding 16,000 new jobs in its e-commerce business[16].

Sainsbury's enjoyed an 81 per cent surge in online sales in the third quarter of 2020, and shipped 1.1 million orders in the 10 days before Christmas, double the number of the previous year. Chief Executive Officer Mike Coupe said: 'Clearly, the longer the lockdown goes on, the more people get used to shopping for their groceries online, the more likely that is to stick'[17].

Marks & Spencer also invested in growing its e-commerce business. It had already indicated its strategic direction with the 2019 purchase of 50 per cent of Ocado, the UK's leading digitally native grocer. This increasingly looked like a wise investment as Ocado's fourth quarter 2020 results showed sales growth of 35 per cent[18].

In September 2020, Ocado switched its main fresh-food partnership from Waitrose to Marks & Spencer and saw very low customer drop-out rates as well as its average basket quantity increase by five items. Marks & Spencer also announced that it was strengthening its clothing e-commerce offer by adding selected third-party brands[19].

The extent of the shift towards online can be seen by looking at the attitudes of grocery discounters like Aldi and Lidl. Historically, they were reluctant to join the e-commerce rush as they felt that their ultra-thin margins would not cover the high delivery costs. However, the Coronavirus crisis caused them to rethink their viewpoint.

In June 2020, the parent group of Lidl – Schwarz Group – took the unusual step of acquiring German online marketplace real.de in a major pivot towards online retailing. Rolf Schumann, Chief Digital Officer of the Schwarz Group, said: 'Real.de is an essential component of our future offering. The combination of brick-and-mortar business and online trading will open up additional opportunities for us'[20].

Aldi had launched a wine e-commerce site as early as 2016, but it was only in April 2020 that its UK operation started selling groceries online, offering home-delivered boxes containing 22 basic products. It seemed that the discounter was pleased with the results, as in September 2020, it announced that it was taking the next step and trying out a click & collect service[21].

As Maxime Delacour, analyst at retail research group IGD, said of Lidl and Aldi: 'The Coronavirus outbreak is likely to accelerate digital transformation. We're expecting to see many more e-commerce developments from both retailers in the immediate future'[22].

Independent retailers

While many large groups were hit by the outbreak of COVID-19, they were well insulated by bridging loans from their banks and help from the government. For many independent retailers, lacking this support, going online fast was purely a question of survival. Necessity being the mother of invention, many independent shopkeepers rapidly updated their websites, speeded up deliveries and started doing live webcasts on Instagram and YouTube – and were quite pleasantly surprised that it worked!

It is estimated that over 85,000 small retailers in the UK went online during the period between April and July 2020. Vice-President of eBay UK, Rob Hattrell, said his company had signed up more than twice the volume of new traders than it would normally expect. A good example of an independent shopkeeper going online is Erika Conti, owner of Solo Mia – a boutique clothing brand for women based in Hampshire, England. Previously, Conti had been adamant that she was not going online but the arrival of lockdown opened her eyes to new ways of selling. She launched a highly successful series of weekly 'Market Nights' live on Facebook every Tuesday at 8.30 p.m., attracting an audience of 1,000 shoppers[23].

Conti also opened a transactional website on Shopify, which enabled her to continue to build her business despite lockdown. 'My customers are so impressed with my new website and it has allowed my business to grow,' she said. 'If I'd have known an e-commerce site could be so easy to use, I would have taken my collections online much sooner'[24].

Another example, this time from the United States, is Susan and Erin Blanton, owners of the Pufferbellies toy store in Staunton, Virginia. They had had a transactional website since 2006, but it was a minor part of their business compared to in-store sales. All that changed as the COVID-19 pandemic hit, and stay-at-home orders took effect. For the Blantons, having an online infrastructure in place gave them a crucial lifeline that kept them connected to their customers. Sales held steady during the crisis, thanks to their ability to process online orders for local deliveries and long-distance shipments[25].

Apart from retailers embracing digital, we also see malls getting in on the act, by opening multi-brand transactional websites. A good example of this is Simon Properties in the US, which has recently opened ShopPremiumOutlets.com, a website featuring 2,000 brands and over 300,000 products. Malls have the potential to amass a lot of customer data quickly, by harvesting the huge numbers of clients passing through their doors[26].

Thus, we can see that the impact of COVID-19 has been to cause a major shift in the retail industry's thinking about their store and Web channels. It has led them to realize how much more robust their direct delivery channel is, as against their physical shops channel. More and more, they are starting to see e-commerce as the transactional backbone of their future businesses, with their stores as the value-added element. We shall explore the role of the store in this brave new world in Chapter 27.

CHAPTER TWENTY THREE

Back from the Dead

Just as the surviving retailers are finally waking up to the necessity of embracing e-commerce as the low-cost transactional core of their businesses, some of their ghostly ex-colleagues are putting in an appearance. A large number of former retail brands, which had declared bankruptcy and closed all their stores, are reinventing themselves as online-only players. This has enabled them to leverage their legacy customer bases (whose data has usually been captured via their Web channels and/or store loyalty schemes) over a much lower cost framework.

For example, Forever 21, which was in the process of closing all its stores outside the United States, as part of its 2020 bankruptcy process, announced that it would continue to trade internationally via e-commerce. BHS, which went bankrupt in 2016, with 15,000 job losses, was relaunched online in 2019 and decided to focus on the homeware and lighting sectors, for which it was always renowned. American Apparel, which went under in 2016, has also come back as an online-only business[1].

Thomas Cook – the venerable British travel agency – which went bankrupt in 2019, has reinvented itself as an e-commerce operation. The brand name was bought by Chinese company Fosun International Limited, who applied for a travel agency licence. And, as we have seen, Toys "R" Us is also coming back as an online operation[2].

British consumer electronics chain Maplin, which went bankrupt in 2018, has continued to operate successfully as an online-only business. The main reason was the much lower cost base. As Ollie Marshall, the brand's IT Director put it: 'Now we don't have the stores and legacy.... we've aimed to set up [the] business in a very capital light manner[3]'.

Jimmy Choo founder Tamara Mellon relaunched her eponymous brand of shoes as a pure online play, having gone bankrupt as a wholesale/retail business. As she put it: 'This is how I think the next generation of luxury brands are going to be built. I don't believe the next billion-dollar brand will be built in the way I built Jimmy Choo.

'The way we used to build brands was wholesale and retail,' she added. 'Now today our customer lives in digital, and unfortunately as an industry, we operate in analogue, in a 50-year-old, 60-year-old business model, and the customer doesn't want to shop that way anymore'[4].

In many cases, retail brands also continue to enjoy franchising revenue from their overseas stores, which were opened by their franchise partners in better times. For example, Mothercare plc, which went bankrupt in 2019 and closed all its UK stores, continued in 2020 to receive income related to its 791 stores in 40 countries around the world. The company also joined another trend – that of erstwhile retailers launching into wholesaling – by signing a deal with Boots to stock its bestselling lines[5].

From stores to brands

This illustrates a subtle shift in thinking among retailers away from defining themselves as 'stores' and towards defining themselves as 'brands' that can live independently of their own shops in various channels, including proprietary e-commerce, third party e-commerce (e.g. Amazon), wholesale and international franchise.

Some shrewd investors are capitalizing on this trend by putting together stables of erstwhile brands with a shared overhead.

For example, Retail Ecommerce Investors is buying up the assets of bankrupt retail brands and relaunching them as online-only plays. In August 2020, it bought the intellectual property rights to the Modell's sports brand, which was, at the time, in the process of closing its 100 stores. The assets included Modell's trademarks, domain names, social media assets and customer transaction data for about 5.6 million clients, as well as the 'Gotta Go to Mo's' jingle. Retail

Ecommerce Investors paid $3.64 million for the assets, or less than $1.00 per customer data point – a lot lower than it would have cost them to acquire such customers via Facebook or Google advertising. This followed on from their acquisition of the dressbarn brand from Ascena Retail Group, Inc. (after the latter announced they were closing the dressbarn stores) and Pier 1, following its bankruptcy in May 2020[6].

In a similar vein, e-commerce fashion company boohoo acquired the online interests of brands such as Debenhams, Dorothy Perkins, Wallis, Burton, Karen Millen, Coast, Warehouse and Oasis after the bankruptcy of their store businesses. And this tendency to close stores and go exclusively online was affecting many retailers who were still in business. A 2020 survey from digital signage company Raydiant of 400 American bricks and mortar retailers showed that 29 per cent of them planned to close their physical locations to go online only[7].

Another major example of a group which is buying up defunct retail brands, and combining them around a common multi-channel platform is Authentic Brands Group – the $14 Billion empire built by entrepreneurs Jamie Salter and Nigel Woodhouse, and backed by investors BlackRock, General Atlantic, Leonard Green & Partners and Lion Capital. They own 50 of the world's best-known brands, including Barneys, Juicy Couture and Nine West. They recently bought Lucky Brand and Brooks Brothers and were one of the bidders for Topshop in January 2021[8].

A newer group with ambitions to build a portfolio of British brands around a centralized shared online services platform, is Torque Brands, started by direct-to-consumer entrepreneur James Cox, who founded Itch Pet, Carbon Theory (skincare) and Simba Sleep. Torque acquired the assets of bankrupt retailer TM Lewin (menswear) in May 2020[9].

Thus, we can see that many brands, having gone bankrupt as physical retailers, are coming back as online-only operations. This heartening process of rebirth shows the power of leveraging the commercial pull of famous brand names, with all their customer data, over low-cost e-commerce platforms. The only pity is that this could not have been done while the businesses were still alive.

CHAPTER TWENTY FOUR

Have You Seen the Middleman?

In the preceding chapters, we have mainly focused on how the rapid acceleration of the retail crisis, post-Covid, is causing brands and store groups finally to accept the reality of multi-channel retailing, the importance of using data to drive personalization and the need for having a higher purpose. All in the process of trying to move from a transactional philosophy towards a value-added ethic. However, this will not be enough on its own. It is also imperative that they review the transactional side of their businesses in order to take out cost. It is possible to add value on the basis of having comparable transactional costs, but not on the basis of having totally uncompetitive transactional costs.

As we have seen in Chapter 1 (*see also* pages 9–16), the three revolutions in manufacturing, brand communications and e-commerce are collapsing traditional brand/retail supply chains. Lean, savvy, direct-to-consumer brands, websites like AliExpress (which sell straight from the loading bays of China's low-cost factories) and platforms like Amazon with their growing private label offerings are finding a shorter route through the supply chain and undermining prices and margins as they go. For the incumbent brands and retailers, with their long supply chains and high mark-ups, this is an existential threat. In order to survive, they have to shorten their supply chains. And that means, in the nicest possible way, taking each other out.

In March 2020, I was speaking at a consumer electronics conference organized by the relevant trade sector body. Its purpose was to examine the future of their industry. Attending the event were all the leading wholesale brands and retailers, and, as had been the case in my old industry, they all appeared to know each other very well and enjoy each other's company.

At the end of my presentation, I asked them who their biggest competitors were, and their answers were predictable. The brands called out other brand names and the retailers called out other retailers. I ventured the point-of-view that actually their main competitors in the future would be their branded suppliers (if they were retailers) and their retail customers (if they were brands).

'Take a good look around the room at your customers or your suppliers,' I said. 'I am sure that you all get on well, but in ten years' time there will only be room for one of you in the supply chain.'

This somewhat provocative opinion was designed to illustrate the point that the combined effect of the revolutions described above has been to take whole stages out of the traditional brand/retail supply chain, causing painful dislocation. This process can happen in two directions:

1) Brands going direct to the consumer and cutting out the retailers.
2) Retailers cutting out brands and replacing them with their own private label products.

This chapter will deal with brands going direct, while the next covers the retailers cutting out the brands.

Brands going direct

The retail crisis that has been unrolling since 2015 has caused a lot of soul-searching in the boardrooms of many branded wholesalers around the world. And the advent of COVID-19 only accelerated this process.

For years they had sat back and watched industry after industry being disrupted by aggressive new direct-to-consumer brands. The direct-to-consumer revolution, which occurred during the period after 2010, was different from the original e-commerce revolution, in that the new direct-to-consumer businesses were not platforms for selling other people's products like Amazon or Alibaba, but vertically integrated brands selling their own products over the Web.

The earliest ones are now famous – brands like Warby Parker in eyewear, Dollar Shave Club in personal grooming and Glossier in beauty – and many of them have attracted billion dollar-plus valuations. But there are literally tens of thousands of direct-to-consumer brands and they have invaded and disrupted sector after sector[1].

The key to the success of the direct-to-consumer model has been threefold. Firstly, by cutting out all the costs of traditional brands (wholesale salesforces, traditional advertising, etc.) and retailing (stores, staff, rents, etc.), they have been able to avoid the multiple mark-ups charged in the traditional brand/retail supply chain and offer the consumer substantially better value for money. Thus, Warby Parker offered the type of luxury eyewear marketed by top designer brands at $300-plus, at the much more accessible price of $95[2].

Secondly, they have mastered the art of one-to-one personalized marketing and use of customer data better than the incumbent brands and retailers. Whereas traditional brands used mass advertising and hoped that customers would show up in store, these brands were able to target their advertising and measure its effectiveness most precisely (as described in Chapter 19, *see also* pages 112–117).

Thirdly, they used modern social media to build strong online communities, converting happy customers into promoters and encouraging the viral spread of their messaging from peer to peer. It is no coincidence that their rise coincided with the growth of smartphones, social media and influencers, which effectively turbo-charged e-commerce after 2007. The combination of these factors allowed rapidly growing online brands to spread into vertical after vertical, giving us names like

- Allbirds in footwear;
- Everlane in womenswear;

- Bonobos in menswear;
- Away in luggage;
- Casper in mattresses;
- Blue Apron in meal-kits;
- Third Love in underwear;
- Birchbox in beauty;
- Harry's in shaving;
- FARFETCH in designer clothing;
- boohoo in fashion;
- Minted in gifts; and
- Huel in nutritional supplements.

These new brands have grown rapidly, backed by billions of dollars in venture capital money, and have become a huge threat to established brands. In fact, there has never been a time before where large established brands, with high name awareness and dominant market shares, have seen consumers switching to new upstarts in this way.

Twenty years before, this would have been impossible. The major brands would have exercised a stranglehold over shelf space, with their heavy advertising spends and established retailer relationships. In that era, launching a new brand would have required a lot of resources and nine out of 10 new brands would typically have failed. However, the development of mobile e-commerce and social media changed the playing field. Suddenly it became much easier and cheaper to start a new online brand from one's garage and to gain traction with consumers directly.

Part of the reason for this lies in the change in consumer sentiment over the past 20 years. As we saw in Chapter 1 (*see also* pages 9–16), young consumers have become relatively impoverished and therefore forced to search for better value options online. In addition, the spread of peer-to-peer reviews, social media and blogger-influencers has provided an objective way for consumers to evaluate new products and spread the good news when something genuinely innovative comes along.

A good example of this is Dollar Shave Club, whose founder, Michael Dubin, created a hilarious YouTube advertisement, which went viral and was seen by over 27 million people. The brand grew incredibly swiftly and was acquired by Unilever in 2016 for $1 billion[3].

In 2009, 39 per cent of online consumers were willing to try out new brands and products. Today, that number has increased significantly to 56 per cent, according to data from research company Forrester: 'We've reached this tipping point,' said Anjali Lai, a senior analyst at Forrester. 'Consumers are desperate for something new'[4].

A profitable model

Many of these direct-to-consumer brands have been very successful. Warby Parker said in March 2018 that it had reached profitability and that it had been growing rapidly as a private company without the need to go public. The company's valuation at its last round of funding in 2020 was $3 billion[5].

As we have seen, Dollar Shave Club was acquired by Unilever in 2016 for $1 billion and has since expanded to have a team of over 600 employees globally and more than 4 million subscribers. In 2020, it announced that it was going multi-channel via a wholesale deal with Walmart[6].

Huel, the British nutritional supplement brand, has enjoyed rapid growth over the past few years to record £72 million of revenues in 2019–20. Moreover, four out of its first five years were profitable and it received £20 million of investment in 2018, valuing it at £170 million (*see also* Chapter 44, pages 243–7 for a full case study on this interesting brand)[7].

Glossier, the direct-to-consumer beauty brand has achieved a valuation of $1.2 billion on reported revenues of $100 million in 2018. The company is said to be eyeing an IPO. Allbirds, the sustainable direct-to-consumer sneaker company, has achieved a valuation of $1.4 billion[8].

Third Love, a direct-to-consumer brand marketing underwear in a millennial-friendly (non-Victoria's Secret) way, achieved sales of over $100 million in 2019 and received $55 million of funding in February of that year, valuing it at over $750 million. It became profitable in 2018[9].

Boohoo – the fashion etailer – has grown from one brand to 12, absorbing PrettyLittleThing, Nasty Gal, MissPap, Karen Millen, Coast, Warehouse, Oasis, Debenhams, Dorothy Perkins, Wallis and Burton, and its most recent results for the half-year ended August 2020 showed revenue growth of 45 per cent (to £817 million) and pre-tax profit growth of 51 per cent to £68 million[10].

The growth of these direct-to-consumer brands has represented a very substantial threat to established wholesale brands. They could see that their retailer base was gradually being eroded and were only too aware of their high cost-to-market and lack of visibility of the final consumer. The logical response would have been for them to develop their own direct-to-consumer businesses.

One brand that showed great vision in doing this was Nike, who, in a stunning and prescient move, announced in 2017 a 'Consumer Direct Offense', which involved the company focusing on selling direct to consumers on a one-to-one basis. We will examine the Nike case in more detail in Chapter 48 (*see also* pages 262–266). However, most major wholesale brands were wary of going direct too aggressively, for fear of creating channel conflict with their retail customers. As we saw in Chapter 6 (pages 46–54), prior to the outbreak of the Coronavirus pandemic, most of them had only developed sales in the range of 1–5 per cent of their total businesses[11].

Wholesale brands go direct (finally)

It would appear that the sight of their retail customers all being shut down during lockdown has had a salutary effect on their courage, however, and many of the wholesale brands now seem ready to start to cut the Gordian Knot of their dependency on their retail customers.

Since March 2020, a large number of Fast Moving Consumer Goods (FMCG) and Consumer Packaged Goods (CPG) companies have announced huge expansions in their direct-to-consumer businesses.

For example, Procter & Gamble (P&G) is investing in direct-to-consumer start-ups to learn more about the sector. 'E-commerce and direct-to-consumer are growing,' P&G Chief Brand Officer Marc Pritchard said in 2019. 'We think the small can help the big get faster, and the big can help the small grow faster'[12].

Acquiring direct-to-consumer brands has helped P&G grow its business in new areas, learn about new methods of advertising (like performance marketing) and to reorganize its brand teams to mirror those of start-ups. For example, in 2017, P&G acquired San Francisco-based natural deodorant brand, Native, for $100 million in cash, followed in February 2018, by New Zealand-based natural skincare brand Snowberry. Then, in July 2018, it picked up First Aid Beauty, a cult digital brand specializing in skincare for sensitive complexions, for $250 million[13].

In December 2018, P&G went on to acquire direct-to-consumer haircare and grooming brands Bevel and Form, which aim to 'Make health and beauty simple for people of colour'. And finally, in February 2019, it acquired 'This is L.', a feminine hygiene start-up that manufactures organic pads and tampons, at a reported price tag of $100 million[14].

P&G has also partnered with venture capital firm, M13, to find, fund and launch direct-to-consumer businesses. The first brand launched under this partnership was Kindra, which provides oestrogen-free solutions, personalized resources and a community for those managing menopause[15].

Growing direct-to-consumer brands is very important to P&G. As brand consultant Allen Alexander puts it: 'They've always dominated the traditional sales channels, but the world is moving to online. And if they don't have their own way to directly connect with consumers, they're going to be playing at a disadvantage'[16].

As we have seen earlier, Unilever was quite early to the direct-to-consumer party, buying Dollar Shave Club in 2016 for $1 billion in cash. It also invested in healthy meal-kit brand Sun Basket in 2017 and acquired the Graze snack food brand in 2019 for a reported £150 million. In addition, it sells some of its major brands directly to the consumer, such as Ben & Jerry's ice cream and Maille condiments[17].

According to then Chief Executive Officer Paul Polman, speaking in 2018, there was no reason why direct-to-consumer sales could not be doubled from the then figure of 5 per cent: 'Every shopping journey now has a digital component. We've learnt a lot from Dollar Shave Club. We've been able to take that knowledge and expand it to other parts of the business. We are now also seeing our online business taking off... and with our prestige businesses we see more opportunities to go direct to consumers'[18].

L'Oréal has increased the share of its marketing expenditure going towards digital channels from 50 to 70 per cent since the start of the Coronavirus pandemic, Chief Digital Officer Lubomira Rochet told the *Financial Times* in 2020. The change in focus matches an accelerating shift in the company's revenues, with e-commerce accounting for 25 per cent of the total in 2020, and growing 60 per cent in that year. The company has also launched Color&Co, a direct-to-consumer personalized hair-colour website, which provides online consultations from expert colourists[19].

The Kraft Heinz Company is also venturing into selling direct. In January 2019, they acquired Primal Kitchen, a healthy food direct-to-consumer brand primarily focused on condiments, sauces and dressings. Then, in April 2020, they also launched Heinz to Home, selling Heinz products direct for the first time, spurred on by the Coronavirus crisis[20].

PepsiCo has recently expanded its direct business. In 2018 they acquired SodaStream, a personalized soda-making company, which has a very strong online business for $3.2 billion, and in May 2020, they launched two new e-commerce platforms – snacks.com and pantryshop.com, selling their mainline products direct to the consumer for the first time[21].

Nestlé has invested in its Nespresso direct-to-consumer website and also in its ReadyRefresh water dispenser site. Mondelez has gone direct with some of its brands, such as Sour Patch Kids, Oreo and Tate's Bake Shop[22].

Traditional brands are also increasingly concerned about the relentless rise of retail private label (whereby stores groups replace brands with their own products), which was already a long-term issue pre-Covid, and which, as we will see in the next chapter, received a powerful boost from the Coronavirus pandemic.

Thus, we can see that the pandemic has prompted a major move among traditional wholesale brands to start selling direct. The impact of the Coronavirus crisis has caused them to start to plan for a future where retail distribution is much reduced through store closures, and their retail customers themselves increasingly abandon them for private label.

CHAPTER TWENTY FIVE

Going Private

Just as brands are trying to go direct to the consumer and cut out the retailers, so retailers are working to cut out brands, by growing their private label product ranges. Private label has long been part of the retail playbook, but store groups often saw it as being limited to the lower-price end of their ranges. However, now, with the collapse of supply chains and falling prices and margins, which has been accelerated by COVID-19, they are ramping up their own-brand developments very rapidly and also going into the higher-quality end of the market. Apart from providing better value for a given price point, private label also has the additional advantage of creating exclusivity in an age where major brands can be found on thousands of websites.

Private label is very well developed in Europe, with an IRI Survey from July 2020 showing that it enjoyed nearly 40 per cent of the EU grocery market. In the US, it has historically had a lower market share, with one out of every four products sold being store brands, according to the Private Label Manufacturers Association[1].

The crisis spurs retailers to invest in private label

Private label sales got a major boost from the COVID-19 pandemic. According to Nielsen, sales of private label products across all retail outlets in the US climbed nearly 15 per cent during the first quarter of 2020, up $4.9 billion. Total dollar sales of store brands in the first quarter of the year were $38.4 billion (or 13.2 billion units)[2].

Shortages also caused consumers to switch brands more easily. In addition, the economic uncertainties created by the crisis led many to cut back on their budgets, favouring cheaper store brands. Historically, private label has always done well during recessions. For example, Target has invested heavily in its unique private label lines and now has six of its own brands, which do more than $1 billion each. We examine the Target case in more detail in Chapter 37 (*see also* pages 215–218)[3].

Swiss bank UBS valued Costco's Kirkland Signature private label brand at $75 billion in February 2020. The brand brought in $39 billion in sales in 2018, accounting for nearly 28 per cent of the Costco's sales[4].

Kohl's has invested heavily in building up its private label sales, which now account for 42 per cent of the total. This push has been particularly evident in women's apparel, where it has three private brands – Sonoma Goods for Life, Apt.9 and Croft & Barrow – as well as a number of exclusive deals with designers like Vera Wang and Lauren Conrad, which collectively account for 70 per cent of sales in the category[5].

Bed Bath & Beyond has also been investing in private label. In 2019, it hired former Target merchandizing executive Mark Tritton as its new chief executive, with the objective of repeating the success of Target's own-brand offering[6].

In late 2019, Tritton announced the launch of the company's first-ever private-label brand, Bee & Willow Home. He then hired Neil Lick, who had built the high-quality Williams Sonoma product range, and in July 2020, announced that Bed Bath & Beyond would be launching six more private label lines in the next two years. The company's share price promptly tripled, and by January 2021, stood at nearly seven times its 2020 nadir[7].

Best Buy has also successfully grown its store brand offerings in recent years. It has five private label brands – Insignia, Rocketfish, Platinum, Modal and Dynex – which collectively account for a substantial percentage of sales. We will look at Best Buy in more detail in Chapter 38 (*see also* pages 219–222)[8].

Walmart has around 30,000 private label products, some grouped under their 'Great Value' brand and some under other in-house brands. Great Value does more than $27 billion per year in revenues and 18 of the private label brands do more than $1 billion each[9].

Walmart Chief Financial Officer Brett Biggs said that, in grocery, private-label penetration has grown more than he ever thought it would in the US as a whole. Walmart has even launched its own tablet that competes with Apple's products, proving that retailers are also increasingly interested in adding private-label products even in spaces that have long been dominated by big brands[10].

Kroger's house brands take over $23 billion in annual sales. Its Simple Truth organic label has 1,500 products, many of which are rated more highly than leading manufacturers' brands in terms of consumer quality perceptions. It did $2.3 billion in sales in 2019, making it the biggest natural and organic brand in the market. Among Kroger's many other private labels are Home Chef, a meal kit brand and Dip, which extends across apparel, home goods and furniture. Kroger's share price has held up reasonably well during the retail crisis, standing at nearly 70 per cent above its 2019 nadir in the middle of January 2021[11].

Amazon-owned Whole Foods has a range of in-house labels including Whole Foods Market, Whole Trade, Engine 2 and 365. Trader Joe's, Publix, Wegman's, Walgreens, CVS and Rite Aid all sell products under their own names[12].

Generally, those retailers who have aggressively developed their private label brands have traded better than those that have not. For example, Macy's, which had only 20 per cent of its sales in private label in 2018, saw its share price fall to around 17 per cent of its peak in January 2021[13].

JCPenney does not release its private label share of sales, but the retailer has been dogged by rumours of failures and very high stock levels in its own-brand apparel and this must have had some bearing on its 2020 bankruptcy[14].

Countering direct-to-consumer moves by brands

In addition, where major brands are aggressively pursuing direct-to-consumer strategies, there is some risk that they will withdraw from previous retail partnerships, leaving the retailers exposed. This could be the case in the sports market, where Nike has made no secret of the fact that it intends to cut back the numbers of its retail customers. In this instance it may make sense for sports retailers to develop their own private labels. It is thus no surprise to see Dick's Sporting Goods adding rapidly to its own-brand offer. Recently, it announced the launch of 'DSG', a private label clothing and equipment line with items priced at between $15 and $40, and exclusively sold at Dick's stores nationwide and on its website[15].

'We saw an opportunity to better serve more athletes by designing quality products at a value that fits everyone,' said Nina Barjesteh, Dick's Senior Vice President of Product Development. 'DSG is a brand with a purpose that is born from sport, and has something to offer every athlete, no matter their size, skill, age or budget'[16].

The company also announced that it will expand its home-grown athletic wear brand, Calia, to 80 stores. In addition, it has a line of private label fitness equipment under the brand name Ethos[17].

In total, Dick's Sporting Goods aims to generate $2 billion in sales from its private label brands and to hit that target, Chief Executive Officer Ed Stack said that it will dedicate 'Meaningful floor space' to its new private label brands, which will be 'Opening price point products'[18].

Asked at a 2020 earnings announcement about the potential reaction from key partner brands as Dick's expands its private-label offerings, Stack said, 'Kind of the same reaction that they get from us when they continue to accelerate their direct-to-consumer business. I think we all know there's a quid pro quo out there'[19].

In the UK, two of the better-performing retailers – Marks & Spencer and John Lewis – have very large private label businesses, something that has helped shield them from the bankruptcies that have affected competitors like Debenhams and House of Fraser[20].

E-commerce platforms join the private label party

Apart from the stores retailers pushing private label, there is also a move by the large e-commerce platforms like Amazon and Alibaba towards going direct, by cutting out national brands and focusing on their own products. In doing this they are benefiting from the vast array of data that they have collected from their third-party business and are using it to guide their own product development efforts.

They have their own teams for product design, development, manufacturer selection, marketing, logistics and after-sales service, and work closely with the same manufacturers that supply global brands to ensure the product quality is correct. They can also leverage their platforms by featuring their own products high up in the search lists and promoting them through their marketing, much as stores retailers have been doing for decades.

Amazon more than tripled the number of private label products it sells, from 6,825 in June 2018 to 22,617 in June 2020. It groups them together under 111 brands, including such names as Amazon Basics for commodity items like batteries and light bulbs, Amazon Collection (jewellery) and Lark & Ro (women's fashion). In basic areas like household goods, Amazon private label products account for as much as 14 per cent of their sales[21].

Alibaba has used its eBay-like consumer-to-consumer website – Taobao.com – to launch its private label brand – Taobao Xinxuan (literally 'Taobao selected'), which sells affordable quality lifestyle and functional daily-necessity goods, including underwear, home fragrances, smart power sockets and sonic-control toothbrushes[22].

JD.com, another huge Chinese e-commerce platform, has introduced private label brand JD Jingzao (meaning 'Made by JD'), which has over 1,000 products on its platform, covering home products, home electronics, kitchenware, apparel, travel goods, food and daily necessities[23].

Chinese gaming company NetEase launched Yanxuan.com in 2016, which pioneered what it calls a 'M2C' (or Manufacturer-to-Consumer) model, by going direct to Chinese factories and creating products for established global brands. Flipkart – the Walmart-owned e-commerce platform in India – sells a wide variety of private label products under its Flipkart Smartbuy brand[24].

Private label is even reaching the world of online luxury. Yoox Net-A-Porter Group has launched '8 by Yoox' – its first private label brand, while Moda Operandi – another successful digital luxury platform – plans to launch private label and has started working with early-stage luxury brands in preparation[25].

'You have to do it in stages,' says Chief Executive Deborah Nicodemus. 'The first stage is working with the emerging talent and building out our own design network and manufacturing network'[26].

In summary, we can see a battle royal taking shape between the brands who want to miss out the retailers and the retailers who want to cut out the brands. What is certain is that in the long term, there is only room for one player in the supply chain of the future.

CHAPTER TWENTY SIX

The Endless Aisle

Apart from the impact that the e-commerce and communications revolutions have had in taking out stages in the supply chain, they have also had a huge effect on the choice of products available. As we have seen, a major advantage of internet companies was the low cost of adding product. It just required some extra pages on their websites in contrast to the high costs of accommodating additional product lines within a store.

In the early years of the Net, pioneers like Amazon tried to stock all the items they sold on their websites themselves, so although they avoided the 'space' costs of retailers, they still had the stock-holding and warehousing costs of all those products.

The marketplace model

In 2000, however, Amazon made a huge conceptual breakthrough with the launch of 'Amazon Marketplace'. Their simple, but genius-like realization was that they did not have to stock all the products themselves, but merely act as a sales platform for other brands to use. The brands did the hard work of stocking and delivering the product, while Amazon kept the really valuable bits of the transaction – fat commissions on the sale itself and masses of crucial customer data[1].

The launch of Amazon Marketplace paved the way for a vast expansion of their range to the 350 million products that we see today. This dwarfs the 12 million products that Amazon actually stocks. Most of the world's leading e-commerce companies have followed the same route, including Alibaba and Ten Cent in China, Rakuten in Asia, Zalando in Europe and Mercado Libre in South America[2].

Having bigger ranges tends to improve two of the key metrics which drive website profitability – namely conversion and basket size. The more choice, the higher the chance that the visitor will find what they want and convert into being a customer, and the more they buy per visit, the lower the delivery cost as a percentage of the sales value.

For retailers raised on having to be careful about fitting their selections within the 'four walls' of their expensive physical stores, this was a rather foreign notion. They imported the mental limitations of their stores into their Web businesses and continued to believe that their relatively puny product ranges could compete with the vast mass of choice available from their online rivals. Even as they saw their businesses drain away, they comforted themselves with platitudes like 'There is such a thing as too much choice'. Or, if they understood the problem, they adopted a defeatist attitude, saying things like: 'How can we possibly compete with Amazon, anyway?' They seem to have missed the point that *they* used to be the big players and that they could have been the 'Amazons' of the industry had they been sufficiently fast and aggressive. All they needed to do was adopt the platform strategy that Amazon was following.

I remember talking to an international client, in a market where Amazon was not yet well established. They were the leading retailer in their category, and I said to them: 'Why can't you be the Amazon of the region?' They looked at me in disbelief, mentally defeated, before they had even started.

Retailers embrace platforming

Intelligent retailers, however, have now hit on the idea that their websites can act as 'platforms' for selling a far wider variety of goods than are physically represented in the stores themselves. This can enable them to fill gaps in their ranges without the risk and cost of carrying all the stock themselves. This realization has been accelerated by the huge leap forward that online has experienced during the COVID-19 outbreak and the continued challenge to their stores businesses from the ongoing health issues. There is a now a high degree of interest in the platform idea: a 2018 survey by *Retail Week* indicated that 44 per cent of retailers were interested in introducing this model[3].

The leading retailer to follow this route has been Walmart, which, fairly early on, took the strategic decision to take on Amazon head-to-head, by massively expanding its product range. It launched its own online marketplace in 2009 and has since grown its range to 52 million products (of which 80 per cent are third-party brands)[4].

H&M is also testing the marketplace model and started to offer third-party brands on its website from 2019 onwards. As the company put it: 'We will start offering selected external brands and products at H&M. We will be adding a curated selection of products that complement our customer offer'[5].

Myer's – a prestigious Australian department store – has created The Myer Market as a marketplace featuring a very broad selection of third-party premium Australian brands. Marks & Spencer also announced that it was strengthening its clothing e-commerce offer by adding selected third-party brands. Other retailers who took the same route include Next, Best Buy Canada, Office Depot, Kroger, Auchan and Darty[6].

Monetizing audiences

It is not just conventional retailers who are adopting the marketplace model. Anyone with a large audience is potentially capable of leveraging it to sell relevant third-party products. Thus, influencers are getting in on the action as top stars like Michelle Phan, Kylie Jenner and Huda Kattan have all recently launched beauty marketplaces selling third-party products[7].

Some marketplaces are coming in from odd angles. For example, media company BuzzFeed, which has 20 million subscribers, launched a marketplace in July 2020, starting with a few beauty brands, but planning to expand to other categories as soon as possible[8].

In launching its marketplace, BuzzFeed worked with Bonsai, a company that focuses on creating marketplaces for media companies. Bonsai founder Saad Siddiqui said the number of companies currently expressing interest in setting up a marketplace is 'Five to seven times higher than pre-Covid'[9].

'People want to monetize their audiences without expending more capital and holding more inventory,' Siddiqui said, 'and, increasingly, marketplaces are a good way to do that'[10].

Setting up a marketplace has never been easier. Technology companies offering plug-and-play Marketplace applications have sprung up, such as Marketplacer, Code Brew Labs, Arcadier, Dokan, Mirakl, Scalefast, Luminos Labs and Naadam[11].

Matt Scanlan, founder of Naadam, said in July 2020 that he had witnessed a major growth in marketplace interest from a variety of companies. He believed one factor behind this was all the excess stock that brands and retailers had built up during the COVID-19 lockdown.

'The industry is definitely moving toward a marketplace model,' Scanlan said. 'There's a lot of inventory out there, and people are looking to marketplaces to move it for them – especially because traditional wholesale models are struggling so much'[12].

Thus, we can see that many brands, retailers and other players are using the power of the internet and particularly marketplaces to create 'endless aisles' of products that start to level the transactional playing field with the likes of Amazon and Alibaba.

CHAPTER TWENTY SEVEN

Whither the Store?

Thus far, we have focused on how retailers are responding to the Coronavirus crisis by moving aggressively into the digital sphere and re-engineering their supply chains to take out cost and add choice. But as all this is going on, what innovations are we seeing on the stores side? If digital is to form the new backbone of the retail industry, what is the future of the store in the multi-channel mix?

As we have seen, retailers historically thought of stores as mainly vehicles for transacting goods. But, as we have also seen, stores are actually a high-cost way of getting goods to consumers. Filling stores with piles of inventory (duplicated across multiple outlets), paying high rents to 'warehouse' it and employing lots of staff to administer it is more expensive than having low-cost e-commerce operations, with centralized, highly automated distribution centres.

As we have seen, retailers are finally waking up to this fact and are shifting more of the goods-transactions side of their businesses online. COVID-19 has accelerated this process dramatically and caused a kind of 'reset' moment for the industry.

If e-commerce is to become the new transactional channel, what should the role of stores be? Should they continue to exist, or are they obsolete, as horse-drawn carriages were when confronted with the motor car?

Solutions coming from left field

Ironically, some of the most innovative answers to this question have come not from retailers, but from online players. E-commerce platforms like Amazon, Alibaba and Ten Cent and direct-to-consumer brands like Warby Parker, Bonobos and Everlane have been launching new store concepts and they have come at the process from a completely different angle to traditional retailers[1].

Their rationale for opening stores has been their desire to connect more closely with potential customers. The basis for this thought has been that, despite the growth of e-commerce, the vast majority of people, globally, still shop in physical stores. And to access this still-large audience, they want to be able to demonstrate the quality and unique features of their products face-to-face, in a three-dimensional brand environment.

This logic has been underpinned by the rising costs of digital marketing, driven by the duopolistic stranglehold that Facebook and Google exert over the online advertising market. What e-commerce players are finding is that, under the right circumstances, the cost of customer acquisition can be lower in stores than online. Or, as they put it, "'IRL' [In Real Life] can beat URL."

This trend has been hailed by some commentators as showing that the whole 'retail apocalypse' theory was wrong and that retailing was not dying after all. However, the way that these online brands are doing physical retail is very different from the traditional model practised by the industry.

Focusing the store on customer recruitment

The key difference is that they design their stores around the brand experience rather than around stock transactions. In many cases, they are happy to let the digital channel handle the bulk of the stock-holding and goods delivery, and to focus the store on introducing potential customers to the brand and creating the beginnings of a relationship. This may involve sales, but not necessarily. If the consumer learns about the product, engages with the brand and potentially shares some data, this is also seen as a win.

It is worth remembering that they view the customer as being on a journey: from ignorance to awareness, awareness to engagement, engagement to relationship and then on to trial, repeat and loyalty. And lying behind this journey, a potential lifetime customer value many times that of any initial transaction. They are confident that if they can manage this process correctly from the start, so that the relationship gets off on the right foot, they can later convert this connection into a sale at the click of a button.

In addition to reinventing the role of the store, they have used new technology to make shops more efficient, more interactive and more exciting than ever before. We will explore the ways in which they have done this in more detail in the next few chapters and also show how innovative retailers are leaping onto these trends and reinventing their own stores so as to keep them relevant in the future.

People have no 'need' to visit stores anymore, they have to have the 'desire' to go. And this is what inventive retailers are giving them. It is exciting to see all this innovation and it gives us hope of a brighter future for stores within the multi-channel universe.

CHAPTER TWENTY EIGHT

Showrooming

As we saw in the previous chapter, the key innovation is the change in thinking about stores from being transactional to being experiential. Shops are moving from being places where you went to pick up stock to places where you are shown new brands and products: they are, in effect, becoming showrooms.

The term 'showrooming' was originally coined to describe how consumers went into stores to learn about products and then bought them on their mobile phones at lower prices. It was regarded as an invidious process by retailers, who felt they were putting in all the work (and cost), only to have the reward snatched away from them. Yet it was also an instructive process. Consumers were effectively saying: 'I value the store experience, but if you are going to lump all the costs of it on me, I'll take my business elsewhere'[1].

The e-commerce brands who opened stores understood this. Their shops were not designed to transact, but to show. Thus, they did not typically try to put their full range of products in the stores; in many cases, this would have been physically impossible as the bigger players had product ranges numbering in the hundreds of millions.

Small is beautiful

Their stores were typically much smaller than traditional 'big-box' retail outlets. This meant that the rents, store-build expenses, wages and utilities were far lower, to say nothing of the stock-carrying costs. For example, without having so much stock, stores did not need stock rooms, freeing up space for more productive use.

Within the available square metreage, far more space was allocated to customer service areas, with comfortable seating, spacious fitting rooms (in the case of fashion) and other amenities. Key products were given hero-status, with plenty of display space, information and demonstrations – the aim being to get the consumer to experience what was special about the brand.

So, for example, Sonos, the high-end direct-to-consumer audio brand, had luxurious listening booths, where visitors could appreciate the rich sounds in comfort. Ample use was made of technology to show other products not physically stocked in the store. So, there were giant interactive screens, where customers could view any product in the range and order online for speedy home delivery[2].

Zero-inventory stores

One of the early innovators in this space was menswear direct-to-consumer brand Bonobos. We already saw in Chapter 18 how they opened 'Guideshops', which focused on giving customers a high level of personal service, while actually transacting through their website and shipping direct to the home (pages 103–111). They were one of the first 'zero-inventory stores', in that the collections in the store were not for sale, but purely for showing to customers[3].

Many customers, particularly men, appreciated this type of service, because they did not always enjoy the shopping process. For example, Nick Hodson, a principal with global consultancy 'Strategy&' puts it like this: 'If I'm a guy and I'm fairly constant in fitness and weight, I can go and try on my suit and chinos and then just reorder, and I don't have to go to the store anymore. So, then all my transactions might be online. Arguably, I might be willing to make an annual trip to a showroom and then place my orders online'[4].

Other direct-to-consumer brands that have adopted a similar model would include:

- eyewear company Clearly;
- furniture supplier Made.com;
- make-up brand Glossier;
- womenswear business MM.LaFleur and
- online pharmacy Well.ca.

Eyewear brand Clearly started as an e-commerce company, where customers could find high-quality contact lenses and glasses at a much cheaper price than at traditional optometrists. Recently, they have opened physical showrooms in major centres, where customers can have eye exams, get contact fittings and try on glasses. If they choose to order frames and/or lenses, the products are mailed directly to their home rather than being handed to customers in the store itself[5].

Made.com is a London-based furniture brand, which started life in 2010 as an online pureplay and still does the vast majority of its £137 million of revenues (2019) through e-commerce. However, it has recently opened a number of showrooms – some pop-up and some permanent – around Europe, which use technology in interesting ways to showcase the company's products.

Made.com gives iPads to its customers, which they can use to scan 'Near Field Communications' (NFC) tags, containing all the product information, and to record the items of interest. Customers are encouraged to email themselves the list, which helps the company capture their email addresses. They also have a 'Touch Wall' where clients can scan a product and have images of all the other products in that range come up on video screens[6].

Glossier, which emerged from the hugely successful blog 'Into the gloss', fronted by star-influencer Emily Weiss, has a huge following all over the world. Their e-commerce channel does the majority of their global sales, but they also operate two permanent showrooms in New York and Los Angeles, as well as pop-up stores around the world. The purpose of the stores is for visitors to try the products and get expert advice on skincare and make-up, with the final sale being done online and delivery straight to the home. Again, the products in the store are not for sale, but for showing[7].

MM.LaFleur's main business is sending shoppers curated fashion boxes from their e-commerce store, based on online questionnaires and styling sessions. However, if the potential customer is reticent about committing to the clothing without trying it on, the brand operates permanent showrooms and pop-up shops in major cities. In these luxury boutiques, customers are able to sit down with a stylist for hour-long appointments to try on selected styles to see what works best for them. This service gives them the chance to get to know the product range and fittings so they can more easily place online orders in the future[8].

Well.ca is an online Canadian pharmacy. It opened a store in Toronto which featured QR-coded virtual displays of its products as opposed to actual stock (QR – Quick Response – codes can be read by smart phone cameras, enabling consumers to click through to product websites). Shoppers just scanned the images of the desired item in order to purchase it on their smartphones. Once ordered, the chosen products were delivered to their homes while a receipt was sent to their mobile devices[9].

How do you stock 350 million products in a store?

Showrooming is also being developed by some of the leading e-commerce marketplaces. Companies like Amazon and Alibaba are recognizing the power of being able to engage with consumers in person, but also demonstrating the futility of trying to stock their vast ranges within the four walls of a store.

For example, Amazon has launched small-format 'Amazon Four Star' stores, which carry around 2,000 lines, each of which scores at least four stars on the website. The products tend towards the innovative and surprising, and are tailored to local tastes. Access is given to the other 349,998,000 products stocked on Amazon's website, via in-store screens, and customers can also return goods via the store. The format is obviously trading well, as Amazon announced its intention to double the number of these stores in early 2020[10].

AliExpress opened a pop-up store in Paris in 2020, designed to encourage new consumers to learn about the quality of its products. Clearly, the company could show only a small fraction of the 100 million products that it sells online[11].

This is a classic example of the new trend in retailing, which is to use the store as an entry-point into the brand, most of which sits on the Web. When one contemplates the 100 million products, it brings home how impossible it would be to put them all in a store.

In 2016, Alibaba also launched a new store format, called Hema ('Fresh Hippo'), in the Chinese market. Hema is a grocery shop, which stocks 2,000 items in the store itself, but provides access (via digital screens) to over 200,000 online. The store itself focuses on theatrical food displays and cooking demonstrations, with an emphasis on special products that the Chinese love, such as seafood. The atmosphere is convivial, with eateries dotted among the displays. There is an app for ordering, complete with self-checkout, and the goods are shipped within half an hour to the customer's home. The format is obviously working, because Alibaba announced plans to roll it out to 2,000 stores[12].

Retailers finally 'get' showrooming

Thus, we can see that the online players have been showing the way forward for the retail industry. Thankfully, showrooming is now being adopted with enthusiasm by innovative retailers as well. Driven by the severity of the Coronavirus crisis, they are looking to shift more of the transactional side of their business online, cut costs by shrinking their stores and repurpose the remaining space away from stock-holding displays and towards brand-marketing and customer service areas. In other words, they are finally getting the point of showrooming.

For example, in June 2020, Nike announced plans to open 200 small-format stores, based around its 'Nike Live' experimental pop-up store format, which was in Melrose, Los Angeles. The stores were to be smaller than standard Nike shops (around 4,000 square feet) and would be open only to Nike app members. The store encouraged members to interact with staff, posting the store's text number in the window.

Nike's aim with this new format was to break down the barriers between physical and digital services by putting its app at the centre of the store operations. Members would be able to use it to enter the store, unlock exclusive merchandise in vending machines, book appointments, record loyalty points and check out. Nike saw the smaller format as a way to extend its distribution to more niche neighbourhoods and tailored the merchandise according to what was selling online in that area, including some very fast-turnaround products[13].

Similarly, Nordstrom has invested in a new format called Nordstrom Local. This is a much smaller store than a regular Nordstrom – 3,000 square feet as opposed to 150,000 square feet – and carries no regular inventory. Instead it focuses on services such as personal styling (free of charge), manicures, pickup for e-commerce orders (including kerbside pickup), returns, alterations, gift wrapping, shoe repair, charity drop-offs of used items and complimentary refreshments.

The stores have high-end interactive screens, where customers can easily access products from any of the company's full-line stores in the area, and either have them shipped to their homes or available for rapid pickup in the store. These stores have performed very well for Nordstrom. On average, a Nordstrom Local customer spends 2.5 times the amount of a Nordstrom regular client[14].

Ikea is doing the same thing with its Ikea Design Centres, which are far smaller than the company's regular big-box stores. The new format offers a free interior design service, with experts advising clients on different combinations of furniture and using virtual reality to show them what they look like in their homes. Design Centres are located in the heart of major cities, rather than out-of-town retail parks, and they only carry a fraction of the full Ikea range, with the rest being available online via interactive screens. The focus for the physical inventory is on furnishing small-space city-centre apartments[15].

Macy's has launched a new smaller format in 2020 called 'Market by Macy's', which was designed by Rachel Shechtman, founder of the experiential retail boutique Story (acquired by Macy's in 2018). The Market store is about one tenth the size of an average Macy's, at only 20,000 square feet, and offers a small selection of products curated to meet local needs. It contains a bar and restaurant and hosts events, to encourage a sense of community.

Talking about the new stores, Jeff Gennette, Chief Executive Officer of Macy's, said: 'We continue to believe the best malls in the country will thrive, however, we also know that Macy's and Bloomingdale's have high potential off-mall and in smaller formats.' Macy's designated Dallas, Atlanta and Washington, DC, as test markets for the new stores[16].

Apple also developed a new format in 2020 called 'Apple Express' which was far smaller than their regular flagship stores and geared for quick pickup of key products during the COVID-19 outbreak. The stores resembled bank teller stations, with staff protected behind plexiglas, and limited phones and accessories on display. Only one customer was allowed in at a time and many people used the stores as pickup points for online orders. As of October 2020, the company was planning to open 50 of the new stores in the US[17].

Retailers have also reduced their space in existing stores. For example, Kohl's has leased out areas in several of its stores to the Aldi supermarket chain and Planet Fitness. In the UK, John Lewis has said that it is looking to reduce retail space by around 40 per cent at its Oxford Street flagship store by converting at least three floors to office space[18].

Dixons Carphone – the UK electrical retailer – announced in November 2020 that it was going to invest in omnichannel, turning its stores into exciting experiential centres. As part of this plan, it said that it would be reducing its in-store stocks by selling slower-moving products via screens and expanding its range online[19].

Thus, we can see that retailers are finally coming to the realization that they do not need to have huge stores, built to house their entire range, but can use smaller, less expensive spaces as access points into their brands. And, the purpose of the stores is shifting from being mainly about displaying products towards being showrooms, where they can tell their brand story, demonstrate key products and provide excellent service. In the following chapters we will look at the best ways of using these showrooms to attract and impress potential customers.

CHAPTER TWENTY NINE

Spectacle Frame

A key part of the 'showroom' philosophy is to create a 'show': to entertain, to surprise, to delight. Stores need to become frames in which brand 'spectacles' are performed. This experiential element is becoming more and more important due to demographic changes. Younger generations like Millennials and Gen Z are spending less and less of their budgets on goods and much more on experiences. For example, a recent survey of Millennials indicated that as much as 52 per cent of their discretionary spending goes on experience-related purchases[1].

This introduces the concept of 'retailtainment'. The last few years have seen the creation of some amazing concepts. Not all of them are in retail proper, but they give a sense of direction that retail should follow.

The Museum of Ice Cream was one of the first truly experiential concepts. Although it later ran into problems, due to COVID-19 and management issues, it showed the way forward in terms of theatrical retail. Built as a pop-up in New York in 2016, it consisted of 6,000 square feet dedicated to ice cream and other sweets. Visitors paid $30–40 to enter the museum, which contained room after room of stunning displays and experiences. Designed to be highly 'Instagrammable', it was initially an enormous success, with more than 500,000 visitors by November 2017[2].

Another powerful immersive concept was Rosé Mansion – a New York wine bar, amusement park and interactive science museum – which featured a series of spectacular rooms, designed by local artists, and all linked together around the idea of wine education. *See also*

Chapter 41 (pages 230–4) for more information about this remarkable concept store[3].

Another format inspired by the Museum of Ice Cream model is Candytopia, a confectionary wonderland launched in 2018 as an installation in Santa Monica, Los Angeles. This first opening attracted 150,000 people, and the company has since opened stores in Philadelphia, Miami and Scottsdale, Arizona and other pop-up locations[4].

Looking internationally, another such experiential idea is Moreru Mignon – a Tokyo store dedicated to the concepts of 'purikura' (Japanese photobooths) and 'kawaii' (cuteness). It offers a mass of Instagrammable backdrops such as outsize sofas in the form of cupcakes, pink London telephone boxes and enormous pastel green donuts. It is not really a retail space (apart from offering a small, curated beauty range), but does suggest ideas which could be used in retailing[5].

Turning to a more high-tech version of the experiential concept, TeamLab is a consortium of Japanese artists, programmers, engineers, computer-generated animators, mathematicians, architects and graphic designers, who create technological 'artscapes' – using digital technology to release artistic expression from its physical limitations in terms of size, cost, movement and interactivity. They have two galleries in Tokyo – Planets and Borderless – and the experience is totally immersive, involving walls, floor and ceiling; it is also interactive, with the viewer influencing the artwork. These are not retail spaces but give some idea of the possibilities that can be created through technology[6].

On a more commercial level, there is Showfields – a revolutionary retail concept based in New York. It offers a vision of how future retailing might look, combining cutting-edge experiential stores, innovative direct-to-consumer brands, culture and community, all in one spectacular department store. More detail on this highly innovative concept can be found in Chapter 43 (*see also* pages 237–242)[7].

The original showman

Actually, the concept of retailing as showmanship is not really new. Harry Gordon Selfridge (1858–1947) built his eponymous store around the idea that that it should seek to entertain the visitor. Known as 'The Showman of Shopping', he summed up his vision by saying: 'A store should be like a song of which one never tires.' He also understood the idea that a department store should be a community, adding, 'A store should be a social centre, not merely a place for shopping'[8].

Selfridge was amazingly inventive in curating a stream of noteworthy experiences for his customers. For example, he exhibited the rickety aeroplane of Louis Blériot, the first person to cross the channel, to marvelling crowds of 150,000 on the shop floor of his store. In 1925, shortly after the launch of public radio, he installed a radio mast on the roof of the store and started broadcasting music to the people of London. He also understood the idea of espousing causes which were more important than mere shopping. For example, he championed women's suffrage at a time when suffragettes were bombing public buildings to bring attention to their cause. He flew their flag above the shop, published advertisements in their newspapers and carried items in their colours[9].

His theatrical vision still guides Selfridges today. The store recently featured a skateboard bowl on an upper floor, a boating lake on the roof and concerts by famous musicians on the ground floor. It is a vision that holds valuable lessons for today's retailers[10].

Another powerful retail concept, which predates the dot-com age, is 10 Corso Como in Milan. The store was conceived by fashion editor Carla Sozzani in 1990 as a living magazine, where editorial choices in fashion, food, music, art, literature, lifestyle and design were displayed in a magnificent setting.

The space, which includes a gallery, bookshop, exhibition area, library, garden café, research boutique and hotel, attracted opinion-formers across the worlds of retail, media, culture and the arts, and became enormously popular. It was so successful that it was acquired by a public company for €30 million in 2017[11].

Brand exploratoria

Apart from theatrical concepts launched by retailers, there have also been some very interesting ideas coming from individual brands, which have deployed temporary pop-up concepts to really bring their products alive, using what are known as 'brand exploratoria'. For example, Boursin – the famous French cheese brand – recently created a 'sensorium' to launch its new flavours, Shallot & Chive and Black Pepper. The brand used Oculus Rift VR headsets to take customers on a virtual tour of a well-stocked fridge. Throughout the journey, viewers were led through the various indulgent sections of the fridge, past towers of luscious vegetables and a freezer full of champagne, and on to a forest of herbs[12].

In a similar vein, Nestlé-owned chocolate brand, KitKat, opened 'The KitKat Chocolatory' in the Seibu Department Store in Japan, which sold limited edition gourmet chocolate bars in a variety of unique flavours, including Purple Potato, Cinnamon Cookie, European Cheese, Bean Cake, Wasabi, Cherry Blossom Green Tea and Special Chili. The store only stocked 500 of the bars a day as the chocolate work was done by hand. Each bar cost ¥315 (£1.83) and the 500 bars available on the opening day sold out in one hour and 40 minutes. This concept store gave Nestlé a huge amount of positive publicity in the Japanese market and has since been rolled out to other countries, and into a web version[13].

Another example comes from Vans, the skateboarding brand owed by VF Corporation, which launched an experiential concept called 'The House of Vans' in London. This innovative 30,000-square foot space was based around the company motto of being 'off the wall'. The main feature was a huge underground skate park, complete with concrete ramps, tunnels and a street course. The location also featured an art gallery, live music, street culture, a cinema and a café. Nothing better summed up the Vans brand than this very cool space, where young people could not only shop but also spontaneously socialize. The concept was very successful and was subsequently rolled out to eight countries[14].

Turning to media brands, Marvel invested in an impactful retail experience to support the launch of its new Avengers movie series in 2014. The Avengers S.T.A.T.I.O.N. was an immersive exhibit that has toured the world since the first Avengers film. It has appeared in key retail areas such as New York, Seoul, Paris, Beijing, London and Las Vegas and always pulls in huge crowds.

The store featured real-life movie props and interactive displays. Marvel branded items were available for purchase, but the goal of the project was not to sell T-shirts and mugs, but to create an experience for fans and bring the brand to life[15].

Brands can also use technology to improve the customer experience in stores. For example, Sephora uses its 'Beauty Hubs' to offer virtual makeovers to customers. By looking into a 'Magic Mirror', the customer can apply different make-up shades to their own face, so that they can see which options best suit them. Specsavers – a British eyewear retailer – uses a similar technology to enable customers to 'try on' different spectacle frames to see which ones best suit their face[16].

These ideas are just some of the creative uses to which retail space can be put. With the growing use of technology, stores can be turned into fantastic brand experiences. This is so much more interesting than traditional serried rows of stock-fixtures and when combined with a super-efficient Web service for transacting, can really give a brand the edge in today's super-competitive world.

Obviously, many of these theatrical concepts were temporarily shut down thanks to COVID-19, but, as the world opens up again in the future, they should provide inspiration for innovative brands and retailers looking to take part in the Retail Revival.

CHAPTER THIRTY

Edutainment

In a similar vein, retail space can be used to educate consumers about a product or brand. Educational experiences are a very popular leisure activity, as can normally be witnessed by the queues outside museums and art galleries (obviously, this has been somewhat restricted during the COVID-19 crisis, with visitors required to pre-book visits).

Every company has a history and every product has an interesting 'maker-story' behind it. If it is presented in the right way, the store can become a fabulous stage-set for recounting the brand story.

Of course, it is very important that this education is presented in an entertaining way, which is why we use the word 'Edutainment'. As many museums have realized, it is not enough to present information in a dry, academic way – it has to be packaged in an interactive way, which engages the visitor.

We have already seen a great example of this in the previous chapter with Rosé Mansion – the New York-based interactive wine-tasting adventure that combines a wine bar, an Insta-worthy amusement park and an educational museum in one epic dream package. Rosé Mansion has been successful in attracting over 80,000 visitors and carries many important lessons for retailers wishing to enhance the educational side of their stores (*see also* Chapter 41, pages 230–4, for a full case study).

There are many other brands pushing 'Edutainment' as a commercial initiative and reaping the benefits in terms of attracting large numbers of visitors. For example, Timberland set up an in-store program to launch its new Sensorflex walking shoes called 'Flex and the city'. Visitors were invited to participate in a virtual walking tour through an imaginary city, using a treadmill and a Virtual Reality headset.

They were able to personalize their journey and activities on the way and, at the end, received a recommendation regarding which type of Sensorflex shoe was best for their preferred activities[1].

Apple has long been a leader in in-store education. Its free 'Today at Apple' classes showcase leading local photographers, artists, musicians and technologists, who demonstrate how they use the company's products to produce their work. These events are always well attended by enthusiastic customers who are eager to learn more about the technology behind the Apple brand. During the pandemic, Apple took the program online with 'Virtual Creative Sessions'[2].

A number of direct-to-consumer brands have pioneered the use of stores as primarily educational vehicles. For example, Casper – the online mattress brand – launched a store concept called 'The Dreamery', which was designed to educate customers about the special benefits of their high-quality products.

Customers could pay $25 for a 45-minute rest in one of nine curtained 'nap nooks', which were equipped with a Casper bed and furnishings, as well as toiletries from cruelty-free beauty brand Sunday Riley, pyjamas from luxury sleepwear business Sleepy Jones and toothpaste from natural personal care company Hello. Sleep sessions could be booked through a Casper micro-site, as well as the ClassPass and MindBody apps, while walk-in visits were also accepted. At the end of the nap, private washrooms were available to freshen up, as well as free coffee in the lounge area.

Customers could not actually buy a mattress in the store, although there were screens enabling them to do so online. For Casper, however, building the stores was a necessary growth step to educate customers about the product and build their trust so they felt comfortable purchasing such a big-ticket item online.

Pete Trentacoste, Environmental Design Director at Casper, summed up the purpose of The Dreamery as follows: 'We call it playful science – which is something that is inspired by science museums ... It teaches you about our product in a very playful way'[3].

For Indochino, the direct-to-consumer menswear brand, its stores are primarily educational vehicles. They employ senior-level brand experts, who spend up to an hour with clients. As Vice President Dean Handspiker put it: 'Our model for a made-to-measure retailer is probably closer aligned to that of a ready-to-wear retailer but with a twist that we don't have the inventory in the space so we can devote a lot more of the space to experiential, to lounge, to a place of education'[4].

Start-up electronics brand littleBits, based in New York, sells simplified, modular electronics components that can be used to build experimental prototypes, particularly for educational purposes. Most of its sales are online, but it set up a store in the city to give people the chance to experiment with its products in a live environment.

At the littleBits Store, the space is divided into a demonstration area, a shop and a workshop. Some of the projects that people can partake in include making a DIY Keytar (a cross between a keyboard and a guitar), a BitBot car or a robotic drawing machine. To make it easy for people of all ages to participate, the shop has experts to help with technical skills at all levels[5].

The Poseidon Project – a taproom and bottle shop in San Diego, California – has introduced craft beer education classes to create greater customer engagement with their product. They also organize visits from famous brew-masters, book-signings by well-known authors and beer-food pairing courses[6].

Jim Beam – the famous whisky brand – designed an interactive environment at Munich airport to promote the launch of a new product called 'Jim Beam Honey'. The display made the most of the product's honeycomb associations, boasting beekeepers and a hive-inspired station. Boosted by the tagline 'It was worth every sting,' the Jim Beam Honey pop-up offered tastings of the Honey-variety whisky as well as the brand's line-up of original whiskies[7].

The above are all examples of brands and retailers devoting space in-store to educational displays which engage and entertain the visitor. Use can be made of modern technologies such as interactive touch screens and virtual reality to create a special 'Edutainment' experience and draw the potential customer into the brand universe. This is essential in order to provide something over and above what can be obtained online.

Retailers can 'find' this space by reducing the displays of inventory in low-selling categories, or where a high proportion of sales are already online. Most retailers have an 80/20 pattern of product sales, with a few products taking up the lion's share of revenues and a long 'tail' of items which sell very little from week to week. This is where to find space and these products can be offered online instead, using in-store monitors.

Obviously, the full potential of experiential and educational store concepts will almost certainly have to wait until the threat of Coronavirus is past. Nevertheless, they are essential strategies for retailers to pursue as they strive to reinvent their stores to stay relevant in the long term.

CHAPTER THIRTY ONE

Clubhouses

Another potential role for stores in the long term is as 'Clubhouses' for the brand community. Human beings are social creatures and despite the growth of online chatrooms, dating sites and social media interactions, they still appreciate getting together physically. In fact, the growth of online socializing has been linked to increased levels of depression. A study at the University of Pennsylvania found that high usage of Facebook, Snapchat and Instagram increased feelings of loneliness[1].

Maslow's Hierarchy of Needs places 'belonging' at just above physical needs (like food, water and security) in the pyramid. Clearly, as a race, we are facing a veritable crisis of belonging. This has been particularly true during the period of the COVID-19 lockdowns, when many people were completely isolated from their normal communities, including work, friends and family. Figures from the Office for National Statistics suggest that nearly 20 per cent of people in the UK appeared to have depressive symptoms in June 2020 compared with 1 in 10 before the pandemic[2].

It is likely after the lockdowns are finished and it is safe to socialize again, there will be a strong desire among people to connect physically. If one studies history, one finds that periods of war or austerity are followed by periods of exuberance and conviviality, as with the Roaring Twenties after the First World War, or the Sixties cultural explosion, which occurred after the lifting of the post-World War Two austerity. Retailers therefore have a great opportunity to use their physical stores to bring people together in communities linked to their brands.

Building a brand community

Of course, this presupposes that the retail brand has a 'community' in the first place. If all a retailer is to its customers is a place to transact, this does not add up to a community. To create a sense of community around a brand, the brand-owner has got to make it mean more than this.

Much of the content of this book is built around the themes that make retailers into 'real' brands – things that stand for something, that resonate, that create emotion. Things like having a higher cause; like being innovative; like treating people as individuals; like having a relationship with customers; like involving them in the life of the brand; like educating them. Once these things are in place, and the brand has a true community, then the store itself can become the epicentre of collective participation and connection. There are many great examples of retail brands that have done this and reaped the benefits in terms of business success.

A good example of this is Rapha – the cycling retailer – whose community is united in its shared love of riding. The brand has turned its stores into 'Brand Clubhouses', where it brings together its enthusiasts to have coffee, plan trips and look at kit as part of the Rapha Cycling Club[3]. (We cover Rapha in more detail in Chapter 45, *see also* pages 247–251.)

Another great example, to which we have already referred (*see also* page 110), is Lululemon. As we have seen, Lululemon sells athleisure clothing, like other sports shops, but, again, this is not what makes it special. What Lululemon is really about is women celebrating the shared feeling of fitness, empowerment and body positivity. As the brand states on its website: 'We're a mindful movement that believes if we push past our sweaty boundaries, we're able to build the strength to push ourselves in other aspects of life'.

Sports retailing used to be very male-dominated and Lululemon was one of the first companies to create a female-centric brand and hence stands out as a beacon of feminist empowerment. The brand has a strong community, both online (through social media) and offline (through events). However, a key expression of its customers' involvement has been the free yoga sessions that it runs in its stores. It brings in well-known local yoga teachers to lead these workouts and they are very popular. Even during the COVID-19 lockdowns, Lululemon has continued the yoga sessions online. This has helped them to achieve above-average results during the retail crisis, with sales being 22 per cent ahead in the third quarter of 2020, despite some of their stores being closed. Lululemon's share price hit a record high in September 2020[4].

Less well known, Lomography is an Austrian camera brand, specializing in analogue photography. Most of their sales are online, but they have stores, that they use to interact with their brand community, which is held together by a common love of old-fashioned film-based photography.

They have a very relaxed attitude towards their customers, allowing them to rent new cameras to see if they like them before buying, and the stores also feature a photographic gallery of their customers' work. Customers love to spend hours in the store trying out different equipment and discussing their work with knowledgeable staff and fellow enthusiasts.

The company also reaches out to its most passionate customers when hiring for new positions, which helps build a seamless community between brand and loyalists. Lomography is an unlikely success story in a world dominated by digital technology. In 2018, it had 12 stores, revenues of £40 million and sold 500,000 analogue cameras along with 2 million rolls of film[5].

Gymshark is a rapid-growth fitness apparel and accessories brand based in the UK, but supported by millions of passionate followers and customers in 131 countries. Created in 2012 by teenager Ben Francis and a group of his high-school friends, it has expanded from being a screen-printing operation based in a garage to one of the fastest-growing and most recognizable brands in fitness.

Although all its revenue and most of its brand community is online, Gymshark believes strongly in the value of physical get-togethers to reinforce shared brand experiences. It has held regular meet-ups and 'Expos' in major cities around the world, where it has brought together star influencers in the gym and weight-lifting space. Fans of the brand have gathered in large numbers to meet their heroes and join in the mass workout groups.

Gymshark also opened a pop-up store in Covent Garden in London for the month of March 2020 and held in-store workout sessions. During the pandemic, it continued to host workouts and challenges online. The brand is highly profitable, earning a net income of £20 million in 2019. It was valued at over £1 billion in 2020, when it received investment from venture fund General Atlantic. (There is more detail of the Gymshark case in Chapter 40, *see also* pages 226–229.)[6].

The Peloton phenomenon

Peloton is a hugely successful sports equipment and media company, which has revolutionized the world of workouts by taking the gym into people's homes. It sells them stationary bicycles and treadmills equipped with giant video screens, on which, in return for a monthly subscription, they can log into live workout sessions led by celebrity instructors.

Since its launch in 2012, Peloton has become the largest interactive sports platform in the world, with over 2.6 million subscribers. The convenience and privacy of home-use, combined with the motivational effect of participating in 'live' events with top instructors, have apparently had a major effect on many users' lives. In consequence, the brand has developed an almost fanatical following, who have created their own Facebook sub-groups, such as 'Christians who spin' or 'Theater nerds who spin'.

Despite the raison d'être of Peloton being online connections, the brand places huge importance on face-to-face events in order to weld the brand community more tightly together. It holds annual 'Peloton Homecoming' events in New York, where over 3,000 of its most passionate acolytes pay $95.00 a head in order to enjoy three days of events over six venues, including live workouts with celebrity trainers, an outdoor run, talks by the CEO and other Peloton stars and a concert by alternative rock artists such as Beck. It also holds regular events in its studios in New York and London, and fan groups organize their own physical meet-ups around the United States. For example, 'XXL Tribe', which describes itself as a group for 'women of size', holds regular get-togethers of its 6,700 members.

The company obviously had to suspend the 2020 Homecoming due to the lockdown, but held special online events to mark the occasion. Its overall strategy is obviously working as Peloton saw growth of 61 per cent in its second-quarter 2020 revenues and its share price rose to five times its IPO-level in September of that year[7].

Another brand which focuses on community building is Itzy Ritzy – the maternity products brand – which has created a strong customer group built around shared parenting experiences. Parenting is rewarding but can also be challenging and lonely, and many people benefit from sharing their experiences with other families. As a result, parenting communities are some of the largest and most loyal that exist.

Itzy Ritzy makes stylish maternity accessories, such as nappy (diaper) bags that look as though they come from designer brands. Their website also has a lot of educational content on motherhood, such that they have become a go-to destination for information about everything from nursing covers to teething tools.

Their engagement with their community is most evident in the parent profiles featured on their blog. These interview-style posts outline not only what some of their most loyal customers love about their products, but also their own personal parenting experiences. This type of real-life user-generated content helps inspire future customers to join the Itzy Ritzy community.

Itzy Ritzy is a brand rather than a retailer, but it holds a lot of live events, often in retail outlets, such as Target. At these happenings, they engage with their customer community live and also create content for their blog[8]. Again, during lockdown, much of this content moved online.

In a more traditional manner, Southern Co-op is a co-operative society, based in the south of England, which prides itself on its close ties to local communities. Each store is encouraged to build local relationships with its neighbours through donating time and money to help those in need. This has proven to be especially valuable during the COVID-19 crisis, with so many vulnerable people left isolated by the lockdowns. In return, local people have shown great loyalty to their Co-op store, which helps explain why they have been able to continue to grow their business through the Coronavirus crisis. (We cover the Southern Co-op story in more detail in Chapter 46, *see also* pages 252–256.)[9].

A brand built by its own community

A very interesting example of a community-based brand is Outdoorseiten – the German outdoor products brand. What is noteworthy is that it was developed by its community, rather than by a company. Originally, Outdoorseiten.net was a forum where hiking and camping enthusiasts used to share ideas on trips, accommodation and equipment. As members exchanged product tips, eventually someone had the bright idea of developing some of the ideas into prototypes and producing them. Then someone else suggested a logo, and it was voted upon. Eventually, in 2005, a group of core members registered the name and the brand was born. This story illustrates one of the key points about building a brand community – successful communities exist, not to serve the brand organization but to serve the people in that community[10].

If we look at the brand communities mentioned above, they all meet a need in their members. With Rapha, it is the desire to share the love of cycling with others; with Lululemon, it is about personal empowerment; with Peloton, it is linked to improvements in fitness and morale; with Itzy Ritzy, it is about new mothers sharing their challenges with other mothers and thus feeling less isolated; with Lomography, it is a need to pursue an artistic interest with fellow enthusiasts. These needs may be to do with gaining emotional support to meet personal challenges, exploring ways to contribute or cultivating interests and skills with like-minded people.

Often, people are more interested in the social opportunities that come from brand communities than they are in the brands themselves. In such instances, brand loyalty is the prize for meeting people's needs for connectedness, not the reason for the community to come together in the first instance. Thus, as we can see, building strong brand communities is key to moving retail businesses beyond the purely transactional and developing brand loyalty during these challenging times. And we can also observe that, while the online world is where a lot of modern brand communities reside, it is still essential to use stores, pop-ups and other 'In Real Life' events to crystallize this sense of togetherness.

CHAPTER THIRTY TWO

'A good stylist is cheaper than a good therapist'

As described in an article which appeared in money.com in 2017, Joshua Jones was a 'guide' at the Bonobos store in Madison Avenue, New York. 'Cool and charismatic', he certainly did not consider himself a sales associate. He was an expert in menswear, with detailed knowledge of materials, cuts and finishes, and had a client book of loyal customers who depended on his good taste to make the right choices for their wardrobes[1].

'Josh', as he asked visitors to call him, worked by appointment with his customers, typically devoting an hour to each one. He took the time to understand their needs and preferences and would put together curated selections for them to try on in the luxurious fitting rooms at Bonobos. He was also equally happy to discuss the latest music trends, where his clients were going on vacation and what their thoughts were on recent movies. In addition, he used to give them a drink of their choice to enjoy while they were waiting.

Orders would be taken on an iPad and the goods would miraculously appear at their home a few days later, shipped from a warehouse in Massachusetts, New England. Josh used to call customers at home to check they were happy with the fit – 'I make it easy for them,' he said. 'People say all the time, "I normally hate shopping, but you made this enjoyable".'

Josh was well paid – he earned $17.00 per hour as opposed to sales assistants at Macy's, who, at the time, would get $8.00 an hour. His benefits were generous, with nearly unlimited vacation, paternity leave and an annual motivational retreat. He did not work on commission, nor was he under pressure to sell as much as possible to his clients. Highly educated, his ambition was to start his own brand one day. When he was first interviewed at Bonobos, the general manager who hired him asked about his five-year plan.

'I was kind of shocked,' Josh recalls. 'And then he said, "I want to help you get there."'

Josh was not expected do the normal administrative tasks associated with retail. He did not spend much time unpacking, tagging or counting stock, because the store was a 'zero-inventory' shop – in other words, the collection was for showing only, not for sale. He didn't even manage cash, because payments were by credit card on the iPad.

A new breed of retailers

Josh is typical of a new breed of retailers who are transforming customer service. Historically, being a shop assistant was a tough, poorly remunerated and often boring job. 'It's just not pleasant to spend most of your time folding stuff, cleaning displays and having piles of products to maintain,' says Nadia Shouraboura of retail technology company Hointer.

The result of this we already know: given the hard and unrewarding nature of their work, it is hardly surprising that many retail workers do not provide top levels of service. Lack of acknowledgement from retail staff is one of shoppers' top three complaints – and it could be a contributing factor to why one report by Salesforce – a company offering Customer Relationship Management (CRM) services – found that only 32 per cent of store visitors enjoyed the experience. However, the new model offers a clear way forward. As Shouraboura puts it: 'Showrooms help the progression of a numbingly boring job into something more exciting, like being a stylist. The level of labour turnover in showrooms is far lower than in regular stores'[2].

High-level stylists like Josh Jones are the secret weapon of retailers in their battle to stay relevant. The internet has so many advantages that if customers already know what they want, they are likely to buy it online. It is when they do not know what they want, and need advice and personal input, that they need to talk to someone with real expertise. And this is what stores – if configured correctly – can provide.

'Roles are changing,' says Jane Greenthal, a senior retail strategist at the design and consulting firm Gensler. 'It's a different skill set. Employees aren't just there to stock merchandise, they're building relationships'[3].

Another brand which has invested in outstanding customer service is REI Co-op – a Seattle-based outdoor clothing and equipment brand. It has a special philosophy, based on its co-operative structure, and contributes a great deal to nature conservation causes. The company has 169 big-box stores and has successfully bucked the trend in retail, pre-Covid, achieving a record $3.12 billion in sales in 2019, more than 8 per cent above the previous year.

Key to its success is the special service it offers in its stores. Sales associates – themselves passionate hikers and climbers – stand by the front doors of the stores, greeting and saying goodbye to customers. Whenever a customer walks in, they enquire about what the customer needs to do or which type of product they are looking for. The associate then tells them exactly where they need to go and even communicates with the rest of the floor to send a staff member in that direction if the customer needs help[4].

On a smaller scale, Seattle ice cream shop Molly Moon's Homemade Ice Cream is a brand that is known for enthusiastic customer service. Its associates — known as 'Scoopers' — have been trained how to ask the right questions and make every customer experience positive.

There is almost always a line outside the door. 'I always feel genuinely greeted, even though the interactions are quick,' says Chris Guillot, instructional designer of 'Retail Shift: Teaching Success on the Sales Floor'. 'They are so friendly and have fantastic personable personalities. Even though the engagement is quick, I never feel like I'm being rushed'[5].

An employee-owned business where shopping is a pleasure

Another retailer who understands how to turn employee motivation into exceptional customer service is Publix – the Lakeland, Florida-based supermarket chain – which has over 1,200 stores across the southern states of America. The company was founded in 1930, by George Jenkins – apparently after he was treated badly by his manager, while working for another retailer. He vowed that he would treat his employees well and based the company philosophy on that principle. As he put it: 'First, take care of your customers. Second, take care of your associates. They will in turn take care of your customers.'

Publix has famously never laid off an employee. All associates are required to start at the bottom, cleaning floors and stacking shelves. The company only promotes from within and posts 'Advancement Charts' in all its stores, showing each employee's route to store management. Over a third of all employees have signed up for this advancement process.

The company does not sell its shares to outsiders. Instead the Jenkins family, which still owns 20 per cent, has given the remaining 80 per cent to the employees. Once an associate has worked for the company for a year and completed 1,000 hours of service, they are automatically given an additional 8.5 per cent of their salary in the form of stocks. Not surprisingly, the company shows up near the top of the 'Best Companies to Work For' charts. Indeed, it won the top spot in Fortune's 'Most Admired Companies in the Food and Drug Store Sector' in 2018. And, just as the founder said they would, the well-looked-after associates have duly delivered the Publix promise to be the store 'Where shopping is a pleasure'.

The enthusiasm is evident as soon as one enters the store. Members of staff immediately smile and ask if there is anything they can do to help. If a customer asks to find a product, they go and get it themselves, put it in a trolley and bring it to them. Queues are limited to two customers per line and there is always an associate to bag the goods and carry them to the customer's car. One reporter tells the story of how the associate at the meat counter helped her select some cuts for a big dinner party she was nervous about and also wrote out a recipe for the dish. On her next visit, he remembered and asked how the party had gone. This emphasis on great customer service has helped Publix withstand the threat from lower-price chains and online giants and its most recent results in the third quarter of 2020 showed an 18 per cent rise in sales, despite the COVID-19 crisis[6].

Even Walmart – not historically known for its customer service – is investing more in this area. In the past two years, the company has spent $2.7 billion on training programs designed to improve how employees interact with customers. It has also raised wages: the average hourly pay for non-managerial full-time employees was $13.85 in mid-2020, up 17 per cent from three years before. 'The human touch becomes a competitive differentiator,' says Walmart spokesperson Ravi Jariwala[7].

Retailer as hair stylist – a useful analogy

When thinking about how having excellent store staff can help to create long-standing brand relationships, a useful analogy is that of the hair salon stylist. Many stylists have a loyal clientele – so much so that having a ready-made following is considered essential to getting a chair to rent in a salon. Customers go to the same stylist for years and follow them around when they move salons. They share intimate stories with them and develop a close relationship.

Star stylists are extremely well paid – often more than the management of the salons. Indeed, management have to be very careful about how they treat them, because they are so valuable. If retailers think about the kind of people that they need in future, and the kind of relationship that they want them to have with loyal customers, then they could do worse than to think of them in this manner. Hiring high-level staff and investing in the customer service area of the store – giving it more space, installing comfortable seating and pleasant fitting rooms, offering tea, coffee or champagne, making appointments for key customers – these are things that all retailers should be thinking about in the future.

Of course, moving towards such a model requires a higher level of staff sophistication than is available in most retail outlets. To pull it off requires investment in higher pay, more training and greater staff autonomy than are typical. But if savings can be made in other areas, through lower rents, fewer staff tied up with administrative work and lower stock levels (as described in Chapters 27 and 28, *see also* pages 159–161 and 162–169), then this should free up some resources to finance the creation of a high-level personal-shopper team. Above all, it is the only option. So long as retail remains mainly about transacting, with a small fringe of customer service, it is never going to be able to compete with online. The only route forward is for stores, and the teams within them, to offer more.

CHAPTER THIRTY THREE

Phigital

Turning now to the question of the technology used in stores, we need to look at how it can help retailers learn more about their customers. As we have seen, stores retailers have been flying relatively blind regarding the type of customers coming in and out of their shops and their behaviour. This has been in stark contrast to the online players who were able to track every twist and turn of their clients as they interacted with search engines, social media and their websites.

Making stores more like websites

New types of technology, however, are giving retailers the ability to see how customers are reacting to their stores, products and promotions in much greater detail and in real time. In effect, they are making stores more like websites.

Smartphone detectors can now pick up the unique Wi-Fi/Bluetooth search 'pings' sent out by individual phones and, when combined with location beacons, can track the movement of the phones' users from the moment that they approach the store. They can show the footfall past the store and the number of people coming in; they can identify how many customers are leaving quickly without engaging (the 'bounce rate') and how many stay long enough to interact with staff or displays. Additionally, they can measure the average time spent in store, see where people are going, identify 'hot' and 'cool' spots, measure dwell time in front of displays, check interactions with staff and finally, record the level of sales conversions[1].

Ceiling cameras can be used to do much the same kind of thing and can additionally estimate the age and gender of the visitors. However, the holy grail of retail personalization is the ability to recognize individual customers and this is possible only through facial recognition technology[2].

Facial recognition

Facial recognition cameras can identify individual shoppers and send them offers tailored to their needs. The information can also be used to brief store staff about the shopper and their preferences, based on past purchases, thus putting retailers on a level playing field with e-commerce players, who have always been able to track the behaviour of their individual customers. However, there have been concerns about the privacy issues surrounding this technology – for example, there have been lawsuits against retailers (including Macy's, Lowe's and Home Depot) over the use of facial recognition technology. The answer lies in getting customers to opt into the use of this type of data, much as they do when they visit websites. The key thing is to wrap this approval into brand community membership schemes, offering suitable advantages like exclusive products, special promotions and loyalty-related gifts[3].

A good example of a successful opt-in program is that of California-based fashion retailer Ruti, which uses facial recognition to take photographs of customers entering the store and combines them with customer preferences, based on what they buy. This information is buffered in the brand's system, pending confirmation. At the point of purchase, the customer is asked whether they wish to opt-in to the future use of this data and if the answer is positive, it is placed in the store's Customer Relationship Management system. When the customer returns, the system recognizes them and feeds the store stylists the customer's name and a shortlist of styles likely to appeal to them.

This technology has enabled Ruti to boost repeat purchases massively, according to owner, Ruti Zisser. She is a great advocate for the use of facial recognition systems. 'Retail with no technology is not going to work,' she says. 'Some stores don't even have the email addresses of their customers. At a lot of the big retailers like Nordstrom and Bloomingdale's, sales associates are using physical books and when they leave that store [for a new job], they take the book with them. The idea that the company doesn't have all that information is insane.'[4]

The store of the future

Another brand which uses such technology in an innovative way is Farfetch. The company started life as an e-commerce portal for luxury boutiques. Since then it has successfully repositioned itself as a technology provider for brands, combining technology and fashion to provide unique in-store experiences.

José Neves, Chief Executive Officer of Farfetch, has spoken about his concern that physical retail is diminishing. His vision for the future of retail includes advancements in technology to make the consumer experience more human. He produced Farfetch's 'Store of the Future', an augmented retail solution that 'Links the online and offline worlds, using data to enhance the retail experience'.

In its retail store in London, Farfetch provides connected clothing racks, touch-screen-enhanced mirrors and sign-in stations that pull data collected online to use in-store. It also provides customers with a sign-in screen to search their purchase history and wish lists, all of which provides valuable insights for the sales assistants. In addition, there is a smart mirror to request different sizes, ask for alternative products or to pay, without leaving the dressing room. This innovation allows Farfetch's customers to enjoy an effortless experience that harmonizes the best parts of boutique shopping with the speed and convenience of online shopping[5].

New types of retailers, which offer 'Retail as a service', such as Showfields, Neighbourhood Goods and B8ta, offer such technology pre-installed in their spaces. They make the data thus obtained available on real-time dashboards so that brands can see how many people are engaging with individual products and adjust their strategies accordingly. This is dealt with more fully in Chapter 31 (*see also* pages 179–185)[6].

In summary, an important part of the future of retailing lies in having the kind of customer data that has long been the preserve of the online players, through the use of 'Phigital' technology, which makes stores more like websites.

CHAPTER THIRTY FOUR

Techs and the City

The other major trend connected to technology is retailers using it to automate basic administrative tasks. This is enabling them to bring their costs closer to those of the e-commerce players and to free up their staff to focus on customer service. We see this in areas like checkout, stock replenishment, cash management and the handling of point-of-sale information.

Automated check-out

Starting with checkout, many stores now have self-checkout stations, thus economizing on the need for regular till staff, although they still tend to have security people to monitor the process. Going further, some groups are now experimenting with staff-free, automated systems. Amazon Go – the new-format convenience store from the internet giant – has shown the way forward. With its 'Just Walk Out' program, customers download an app and use it to scan-in when they enter the store. Thereafter, they can pick up products and leave without paying, while the app produces a receipt and charges their credit card. This not only reduces labour costs for retailers, but also increases consumer convenience[1].

The technology used is a combination of cameras and artificial intelligence to track individual customers around the store and weight sensors and Radio Frequency Identification Devices (RFID) to track their purchases. The system is remarkably accurate and represents a major step forward in store management. Amazon announced in March 2020 that it was making this technology available to third parties[2].

If other retailers are loath to work with Amazon, similar technologies are on offer from other vendors, including Grabango and AiFi. Grabango was founded in 2016 in California and uses computer vision and machine learning technology mounted in overhead rails to monitor the position of every product in the store, whether on the shelf, in someone's basket or with a shopper leaving the store. Retailers can sign up for the service and it can be installed in any size store (unlike Amazon Go, which is specifically designed for small format stores). Customers download an app, pick up products and simply scan the code on their app to pay[3].

AiFi is a Santa Clara, California-based start-up, which offers two types of solution in this area. One is OASIS – a patented end-to-end platform to build and operate autonomous stores, using computer vision and sensor fusion. The other is the NanoStore – a complete solution-in-a-box, fully automated, container-sized, checkout-free store, which can be shipped to any suitable location and installed quickly[4].

Similar systems have been pioneered in the Far East by groups like Suning.com in Nanjing, China, 7-Eleven, with its unmanned X-Store in Taiwan, and NTT Data, with its Catch & Go stores in several countries, including Japan, Korea and Singapore. Apart from their lower cost and greater convenience, autonomous stores have great relevance in the COVID-19 environment, as they enable shopping without human contact[5].

Robots

Another area of automation is the use of robots in stock and display management. Checking the aisles for products that are out-of-stock, wrongly positioned, incorrectly priced or mis-promoted is one of the most time-consuming and mind-numbing activities in retailing. Yet it is a critical task as it is estimated that out-of-stocks alone cost American retailers 15 per cent of their sales.

The use of robots to carry out these tasks is growing rapidly. For example, Simbe Robotics' autonomous shelf-scanning robot, Tally, has been used in Schnucks Markets and Giant Eagle stores in the US. The low-maintenance robot contains more than 40 sensors that allow it to avoid obstacles as it navigates around the shop-floor, scanning shelves. Tally can check 15,000 to 30,000 products per hour as it audits stocks through the help of cameras, computer vision and machine learning. It is able to identify prices, product placement, availability and special promotions. Store staff can then use the information to ensure that all products are in stock and correctly promoted. Apart from scanning the shelves 24 hours a day, it gives employees a priority list of tasks to do, thus improving efficiency[6].

Bossa Nova Robotics, a start-up based in San Francisco, is working with Albertsons Companies Inc to test its shelf-scanning robot – the Bossa Nova. In the UK, Asda is testing an autonomous robot built by the Tennant Company and powered by a Brain Corp operating system, which is designed to clean up spillages in its grocery stores[7].

Some retailers are also experimenting with using robots as customer service guides. For example, home-improvement retailer Lowe's introduced the LoweBot, a robotic assistant which helps customers find what they are looking for, while Soft Bank Robotics created Pepper, a semi-humanoid robot that can be used to answer basic customer enquiries[8].

In 2018, JD.com opened its own high-tech supermarket, '7Fresh', which included smart shopping carts which follow the customer around, without being pushed, thus creating a hands-free experience. The carts also have screens showing product information about items that the customer has picked up. In addition, grocery stores such as Walmart are installing automated unloaders, which speed up the intake of stock into the back of the store. The machine reads bar codes on the boxes and routes them to the correct departmental unloading-wings, including a location for urgent, out-of-stock items[9].

Safe tech

Technology is also being used to improve the safety of the in-store experience. Robots are being used by restaurants and cafés to reduce the risk of human waiters infecting customers with the Coronavirus. For example, at the Dadawan restaurant in the Dutch city of Maastricht, there are three robot waiters, called Amy, Aker and James, who have been installed to serve drinks to customers. Bar staff load the drinks onto trays carried by the robots and tap in the relevant table number. The 'waiters' then take them to the table. They are not very flexible – for example, customers have to unload their own drinks – and the robots do not have much conversation, other than wishing customers a good meal, but they indicate a potential avenue for development, especially in the post-Covid era[10].

A further retail task, which is being automated rapidly due to the challenges created by COVID-19, is cash management. The need for contact-free payments has largely made cash redundant in most retail outlets, which has removed the time-consuming and stressful process of counting, reconciling and banking cash[11].

Another area of 'safe tech' is that which permits customers to pre-book items for quick instore or kerbside pickup. For example, Safe Queue is an innovative app which reduces queuing. It is designed to allow stores to manage the flow of customers digitally so that they can wait inside their cars until there is space for them to shop. GPS-based, the app knows when the customer is within 1,000 feet of a store. The customer simply taps on a button and the merchant puts them in the Safe Queue virtual line. When they are at the front of the queue, they get a message and can go in and quickly get their transaction done – reducing risks for customer and store staff alike[12].

The Nike flagship store in New York has a service called 'Speed Shop', which enables customers to reserve shoe sizes online. They enter via a separate entrance and unlock a digital locker, try the shoes on and purchase via self-checkout – all without coming into contact with anyone[13].

Product information

Another area where technology can improve retail administration is by automating the provision of point-of-sale information. As we have seen, one advantage that e-commerce has historically enjoyed over retail is the clarity of its product information. In retailing, information about product features and benefits, sizing options, stock availability and user reviews is often lacking at point of sale, whereas on most websites it is very clearly laid out. However, new technology is bringing this kind of information to stores as well. Retailers are equipping products with QR codes which are readable on apps, bringing up a full set of information about the product on the customer's phone. Some retailers also use location beacons which project product images and information onto nearby screens when a customer spends time looking at them[14].

There is also a growth in automating the update of product and pricing information. Sixty-seven per cent of all shopper decisions are taken at the shelf's edge, so it is crucial that the information on shelf ticketing is timely and accurate. With products moving, promotions starting and finishing and prices changing constantly, it is a huge task for store staff to keep all the shelf-edge information up to date at all times. For example, large grocers currently have to change up to 10 million labels a week in the US.

Consumers are increasingly price-sensitive, so it is critical to be able to update prices in real time to react to competitor changes. In addition, today's consumers are used to being able to read reviews easily online and stores may suffer a disadvantage if they cannot provide the same information. Thankfully, there is now a plethora of new technologies to automate all of this data so that it can be updated directly from the retailer's head office. This can be combined with competitor price-checking software to react in real time to any changes.

Firms like Tesco and Morrison's in the UK have tested digital shelf-edge technology, while Walmart, Best Buy and Kroger are doing the same thing in the US. For example, in 2018, Kroger worked with Microsoft to develop a new technology called 'Kroger Edge', which displays pricing and nutritional information digitally, allowing the store to update it in real time and from a remote location. They are also working on an app that creates efficient 'journey plans' for consumers, guiding them around the store, based on their shopping lists[15].

The automation of all these basic store activities will reduce costs considerably, bringing the cost of retailing closer to that of e-commerce. Consulting firm McKinsey & Company estimates that the combination of these technologies can reduce the labour hours necessary to run a typical grocery store by as much as 65 per cent. There is, of course, the risk that the introduction of such technologies will cost jobs. However, automation does not have to be viewed purely in a cost-saving context. It can also be seen as freeing up staff time to concentrate on value-added activities such as in-store customer service or out-of-store activities like installation and maintenance[16].

CHAPTER THIRTY FIVE

Please Re-lease Me

So far, we have been focusing on how brands and retailers are adapting to the longer-term changes in their industry and to the 'burning platform' of COVID-19. But what of the landlords who own the high streets and malls that make up the retail industry?

As we saw in Chapter 7 (*see also* pages 54–58), the commercial property industry has been going through a very challenging time, with store vacancies at an all-time high as anchor tenants go bust or reduce their store portfolios dramatically. Rents are falling or not being paid at all, across large swathes of the retail world, and, as we have seen, some major property groups, such as intu in the UK and CBL in the US have fallen into insolvency. Most others have seen their share prices drop by 65 per cent or more.

There is clearly going to be a shake out of retail space, particularly in the US. America has long been considered to be 'over-retailed', with 23.5 square feet of retail space per person, compared with 16.4 in Canada and 11.1 in Australia – the two next highest globally. And the difference with the rest of the world is even more extreme as US space per person is more than six times that of Europe and Japan[1].

It is likely that around 1 billion square feet of American retail space will need to be rationalized over the coming years, with around 400 out of the total 1,100 enclosed malls in the US closing in the near future. Larger malls will probably continue to do well, but a lot of smaller ones in poorer areas of the country are unlikely to survive[2].

In the UK, many high streets were already partially boarded up prior to the start of 2020 and the arrival of COVID-19 has only worsened the hollowing-out of Britain's town centres[3].

What strategies should the major retail property groups adopt to deal with this crisis?

Doubling down on retail

Some companies are doubling down on the retail sector. For example, Simon Property Group has acquired some of its leading tenant brands – all of which had gone bankrupt – in an attempt to stop them disappearing from its malls. It made its first forays into the retail business when it teamed up with Authentic Brand Group (ABG) – a brand licensing firm – and Brookfield Properties to buy Aeropostale (2016), and then Forever 21 in February 2020. Then, as COVID-19 scythed through the ranks of the retailers, it went further, working with ABG to buy Brooks Brothers and Lucky Brand, paying $325 million for the former and $140 million for the latter. By November 2020, Simon had moved onto even bigger game, again teaming up with Brookfield Asset Management to take control of retail giant JCPenney[4].

Whether this is a good idea or not is moot. Clearly the crisis represents a chance to pick up some venerable names at very low prices. On the other hand, all of these brands have been struggling over the past few years, and Simon has little experience of running retail operations.

If retail is to have a vibrant future, a profound change needs to occur in the mind-set of the landlords.

Making it easier to open a store

Let us start with the realities of the retail marketplace. The traditional retailers are in retreat and they are not going to be opening many new stores over the next few years. So where will the mall and high street brands of the future come from?

The only place they can come from is from among the hundreds of thousands of digitally native brands that have sprung up over the last 20 years. They are dynamic companies, with innovative products and new services. And, as we have seen, they are interested in using physical spaces to interact with potential customers and sign them up for their online communities. However, they are not (for the most part) going to be interested in entering into the kinds of long leases that were typical of the industry in the past. Nor are they going to want to commit to long and expensive store builds which have to be amortized over five years[5].

They see physical retail as a means of recruiting customers so it would make sense for them to use their stores as more like marketing campaigns – in short bursts, rather than for long periods. Just as it would not have made sense in the old days to advertise a new product endlessly in the same magazine, it probably does not make sense to have your customer recruitment store always in the same place.

So long as physical stores were pretty much the only way of buying things, it made sense for them to be in the same location for long periods. This was because it was easier for customers to remember where they were, so that they could return to them to place repeat orders. However, once a brand thinks online-first, then their permanent location for repeat purchases is always in the same place – on the Net. Therefore, if they want to use physical space primarily as a recruitment mechanism for new customers, it would make more sense to move the stores around, so they keep attracting new audiences. For example, if a brand opens a store in a high-traffic location such as King's Cross station in London, then, over a six-month period, it is likely that a substantial proportion of the commuters using that route will have been exposed to the store.

If, at the end of that period, they have not engaged with the brand, it probably means they are not interested in it. Would it not therefore make more sense, at the end of the six months, to move the store to another high-traffic location (for example, Paddington station) to give a fresh set of potential clients a chance? In order to attract this new breed of digital-first brands, it is therefore necessary for the landlords to move away from the traditional long-lease model towards a more flexible set of arrangements.

Reducing set-up costs

The cost and timescale of a full retail fit-out is also something that needs to be addressed. Staying with the same logic, if a brand only wants to trade a location for six months, they are hardly going to wish to spend three to four months and hundreds of thousands of dollars to fit it out. Therefore, the way in which stores are fitted out will need to change. One solution is to use pop-up stores, installed in blank white spaces. However, many pop-ups can be unattractive and makeshift-looking, and they do not always deliver good commercial results.

Fortunately, new technologies such as large-scale digital screens make it possible to create highly branded store environments, which can nevertheless be flipped from brand to brand very quickly and easily. Store window backdrops and interior walls can be lined with digital screens, which can project the brand's imagery in a very premium way. For example, Heathrow airport is testing a new boutique space with digital walls, where the whole look and brand-feel of the store can be transformed at the flick of a switch. However, such digital technology is not cheap to install and again the brands are not going to want to take on the expense of doing so, purely for the sake of enjoying six months of trading.

Plug & play spaces

What makes a lot more sense is for the landlords to pre-install such technology in the spaces. That way the brands can just arrive with their digital marketing chips, plug them in and create the branded effect immediately. This would reduce the downtime currently experienced by brands doing traditional physical fit-outs and make it possible for both brands and the landlord to maximize the use of the space.

The same applies to other technologies – all of the automated labour-saving devices and customer-tracking systems covered in Chapters 33 and 34 (*see also* pages 192–195 and 196–201). Again, it would make sense for the landlord to pre-install these systems so that the brand can focus on customer service, rather than administrative basics, and have access to real-time customer engagement and conversion data.

The landlord would benefit from having highly attractive spaces which would rent out quickly and easily, and would be able to amortize all the technology over a five-year period, during which time there might be 10 to 15 brands passing through the same space. The brands would benefit from having access to these 'plug & play' spaces to use for flexible periods without having all the risk and cost of the traditional leasing model. They could move their 'customer recruitment machines' (also known as their stores) from one high-traffic location to another, thus maximizing their reach.

Who owns the staff?

The same logic might apply to staffing. Most of the e-commerce companies have no experience of running store operations. Things like clock-in and clock-out systems, till operations, cash management procedures, hours rotas, stock booking rules, staff motivation and employee bonus schemes are foreign to them. It would therefore make more sense, again, for the landlord to 'own' the shop staff and related systems. If the landlord were to follow the advice contained in Chapter 32 (*see also* pages 186–191) and hire teams of high-level personal-shopper-type enthusiasts, they could offer them to the brands on a per-day basis. All the latter would have to do would be to have their trainers visit a few days before opening and educate the teams about the values, features and benefits of the brand. The landlord could also move staff flexibly between stores, avoiding the phenomenon so often seen in malls, whereby one brand is overwhelmed with customers while others nearby have staff standing idle, with no clients.

Changing the leasing arrangements to the above system, perhaps initially in one part of a mall or high street, would have the benefit of attracting large numbers of digital brands, thus revitalizing the financial health of the retail property sector. The supplementary benefit of this would be to bring a cornucopia of fresh, innovative and ever-changing new brands to malls and high streets which have, for so long, languished under a stultifying blanket of sameness and mediocrity. This is the kind of revolution that the retail industry needs to make shopping exciting again.

CHAPTER THIRTY SIX

Retail as a Service

Linked to this change in philosophy regarding commercial property, we have seen the rise of a new concept called 'Retail as a Service' or RaaS. RaaS providers are companies which offer solutions for online brands who wish to make the move into physical stores, but lack the resources and skills to do so in the traditional manner[1].

As we have seen in the previous chapter, many online brands want the benefits that physical stores can give them – greater brand engagement, higher levels of customer interaction and more new customer recruitment – but are nervous about investing in traditional shops. The RaaS companies have stepped into this gap, typically by leasing larger spaces, and then subdividing them into smaller modular units and leasing them out to brands on a more flexible basis. They usually equip them with the latest retail technologies and often wrap the whole thing up in a larger community-oriented cultural and entertainment envelope. Many of them talk in terms of making opening a retail store as easy as designing a website and of being the 'Shopify of retail stores' (after the famous Web company which created turnkey e-commerce websites).

The leading players

The leading players in RaaS are Neighborhood Goods, Showfields, Bulletin, B8ta and Anchor Shops. Neighborhood Goods was founded by Matt Alexander in Plano, Texas, in 2018. It aims to be a new type of department store, featuring an ever-changing landscape of thoughtful, exciting and contemporary brands, stories and events. It offers a selection of 32 direct-to-consumer and other innovative brands, in 14,000 square feet of space, which is divided into modular smaller spaces. Leases range from two to 12 months and brands pay a fixed fee per month. In return, the company provides all the staffing and a central checkout mechanism, both online and offline. It also gives brands access to a real-time data dashboard, which records key metrics like customer flow, dwell time and conversion, based on pre-installed technology built into the spaces[2].

Neighborhood Goods also aims to create a community of forward-thinking customers, by adding features like a restaurant/bar – Prim and Proper – and a program of live events and speakers[3].

Brands which have signed up include A.N OTHER (fragrances), Act & Acre (wellness), Aesop (beauty), Akola (accessories), Boy Smells (candles), Dollar Shave Club (shaving), DSTLD (clothing), Kinn (home products), Rockets of Awesome (childrenswear) and Sonos (audio)[4].

Neighborhood Goods has opened three stores in total – the first in Plano, the second in Chelsea Market, New York, and the third in Austin, Texas. With the advent of COVID-19, and the temporary closure of the stores, the company pivoted strongly towards online, adding more than 100 brands to its transactional website[5].

We have already mentioned Manhattan-based start-up Showfields, which is leading the way with an exciting mix of direct-to-consumer brands, theatrical displays and a strong community-based cultural program. Chapter 43 features a full case study on this very interesting brand (*see also* pages 237–242)[6].

Bulletin is a New York-based start-up, which aims to democratize retail for brands and to optimize retail for stores. It works with female-founded digitally native brands, selling them through its three company stores and also acting as an intermediary to help them reach a broader group of high-quality retailers. For its own stores, it charges brands between $300 and $2,000 a month to rent space, as well as a percentage of the sales. In return, it provides them with valuable real-time data on how customers are interacting with their products[7].

Many of the brands have strong social media followings, which they bring to the Bulletin stores for launch events. The brand selection is highly curated, unique and quirky and includes companies like Fat Toad Farm (which sells goats' milk caramel), SHHHOWERCAP (which sells nano-technology shower caps, which dry instantly) and The Bitter Housewife (which sells mixer drinks for whisky).

Bulletin also acts as a curated marketplace, bringing selected brands into contact with pre-vetted, high-quality boutiques. It offers technology that enables retailers to see information about brands, such as products, prices and minimum order quantities, and then place orders online. It also offers brands an automated upload system so that they can get their products onto retailers' till systems rapidly.

B8ta is a San Francisco-based company, started in 2015 by Vibhu Norby, William Mintun, Phillip Raub and Nicholas Mann. Describing itself as 'Retail designed for discovery', it has 22 company stores, where consumer electronics and homeware brands can show off their products. It has created high-technology software, which helps brands monitor consumer engagement, manage checkout and control inventory[8].

B8ta is a subscription service, so the brands get 100 per cent of the sales but pay for the space and services, including staff and real-time data. The staff are known as 'b8ta testers' and are trained by the brands. Alongside each product, b8ta provides a built-in iPad, into which the brands can load their product information.

The company has worked with more than 500 different companies and rotates through 10 to 15 products a month, all on consignment. It sees retail as a 'media and advertising platform', with the store providing brand awareness and data such as impressions, customer engagement, product demonstrations and dwell time.

Sales is not the only performance indicator for b8ta, nor for its brands: 'Most new brands find that about 50 per cent of their brand awareness comes from retail, not public relations, not digital advertising,' says Phillip Raub, President of b8ta. 'People are discovering and learning about their products for the first time in a store environment'[9].

The company has also developed a separate business selling its Ark software to other retailers. It has helped Lowe's open 70 SmartSpot stores, which sell intelligent-technology products, and has also worked with Macy's and Toys "R" Us[10].

Leap Inc is a Chicago-based RaaS provider, which was founded by Amish Tolia and Jared Golden. It offers a turnkey solution to digital brands, including leasing, store design/build, sales operations (including staffing) and technology infrastructure. The technology interlocks seamlessly with the brand's digital architecture, enabling it to track customer footfall, engagement, dwell time and conversion in real time. Leap also offers omni-channel integration, including the option to accept returns at any Leap store (not just the relevant brand's store).

The first store that Leap built was in 2018 for premium sneaker brand Koio in Chicago, which was very successful. This is not surprising as, according to an ICSC 2018 survey, opening a new physical store for emerging brands results in an average 45 per cent increase in overall traffic to that brand's website. In total, by October 2020, Leap had built 12 stores for innovative online brands including Naadam (fashion), Floravere (bridal), Goodlife (apparel), A.L.C. (celebrity fashion), Charlie Holiday (apparel), Public Rec (menswear), Something Navy (apparel) and Oros (outdoor-wear)[11].

Malls embracing RaaS

Some of the more enlightened mall groups are also participating in this trend towards more flexible leasing arrangements. Macerich, the major commercial property group, has launched a new service called Brand Box. It offers short-term leases, modular store designs and help with build-outs to online brands wishing to go from 'pixel to physical', as they put it. They promise to de-skill the store creation process, supporting brands with full-time 'success managers', enabling them to experiment with retail without the risks normally associated with the full store-opening process.

They pre-install the brand spaces with retail technologies and subscription software that would normally be inefficient to put into a regular pop-up store, but can be very helpful for brands in terms of learning about daily footfall, dwell time, customer flow and conversion. They also assist with employee recruitment, training and management systems.

The concept opened at Tysons Corner Center, Virginia, in 2018 and is planned for two other Macerich properties – Santa Monica Place, Los Angeles, and Scottsdale Fashion Square, Arizona. Participating brands included Winky Lux (beauty), Naadam (fashion), Interior Define (furniture) and Nectar (clothing)[12].

Simon Properties has launched a similar concept called 'The Edit' in one of its properties, Roosevelt Field Mall in New York. Simon describes it as 'a first of its kind, scalable, turnkey retail platform'. Brands who have participated include Raden (luggage), Rhone (sportswear), Lively (underwear), goldno.8 (accessories), Jars by Dani (food), Beltology (accessories), Vitaly (jewellery), Yosi Samra (shoes), Skinny Dip London (gifts), Thursday Boots (footwear), KOIO (footwear) and Cuzin's Duzin (food)[13].

Raden founder and Chief Executive Officer Josh Udashkin explained why online brands were interested in these RaaS concepts: 'Raden strongly believes in the power of the mall. There is a lot of foot traffic in malls with different customers to reach. We are a brand that wants to reach new customers, where they are already predisposed to shopping. Simon has malls with lots of traffic. We believe the mall is an under-penetrated market for new brands that should be taking advantage of it'[14].

Two other commercial property groups – GGP and Unibail-Rodamco-Westfield – have launched similar concepts, named 'In Real Life' and 'The Gathering Shops', respectively[15].

Thus, we can see that the long-term retail crisis, accelerated by COVID-19, is finally bringing about substantial changes in the retail property market and spawning innovative solutions, such as Retail as a

Service. These changes are making life easier for existing retailers and encouraging online brands to enter the physical world.

This completes our survey of the trends that are coming together to create the basis for the Retail Recovery. We will now, in Part Three of this book, look at a number of case studies of retailers and brands that are succeeding, despite the crisis, by using a combination of the strategies outlined in this book. Hopefully, they will provide practical examples of how these ideas can be applied and give confidence to those wishing to try them in their own businesses.

At the end of Part Three, there is a conclusion, which will draw together all the themes discussed in this book into a blueprint for the Retail Recovery.

PART THREE

Winning Through Creativity – Retail Success Stories

CHAPTER THIRTY SEVEN

Target

Target is a good example of a successful Retail Recovery story. The American retailer started life as the discount division of the Dayton's Company of Minneapolis, Minnesota, in 1962. It did well in the 1990s and early 2000s, based around the popularity of its low prices combined with good quality. However, it fared less well in the aftermath of the 2008 recession as competition from Amazon and other online players ate into profits. By 2015, revenue growth had more-or-less stopped and net income was more than 40 per cent below 2008 levels. Stores were in disrepair and many commentators were encouraging the company to close loss-making outlets in line with the rest of the retail industry. Instead, Chief Executive Officer Brian Cornell decided to double down on growth by announcing a $7 billion investment program in March 2017. The investor community did not agree with his decision, causing the stock to plummet by over $8.00 on the day of the announcement – its biggest one-day decline ever[1].

Cornell's plan was built around three key elements, all of which have been emphasized in this book: enhancing its digital shopping experience, remodelling its existing stores and opening smaller ones and introducing new private label brands.

Enhancing digital

The first area of focus was to concentrate on developing digital sales. Target realized that it needed to find a source of competitive advantage against Amazon, so it decided to utilize the asset of its store network to reduce delivery costs. In order to speed up its deliveries, in 2017,

Target acquired Grand Junction – a software platform that linked data from retailers' store inventories to a network of more than 700 regional and local carriers. It also paid $550 million to acquire the same-day delivery service, Shipt, which by March 2019, was made available in 1,500 Target stores[2].

Target used these acquisitions to improve its online home deliveries and offer an efficient 'click and collect' service. In both cases, the key was to use the stores' existing inventories as 'mini-warehouses', which were already situated close to where customers lived, rather than relying on central warehousing. This reduced delivery costs by 90 per cent and also ensured rapid fulfilment, so that customers were able to order a product online, then pick it up in a store on the same day. In addition, many customers decided to do some extra shopping during their visit. Target also pioneered the use of order online/kerbside pickup, which was particularly helpful during COVID-19[3].

By successfully integrating these acquisitions, Target was able to offer customers an alternative to Amazon Prime. As Tory Gundelach, VP of Retail Insights at Kantar Consulting, explained: 'Omnichannel means consumers can do business with Target through bricks and mortar, online, voice and mobile. To do this effectively, Target's front-end technology personalizes a customer's experience, so she gets the same message across all channels'[4].

Remodelling stores and opening smaller ones

One of the most controversial elements of Cornell's plan was its new investment in its stores, since many analysts felt, at the time, that stores were not the future of the business. However, he pushed ahead with investment in modernizing the look of Target's shops and, during COVID-19, in the cleanliness of its instore environments. He also opened 100 compact stores (12,000 square feet, as opposed to Target's usual 130,000 square feet) in urban areas and around college campuses. Critically, these were areas where its prime competitor, Walmart, did not operate[5].

These compact stores carried a curated selection of merchandise based on the area served. So, for example, those near to college campuses had large selections of 'grab & go' ready meals; those in residential areas included family-oriented selections like toys, and those in Latino areas had signage in Spanish. Also, although they only stocked limited selections physically, they created pickup centres and ship-to-home services for the company's entire assortment, which could be ordered online. These smaller stores have been a great success, generating nearly $900 per square foot in annual sales – about three times the figure for a typical suburban Target store[6].

Private label

Target was traditionally known for its good-quality private label, which was sold at accessible prices, earning it the tongue-in-cheek mock-French epithet 'Tarzhay'. However, it had lost its direction somewhat, with too many new in-house labels which were not up to the mark, such that it had lost its caché.

Cornell focused on rebuilding Target's private label offer, launching 20 successful new lines over the period 2017–20, including brands covering food (Good & Gather), modern furniture (Threshold), kids' clothes (Cat & Jack), electronics (Heyday) and home goods (Project 62). Most retailers regarded private label as a budget version of national brands, but Target invested in creating higher-quality, differentiated products with unique brand images, which gained traction with consumers[7].

The investment paid off: in 2019, six of Target's private label brands each did more than a billion dollars in annual sales. These labels, together with other brands sold exclusively at Target, contributed nearly a third of the company's overall revenue. And, because of the higher margins obtainable on private label, it contributed an even greater percentage of profits[8].

Target's new strategy has helped carry it through even the toughest part of the COVID-19 outbreak. It announced stellar results for the third quarter of 2020, with sales up 21 per cent, digital sales up 155 per cent and net earnings up 42 per cent. As a result, Target's stock price went up from around $53.00 in March 2017 to nearly $194.00 in February 2021[9].

Target's success story combines many elements discussed in this book, including embracing online and multi-channel, developing private label, opening smaller store formats and investing the in-store customer experience.

CHAPTER THIRTY EIGHT

Best Buy

Best Buy is another good example of a retailer which has brought itself back from the brink of failure to become a highly successful operator in the new digital world. The consumer electronics retailer was originally founded in 1966 as an audio-equipment store called 'Sound of Music' and was only re-branded Best Buy in 1983. Like Target, it did well in the 1990s and early 2000s, but revenues flattened, and profits dropped after 2008[1].

When Hubert Joly took over as CEO in September 2012, Best Buy had suffered three years of declining same-store sales and was losing share steadily to Amazon.com.

'Seven years ago, people thought we were going to die,' he said at the Adobe National Conference in 2019. 'We were not in good shape'[2].

Joly realized that he had to shift the group's emphasis away from a traditional retail focus on the quantities of goods being transacted towards a customer focus based around data, problem-solving, purpose and employee-enablement. As he put it: 'In retail, we've often focused on traffic to stores and conversion rates. The metrics are changing. In Las Vegas, for example, we'd look at how many consumers live in this market, how many are our customers, who we have relationships with, how we are helping them in an ongoing fashion.' He launched a turnaround plan – 'Renew Blue' – which was a comprehensive strategy to address key stakeholders, starting with customers and extending through to employees, partners, shareholders and communities[3].

The centrality of data

The backbone for the relaunch was customer data. As Joly said: 'You can talk about transformation, but if you don't have an enabler, it's just talk. Data has been a key element of transformation from day one, applied to every one of our processes, starting with customer journeys. These go across multiple touchpoints, from the website and the personalization we can do there, to using AI and machine learning in search.

'If you order a TV online, for example, and want to pick up in our store, we have a feature called "on my way", so staff can bring your TV from the back to the front of the store to collect quickly. We then send emails with unpacking and install instructions around your purchase'[4].

In addition, Best Buy personalizes information based on which products a customer owns and it is also using virtual reality to help customers choose products like televisions by visualizing how they will look in their homes.

Digital marketing has been another key priority. In 2012, 80 per cent of Best Buy's advertising spend was in traditional mass media like television. By 2019, 90 per cent of it was devoted to personalized digital communications. For example, the company sends out 40 million versions of its promotional emails[5].

'We have built a huge customer database, with 12,000 attributes,' Joly said. 'It's been a huge undertaking – we had data across the entire company. Being able to put it all together with a single customer identity is a huge foundation. From that, you can do so much more targeted marketing.'[6]

Solving customer problems – end-to-end

Best Buy then equipped all its in-home advisors and technical support staff with information to ensure they knew who the individual customer was and everything they had in their home, making their service more effective.

Armed with this data, Best Buy then set about aiming to solve customer problems end-to-end, rather than just selling them products. As Joly put it: 'We don't see ourselves as a bricks-and-mortar retailer. We are a company obsessed about the customer and in serving them in a way that truly solves their unique problems'[7].

A good example of this is the company's 'Total Tech Support' program, which, at a cost of $200 per year, offers to look after all the technology in the customer's home, no matter what brand, or whether they even bought it from Best Buy. This is a big move forward from a traditional in-home support service, which typically covers only the product purchased and ignores related technologies that might affect its performance. As Joly said, 'No home is mono brand. If Netflix doesn't work, is it Netflix, pipe to the home, Wi-Fi, TV, streaming device? We are the "honey" who comes and fixes it'[8].

This is a great example of 'Servicizing a goods business', in which Best Buy, in effect, replicates the service one would get from an electrician. Given electricians' typical call-out charges of $100-plus per visit, the $200 annual Best Buy charge would seem to offer good value. It also ensures the creation of a much closer relationship, whereby the support staff get to learn about the customer's needs in a more relaxed setting and can cross-sell new products.

The importance of purpose

Linked to this emphasis on meeting overall customer needs was the search for a new purpose for the business. 'We said we're not in the business of selling products or doing transactions, we have our purpose, which is to enrich lives with the help of technology,' Joly explained. 'We're making big changes in people's lives by addressing key needs – from entertainment to health and security. This sense of purpose is mobilizing everyone and we're innovating in support of that'[9].

Apart from the regular programs to support customers outside the store, the retailer also has a unique initiative focused on supporting ageing seniors and ensuring they can stay in their homes, independently, for longer. In this vein, Best Buy acquired Jitterbug in 2018 – a company focused on utilizing technology to support the elderly living at home.

'We put devices in the home, monitor activities of daily living of ageing seniors. Through AI, monitoring and humans, we can detect if something wrong is happening or about to happen, and enact an intervention,' Joly said[10].

Linked to this sense of idealism, the company is also working to build a reputation as a good corporate citizen. Initiatives along this line include reducing Best Buy's carbon footprint and launching 'Teen Tech Centers' – interactive spaces assisting teenagers to better understand technology and its role in modern lives[11].

This sense of purpose is also key to engaging the 25,000 Best Buy employees to be passionate about their work. As Joly said: 'We invested in experience in-store and invested in employees, which has seen turnover now reduce to under 30 per cent.

'Whether it's digital or physical, we are a human organization made of individuals working together in pursuit of a particular goal. If you can connect purpose of individuals working for you with purpose of the company, magic happens.

'The imperative is to make money but it's not the purpose. In our case, the purpose is to enrich lives through technology. How you orchestrate at scale makes it a privilege to work at Best Buy.'

The combined effects of this change process have transformed Best Buy's results. In the teeth of the pandemic, it managed to increase Enterprise Comparable Sales by 23 per cent in the third quarter of 2020. As a result, Best Buy's share price has appreciated from $15.78 in January 2013 to nearly $112.00 in January 2021.[12] In the context of so many retailers going to the wall, this is truly a great example of a Retail Recovery which exceeded expectations[13].

CHAPTER THIRTY NINE

Aerie

Aerie is a women's underwear retailer, which was launched as a sub-brand of American Eagle Outfitters Inc. in 2006. In its early years, it failed to make much traction, such that by 2011, it only had 2 per cent of the US lingerie market, compared to market leader Victoria's Secret which had more than 35 per cent.

However, all that changed in January 2014, when Aerie launched a revolutionary marketing campaign entitled '#AerieREAL', which, in one brilliant stroke, outmanoeuvred Victoria's Secret, by making it look artificial, dated and sexist[1].

As we have seen, in the period leading up to this date, younger generations such as Millennials and Gen Z were coming into the market, with different values from their predecessors. Diversity of all types was increasing, with 42 per cent of female teenagers characterizing themselves as being a 'non-typical' size. Young people were becoming increasingly disenchanted with the stereotypical images peddled by brands like Victoria's Secret, which had pushed an idealized version of feminine beauty, as exemplified by the VS 'Angels', who starred in its extravagant fashion shows – six foot tall, impossibly slim supermodels, decked out in cantilevered push-up bras.

The voice of a new generation

Jennifer Foyle, Aerie's global brand president, spotted the opportunity to re-position the brand as the voice of this new generation, pushing values like authenticity, inclusiveness and body positivity. As she put it: 'We felt like girls today are more independent and stronger than ever. We just knew that it [the new campaign] would really resonate with this generation.'

'#AerieREAL' used un-retouched images of real women, in all their diversity – women of every shape, size and colour; women with freckles, moles, stretch marks, scars and cellulite; women with prosthetic limbs and insulin pumps. What united them all was their obvious enjoyment of their lives and of the product.

The brand message was clear – that beauty had many forms, and that Aerie celebrated this beauty and diversity as a life-affirming force that could change society for the better. As they put it: 'Stop retouching and keep it real; focus on real change; real change happens together and real change starts with you'[2].

Alongside the marketing came products that suited the core audience's needs and were compatible with the brand's DNA. Out went push-up bras, shaper briefs and glamorous lacy lingerie, and in came relaxed-fit bralettes, sporty looks, period briefs and casual loungewear. The brand worked with soft, comfortable fabrics and carried a very large range of sizes.

The power of community

A major driver of Aerie's success was the creation of a powerful community built around the brand's values. Known as the 'Aerie Fam', it consisted of a huge group of enthusiasts on social media, effectively creating a platform for young activists to have a voice.

Much of the activity involved people posting user-generated content – pictures of themselves wearing the products – which massively increased the brand's reach. For example, in 2020, Aerie benefited from more than two billion organic impressions on social media[3].

The community was led by three groups of activists – Role Models, Changemakers and Brand Ambassadors. Role Models were successful women such as scientists, actresses, disabled athletes and blind YouTube influencers, whose personal stories were inspiring to the community. Changemakers were activists who were trying to improve society by doing things like building libraries, empowering incarcerated youth and writing books on subjects like body positivity. Aerie awarded 20 grants of $20,000 per year to support their efforts. Lastly, Brand Ambassadors were young people who led the brand-outreach program to colleges and other communities. They executed on-campus events, drove sales by offering coupons and highlighted brand campaigns on social media. They also ran AerieREAL pop up tours – a road show which traversed the US[4].

Contribution

Aerie also has a powerful 'Better World' contribution program, which supports organizations like the US National Eating Disorders Association (NEDA), Bright Pink (a non-profit dedicated to fighting breast and ovarian cancer) and First Mile (which recycles plastic bottles into textile fibres)[5].

Although Aerie has a thriving online business (representing 40 per cent of sales), it also invests heavily in its retail stores. The brand has partnered with NEDA to train staff by giving them the tools and language necessary to make all women feel confident in the fitting room. The whole Aerie team is united in their crusade to empower women. As Stacey McCormick, Aerie SVP Brand Marketing, put it: 'To know that what we're doing has shifted the culture in a much bigger way – much bigger than marketing, much bigger than retail – that's the reward for us'[6].

Massive success

This clear-sighted and faultlessly executed strategy has propelled Aerie into the big league. Revenues have exploded from $310 million in 2015 to over $800 million in 2019. In contrast, Victoria's Secret experienced a decline in sales from $ 7.7 billion in 2015 to $6.8 billion over the same period.

Even during COVID-19, Aerie continued to create stellar results – with revenues hitting nearly $1 billion in 2020. American Eagle announced plans to double sales by 2022, making Aerie a $2 billion brand[7].

Aerie's strategic repositioning and subsequent success is an inspiring example of what can be achieved with vision and executional excellence, even in a large corporation. It is a near-perfect case study of how focusing on values rather than transactions can inspire a passionate community, and create an iconic brand in the midst of an otherwise commodity market.

CHAPTER FORTY

Gymshark

Gymshark is a highly successful British direct-to-consumer sportswear brand, which has exploded from its foundation in 2012 to being worth over £1 billion in 2020. It is a textbook example of how to combine online expertise, social media skills, community-building and physical events to create a huge business in a very short time span.

The genius behind Gymshark – a former pizza-delivery boy called Ben Francis – started the company in his parents' garage when he was only 19 years old. He was a gym enthusiast, who felt that he could not find any sportswear that appealed to him, or his generation, as it seemed to be largely made for older consumers[1].

At the time, brands were either selling loose-fitting body-building gear targeted towards more mature customers, or high-end fitness clothes that were too expensive for younger Millennials and Gen Z. With the help of his brother, and a small group of friends, Francis bought a sewing machine and screen printer and started to make highly innovative gym vests, T-shirts and technical leggings, which he sold exclusively on the Gymshark website. By keeping design and manufacturing in-house and avoiding the cost of traditional brands and shops, he was able to sell products with premium designs and technology for a much more affordable price. For example, Gymshark's shape-boosting leggings retailed for $25.00–$65.00 versus similar products from Alo Yoga or Athleta at $80.00-plus[2].

Influencer marketing

From the very start, Francis sent products to social media influencers who expressed their delight with the brand's radically designed products. He then spent every penny that he had to get a booth at the main UK fitness expo, BodyPower, paying the influencers to spend time on his stand. It was there that he had a major realization – people who had never heard of his brand were flocking to meet their blogger heroes.

Each influencer had a large following and based on their endorsement, the brand's popularity started to explode. For example, after the show, Gymshark's Luxe tracksuit went viral on Facebook, generating £30,000 of sales within 30 minutes. Over time, the brand built its sponsorship program to include 18 major influencers, with a combined following of over 20 million[3].

Building a community

Ben Francis also worked hard to create a community around Gymshark, using a lot of user-generated content, and encouraging people to 'Be a visionary' and to get beyond their 'I will do it tomorrow' mentalities. Brand enthusiasts were encouraged to share their personal fitness journeys and the company celebrated their progress.

As we saw in the previous discussion of brand communities, success depends on them delivering real benefits for their members and Gymshark managed to do this in a very powerful manner. For example, on 1 January 2020, the brand started a viral movement linked to New Year's Resolutions under the hashtag '#Gymshark66', which encouraged followers to work out for 66 days in a row, with a video showing ordinary people overcoming their workout fears. The hashtag gained nearly 45 million views and encouraged millions to join the '#Gymshark66' challenge[4].

As Calum Watson, Head of Sponsorship at Gymshark, put it: 'Creative storytelling was a way to stand out of the crowd. People buy into Gymshark because they want to be part of the community. Investing in the creative side helps us evoke emotion and helps people find a connection with the brand'[5].

The importance of physical interaction

Although the business was all online, Gymshark also invested heavily in major physical events, called 'meet-ups' and 'expos', which were attended by celebrity influencers like YouTube body-builders Nikki Blackketter and Lex Griffin. Gymshark enthusiasts flocked to these events to meet these stars.

The brand expanded this concept to an 'expo world tour', taking its events to locations in Germany, America and Australia – all documented on social channels, creating influencer-style 'vlogs' on YouTube. Eventually the numbers became so huge that the events became chaotic and so the brand decided to open a physical store in London's Covent Garden instead[6].

In 2016, the company was named fastest-growing retailer in the UK and Francis was included in Forbes' '30 under 30' list, which acknowledged the brand's exceptional success in a market dominated by huge global players. It was also adopted by celebrities like supermodel Alessandra Ambrosio and actresses Gabrielle Union, Jennifer Garner, Sarah Hyland and Vanessa Hudgens[7].

By 2020, Gymshark had built a following of 4.8 million on Instagram and sales of £258 million (up from £176 million in 2019). It had businesses in 180 countries, offices in the UK, Hong Kong and Denver, and 499 staff. Sales continued to grow during the Coronavirus crisis as people focused on their health and fitness, and shopped online more than ever before. As Francis put it: 'Commercially, it's been quite good in the sense that people are shopping more online and people are running, cycling and doing home workouts more than ever before'[8].

In August 2020, US private equity firm General Atlantic purchased a 21 per cent stake in the brand in a deal which valued the company in excess of £1 billion. Francis wants to use the investment to continue to build the brand internationally. 'This is my one true passion and the thing that I've truly dedicated my life to,' he said. 'So, all of my mind-set right now is about continuing to develop this brand into a truly, truly global phenomenon'[9].

The Gymshark story shows what can be achieved in a relatively short period using ultra-modern digital marketing strategies built around a strong founder/brand story, viral social media campaigns, powerful influencer alliances and online/offline community building. It also shows how easily a market long dominated by powerful incumbent brands can be disrupted by targeting a new generation of consumers, who play by different rules.

CHAPTER FORTY ONE

Rosé Mansion

When we looked at the roles that stores could continue to play in the digital era, one of the themes that we covered was the idea of 'Edutainment' – providing experiences, related to the product category, that were entertaining but also educational (*see also* Chapter 30, pages 175–9). Critically, these were experiences that could not be replicated online.

The logic for this is clear: after all, people are willing to spend large quantities of time and money on various forms of education – witness the huge industry that exists around museums, galleries and historical-tour visits – so why not offer this, packaged in an entertaining way, as part of the retail experience?

One company that really epitomizes the use of Edutainment is Rosé Mansion, the New York-based start-up, which has already been mentioned in previous chapters. Rosé Mansion is an interactive wine-tasting adventure that combines a wine bar, a fun-packed amusement arcade and an educational museum in one epic experience. It was launched in June 2018 by serial entrepreneurs Morgan First and Tyler Balliet[1].

Morgan First originally had the idea of creating educationally related concepts when she was building her first business – a crossover calendar planner and local adventure guidebook called 'MAP Boston' – which she launched in 2006. 'I noticed that people need a "prompt" to have fun,' she said, 'something related to educating themselves'[2].

In 2008, she met Tyler Balliet, who had started a wine-event company called 'Second Glass'. Balliet had been working in a wine shop in Boston and had realized that nobody was marketing wine to his generation. 'All these young people were coming in and they had a ton of questions,' he says, 'but it was not like, "Tell me about the '04 Burgundy season", it was "What the hell is Burgundy?"'

Together, the pair started promoting Second Glass events at wine stores. These were educational wine tastings, but rather than follow the usual, somewhat pretentious format of such gatherings, they infused them with fun. For example, they held 'Smackdown' series – competitions between, for example, French and Californian wines. They would add in stand-up comedy and food, and sell the tickets for $15.00–20.00.

These events were a great success and the pair started booking larger spaces, like the Chicago Union Station, which were capable of hosting between 2,500 and 6,000 people, and putting on huge extravaganzas called 'Wine Riots'. With 250 wines on offer, wine producers got on board and started donating product in return for having booths on-site. The founders added other features such as DJs, photobooths, wine-tattoo stations, an app and a print publication. Wine Riots were held in New York, Chicago, Washington, Los Angeles and Boston[3].

In 2017, First and Balliet sold the business and were looking for new opportunities to take their Edutainment concept forward with a more permanent installation. At that time, there were some interesting experiential concepts which were starting to pop up, such as the 'Museum of Ice Cream', '29 Rooms' and 'Body Worlds', which were enjoying some success.

Educating a new generation about wine

The idea was to create a permanent venue based around wine education for a new generation. The challenge was to find a simple concept that avoided the complexities of the overall wine industry. Analysing the demographics of Wine Riot, they realized that 75 per cent of their customers had been young women, aged 21–35 years old. At that time, the fastest-growing drinks craze among this group was rosé wine and so the idea for 'Rosé Mansion' was born.

The concept was to provide young women with a place to go out for celebratory events like promotions, bachelorette parties or birthdays – which were a little more special than just going to a bar or nightclub. As Morgan First says: 'American culture is still against women just going out drinking – it is kind of taboo. Women need another activity or excuse to motivate them. Having the additional element of learning about wine adds a sense of purpose to the event. It is like a kind of Disneyland for adults!'[4].

Rosé Mansion was launched as a pop-up on Fifth Avenue in Manhattan from July to October 2018 and then returned in an expanded (32,000 square feet) form in Manhattan Mall in Midtown from April to October 2019. It featured a Millennial-friendly pink entrance area and multiple rooms, each featuring impressive and immersive wine-related experiences. The rooms were designed by avant-garde New York artists such as Sandrine Saint-Louis, Kasey Jones, INK and Dirty Rascal.[5]

Rooms with a view

Each room had an educational message. For example, in the 'Vision Room' – a minimalist 'infinity' space – participants were offered a sheet of grape stickers, which they were invited to affix on the white walls in order to 'soak the room' with wine. The underlying message was that rosé is actually made from red grapes, but the light pink colour stems from the fact that the red skins are only left in the wine for a short time.

Another room was the 'Roman Room' featuring wine made from the original grapes that were used in Roman times, in order to illustrate the fact that rosé has been made since the classical era.

A third room was decked out like a 1950s travel agency, complete with an antique aircraft fuselage. Visitors were invited to put a pin in a map showing which country they were from, making the point that rosé can be produced almost everywhere in the world.

Another area was the 'Science of Sweet' room, which focused on sweet rosé wines and featured a candy cart and scratch-and-sniff panels on the wall. Yet another space was decked out like a science lab and invited guests to blend their own wine. There was also Cleopatra's secret drinking club, which made the point that the famous queen of ancient Egypt liked to drink rosé wine.

Other features were a huge ball pit full of bubbles, inviting you to swim in a glass of rosé, a bathtub filled with rose petals, a rosé champagne cascade and a Secret Garden with a chandelier swing[6].

As visitors progressed around the exhibits, they were treated to eight tasting glasses of rosé, by enthusiastic former-actor guides, who helped support the educational process. At the end, guests could linger into the night in 'Roséland', a bar offering the largest selection of rosé wines in the US, along with fashionable finger foods and sessions with a tarot reader. The concept was extremely successful, with Rosé Mansion selling 80,000 tickets at $45.00 each. Happy Hour sessions, at lower prices, were added to extend the trading period into the late afternoon. Unfortunately, the advent of COVID-19 put plans for an expansion in 2020 on hold: however, the founders responded by taking their wine sales online and were also potentially planning to move the venue to an outdoor format[7].

Clearly, the full potential of Rosé Mansion will have to wait until the end of the Coronavirus crisis, although the idea of mixing education with entertainment in an immersive three-dimensional environment is excellent and should be instructive for all retailers wishing to elevate their in-store experience above that of purely transacting goods.

CHAPTER FORTY TWO

Walmart

Walmart is the largest stores retailer in the world, with $523 billion of revenues, 11,500 stores and over 2 million employees worldwide in 2020. However, back in 2014, its new Chief Executive, Doug McMillon, recognized that, despite its dominance in the physical world, it was losing the battle against Amazon in the fastest-growing channel – the internet. In that year, Amazon controlled 23 per cent of the American e-commerce market, dwarfing Walmart's share, which was 3 per cent, and Walmart's digital sales growth had slowed to 7 per cent per annum[1].

Doubling down on digital

McMillon decided that Walmart must step up and face Amazon head-on in the e-commerce market. He invested heavily in the technology and people needed to undertake this Herculean task, expanding Walmart Labs – a technology research unit – and acquiring Jet.com – a fast-growing e-commerce upstart – for $3.3 billion in 2016.

With Jet.com came its founder – Marc Lore – an e-commerce genius to rival Amazon's Jeff Bezos. McMillon put Lore in charge of all Walmart's e-commerce operations and granted him a high degree of autonomy. Lore proceeded to develop Walmart's digital business very rapidly, causing it to grow from $15 billion in 2016 to an estimated $38 billion in 2020 – a growth of 253 per cent. Lore eventually retired from Walmart in January 2021, but not until after he had transformed the company's e-commerce culture[2].

To achieve this growth, Walmart innovated in a number of areas. It massively expanded its product line by turning itself into a marketplace platform, following the lead set by Amazon. The addition of third-party brands gave it a range of over 50 million products – still not as large as Amazon's 350 million, but far larger than the 7 million that it had had in 2016. It also invested in creating seamless sales and stock mechanisms enabling customers to shop any way that they wanted. As McMillon put it: 'We will be the first to deliver a seamless shopping experience at scale. No matter how you choose to shop with us, through your mobile device, online, in a store, or a combination, it will be fast and easy'[3].

Walmart also doubled down on customer data collection and relationship management, drawing lessons from Jet.com. In September 2020, it launched 'Walmart +', a free one-day delivery loyalty program (for an annual membership fee of $98) to compete with Amazon's Prime offer. During this period McMillon came under fire because of the high losses accompanying this investment. Walmart's e-commerce business was apparently loss-making to the tune of $2 billion in 2019. Still, McMillon stuck with the strategy, daring to step up and challenge Amazon directly – almost the only major American retailer to do so[4].

The importance of the stores

In pursuing this daring strategy, McMillon relied on the one advantage that Amazon cannot replicate – Walmart's network of stores, which puts 90 per cent of Americans within a 10-mile radius of a store. Given the high distribution costs endured by Amazon (which, as of January 2020, had only 110 fulfilment centres in the US), this meant that Walmart had a considerable advantage over Amazon in terms of delivery costs.

Despite the emphasis on digital, Walmart did not neglect its stores, choosing to invest in them at a time when it was not fashionable to do so. As we have seen in previous chapters, it installed new technology to automate many store operations, including robotic floor cleaners and shelf scanners, machines that scan and sort items unloaded from trucks and pickup towers/vending machines that dispense online orders within stores. It also pioneered kerbside pickup (even before the advent of COVID-19)[5].

The arrival of the Coronavirus made McMillon's strategy look percipient. In the quarter ending September 2020, the company grew total revenues by 5 per cent on the back of e-commerce growth of 79 per cent and operating income grew by 23 per cent from $4.7 billion to $5.8 billion. This is a tremendous example of a retailer which took the right strategic decision at the right time and invested in multi-channel development, strong customer data/loyalty programs, product line expansion and instore technology in order to compete directly with Amazon. It is a tribute to Doug McMillon that he persevered with the strategy despite criticisms from the financial community and he has been vindicated by the company's strong performance during the COVID-19 crisis[6].

CHAPTER FORTY THREE

Showfields

One of the themes covered in this book is the changing nature of the retail property market in the wake of the collapse of so many anchor store groups. The classical leasing model, whereby retailers invested heavily in building permanent stores on 10-year-plus leases, has come under pressure recently as brands and retailers have sought more flexible arrangements.

As we have seen in Chapter 36 (*see also* pages 207–212), part of this movement has been the emergence of the new concept of 'Retail as a Service' (RaaS), which aims to offer an innovative model for how retailing can work in the future. One of the leaders in this area is Showfields, an American start-up based in New York, which bills itself as 'The most interesting store in the world', The company's mission is to be 'The ultimate curator, bringing together the most mission-driven, design-oriented, innovative, unconventional, and relevant brands, artists and communities from around the globe'[1].

Showfields was launched in 2018 by tech entrepreneur Tal Zvi Nathanel, real estate veteran Amir Zwickel and investor Katie Hunt. It is a Manhattan-based department store, covering four floors and 15,000 square feet[2].

The founders were intrigued by an apparent paradox. 'We noticed a huge gap between the fact that there is more innovation out there – more cool brands – in the online world than at any time in history, and yet the streets are more boring and dull than at any time,' says Amir Zwickel. 'The reason for this gap is that it is really easy to start your business online, but opening your own physical store is something that is almost impossible for most of the brands in the world'[3].

Simplifying store opening

The Showfields team posed a simple question: 'What if creating a retail space was as simple as developing a website?' As an answer, they set about lowering the barriers to entry from clicks to bricks, targeting digitally native direct-to-consumer brands. These companies were interested in experimenting with physical retailing, but did not want to commit to major investments and long leases, and lacked the skills to design and run stores[4].

Showfields offers these brands a much more flexible option, with short-term contracts (as little as three months) and new technologies and strategies to support the opening process. The first stage of this is onboarding, which is done through a six-step online procedure that can be completed remotely. 'We have brands from Latin America, Asia, Europe and Australia that have activated stores without ever setting foot in the US,' says Zwickel[5].

The next stage is for Showfields' team of designers and store-build experts to help the brands create highly impactful retail spaces. As regards operations, Showfields supports brands with technology which acts as an extension of their Shopify websites, giving them access to sales and stock information. The spaces are also pre-equipped with all the modern store technology described in Chapter 33 (*see also* pages 192–195), such as cameras and location beacons. Brands have access to dashboards with real-time data on metrics like footfall, product engagement, dwell time and conversion. Showfields also employs brand hosts – who are high-level 'story-tellers' as opposed to regular shop employees – to staff the stores, meaning the brands do not have to create their own teams[6].

The company thinks in terms of five factors which drive a successful physical touchpoint for online brands – what Amir Zwickel calls the five 'Cs' – Curation, Convenience, Community, Content and Connection, which together create a magical experience for the consumer[7].

Thinking beyond the sale

Although products are for sale in the store, and many brands experience high levels of transactions, that is not the sole point of the venture. The company encourages brands to think beyond the immediate sale and to focus on the quality of the customer experience.

Says Zwickel, 'If their main R.O.I. is sales, that does not mean that they have to get everything in store. We can easily calibrate the online sales that occur due to exposure in Showfields and we have many case studies showing that it works. For example, we had a brand that sells mattresses, which activated a space in Showfields last year, serving their New York customers, and we found out that 75 per cent of their online clients in the area were first exposed to the product at Showfields'[8].

Showfields' economic model is that product sales go directly to the brand, with Showfields collecting membership fees from them. Fees vary between $5,000 and $25,000 per month, depending on the size of the space and the level of exposure (for example, if they have window locations)[9].

The importance of curation

Showfields features up to 50 brands at a time and aims to curate the most interesting selection of products available on the market. The company pushes brands to innovate in the way that they present themselves. As co-founder Katie Hunt puts it: 'We really want to push people to break the mould of what traditional retail is and no longer line things up on a rack. It needs to feel new and fresh and delightful to the consumer. If you're a legacy brand, that becomes a discussion of, "What are you doing that's new and cool? How can someone experience your brand in a way they've never experienced it before?"' As the store's slogan puts it, it is 'Where art meets retail'[10].

The curation process is very important, adds Zwickel: 'We are moving from the age of creation, which is the reason why we see all this huge innovation and variety of brands out there, to the age of curation, which is why curated environments succeed today and why we see all these influencers out there – each one of them is a curator in their own field'[11].

The key difference with a traditional department store is that the level of brand innovation is far greater. The question being asked is not 'Will it sell?', which tends to lead to a risk-averse selection of brands, but 'Will it be interesting for our local customers?', which produces a far more radical mix of products.

Among the brands showcased in the store have been Brand Assembly (fashion and lifestyle), Gravity Blanket (sleep products), Ethos (alternative holidays), GEM (nutrition) and Better Natured (hair products). All of them share a highly innovative product or service and a strong mission-driven philosophy[12].

Culture club

Showfields also provides other activities which complement the brand spaces, such as a stylish bar and event area on the fourth floor, called The Loft – complete with roof deck – which offers art exhibitions, cultural events, food and drink and community programming, such as yoga, during the day. At night, it turns into an invitation-only venue for creative types. Many of the brands choose The Loft to hold their offline launch events, which adds to the buzz around the space[13].

The culture is as important as the brands in the Showfields mix. '50 per cent of the space is dedicated to what we call "Show" and the other 50 per cent is dedicated to what we call "Fields", says Zwickel. 'The Show part is where the art comes into play, where the experience is, where Showfields builds its own community and where we inspire your mind to be in a discovery mood. The Fields part is where the brands come into play – and each field is an entire holistic experience, built around a certain brand'[14].

Every six months both the Show and the Fields change over and an entire new show curation is launched, telling a different story, aligned with a new set of brands.

Zwickel adds that the content of these themes is becoming increasingly sophisticated: 'Creating more and more Instagrammable moments is just not enough anymore. People look for something with a bit more intellectual depth to it.' As an example, he refers to a recent event that Showfields held with Polaroid and Rave the Vote to encourage people to register in the run-up to the 2020 US election. Visitors were asked to take pictures with Polaroid cameras and post them on photo walls within the store, along with descriptions of what personally inspired them to vote[15].

In terms of funding, Showfields raised $15 million up until November 2020, from investors like Hanaco Ventures, SWaN & Legend Venture Partners, Rainfall Ventures, Communitas Capital and Richard Gelfond[16].

The company opened its doors in March 2019 to rave reviews and garnered more than 100,000 visitors in its first year of operation. Brands experienced sales growth of over 50 per cent and major increases in awareness, particularly among opinion formers[17].

Innovating through Covid

Like the rest of New York's non-essential retail, Showfields was forced to close down in March 2020. However, it used the lockdown to accelerate its digital capabilities, offering virtual tours and online artistic events and developing its e-commerce business, which enabled it to continue trading. This speedy and flexible response helped the company to attract new brands and it says that it has onboarded over 100 of them since the crisis started[18].

Once it reopened the store in July 2020, it added safety features like kerbside pickup and an app called 'The Magic Wand', which enabled shoppers to explore the store – phone in hand – and get product information, enjoy audio tours and order items online, all without touching anything.

There were also interactive touchscreens, which helped customers gain more information on products, pay through self-checkout and order online items for home shipment. In addition, the store offered brands a service called 'Go Live', whereby visitors to the brand websites could press a button and be connected with hosts on the floor of Showfields[19].

'Something good happened to us with Covid,' says Zwickel, 'because the opportunity around flexible retail became bigger than at any time before. Pre-Covid, we were mostly targeting direct-to-consumer brands; post-Covid, even the Gaps of this world are no longer looking to sign up on a new $45 million lease in Times Square. They are looking for something with way less risk, but something that is still elegant and respects their brand. If that's what you are looking to do, then the Showfields offering is one of the best out there.'

He says that it has led to an increase in the level of interest: 'We feel it already in the brands that we are speaking with. We have more conversations than we have had at any time before and higher conversion levels. We also have more brands renewing their contracts – we signed nearly double the number of extensions in the last two weeks with our current brands, compared with the curation before'[20].

After it reopened at the beginning of July 2020, Showfields saw a good recovery in customer traffic. Plans for expansion are ongoing, with the opening of a second location in Miami in late 2020, and more scheduled in the future. The aim is to bring its flagship model to every major city in the world[21].

Showfields' concept of curating innovative brands, offering them flexible leases and wrapping the whole experience in a highly theatrical and artistic envelope, is absolutely right for the long-term future of retailing. As Amir Zwickel says: 'It is bringing the discovery back into retail'[22].

CHAPTER FORTY FOUR

Huel

Huel is a British direct-to-consumer brand, selling nutritional food supplements mainly via its Web channel. It was founded in 2015 in Aylesbury, Buckinghamshire, by serial entrepreneur Julian Hearn and experienced nutritionist James Collier[1].

Huel's main product is a powdered food, which can be mixed with water or plant-based milk in a portable beaker. Its ingredients include oats, pea protein, flaxseed, brown rice protein and a blend of key vitamins and minerals. Flavour boosts can be added, such as strawberry, banana, chocolate, cappuccino and chocolate mint[2].

Huel's name comes from a contraction of 'Human Fuel' and its vision is: 'To make nutritionally complete, convenient, affordable food, with minimal impact on animals and the environment'. The original idea was to provide nutrition to for busy people. As Hearn put it in early 2020: 'Our core customer works in an office and is time-poor during the week. They may have a Huel on the way to work or one at their desk during lunch time and then have a traditional family meal in the evening.' He believes that for too long we have focused on the taste of our food, as opposed to its nutritional value: 'As a population we have made food so delicious that we crave it, get addicted to it, and over-consume it,' he says.

'People overcomplicate nutrition,' says Collier, 'It's not rocket science. For the lay consumer, getting your nutrition right needn't be that hard'[3].

Huel is very healthy and it is also affordable as the brand leverages its lean direct-to-consumer supply chain to get these meals to people at a cost of only $1.50 per serving. It thus appeals to health-obsessed, gym-going millennials, who are also on tight budgets[4].

Values-added

In addition, Huel is lactose-free, vegan and non-GMO. This is important to consumers who care about animal welfare and the environment. The meat and dairy industry has a disproportionate impact on the world's ecosystem, creating 60 per cent of the greenhouse gases coming from global agriculture, despite only representing 18 per cent of calories consumed[5].

With 600,000 Vegans in the UK, 22 million 'Flexitarians' (those trying to reduce meat and dairy consumption) and millions more deeply concerned about global warming, there is clearly a substantial audience for concepts like Huel[6].

Based on this strong product appeal, the company has grown extremely fast, expanding its product range to include Huel Ready-To-Drink, Huel Bars, Huel Granola and Huel Hot & Savoury ready meals. It has been expert in the way that it has used digital performance marketing to build a solid base of subscriptions, thus enhancing the lifetime value of its customers. Its cool minimalist branding – as seen on the Huel shaker bottles that have seemed ubiquitous at dot-com start-ups over the last few years – has also made it stand out[7].

Huel has leveraged social media to create a strong brand community based around a common enthusiasm for its values. Although mainly an online brand, it has regular physical events to reinforce this sense of community. For example, recently it held an event in London for the launch of one of its new products where committed members came from as far away as Denmark[8].

This enthusiasm extends to the Huel team, who share the brand's values. The culture is informal and humorous, as shown by its slogan, proudly displayed on the office wall: 'Don't be a dick'[9].

The company also has a strong contribution program – for example, it worked with a charity called Vitamin Angels to give a year's supply of Huel to 33,000 malnourished kids per annum. Vitamin Angels is an American-based charity that provides lifesaving vitamins to mothers and children under-five at risk of malnutrition[10].

Hueligans

The brand's loyal enthusiasts – also referred to as 'Hueligans' – have catapulted Huel to be the best-selling complete food brand in the world. It received investment of £20 million from venture capital firm Highland Europe in October 2018, with the mission of turning it into a major global brand[11].

Huel's 2018/19 sales were £40 million and in that year, it grew customers by 150 per cent. As of early 2020, it had sold cumulatively 100 million meals in 100 countries and 1.5 million customers used it on a monthly basis. It had been profitable for three out of its first four years and had 100 staff in four offices, including the UK, Berlin and Los Angeles[12].

When COVID-19 hit, Julian Hearn was initially concerned that the lockdown would undermine the logic for using Huel – based (as it was thought to be) on the needs of time-poor office executives. As he put it: 'Huel is a convenient food product that's perfect when on-the-go, so with the world in lockdown we were unsure what place Huel would have in people's homes.' However, in the event, Huel's subscription-based model held up during the pandemic and indeed, sales growth accelerated as people shopped more online and became increasingly concerned about their health: 'Being direct-to-consumer meant that during lockdown, we were able to deliver nutritious food straight to people's homes,' Hearn added. Such was the demand that in September 2020, Huel was able to announce 2019/20 revenues of £72 million – a 43 per cent increase on the previous year, representing a fifth consecutive year of growth.

Assuming the company continues to grow at its current rate, it is expected to be worth $1.25 billion by 2022.

Huel is another example, like Gymshark (*see also* Chapter 40, pages 226–30), of how a new brand can explode very rapidly by creating a highly innovative product for a new target audience and using new channels and marketing techniques to create a compelling brand story[13]. It is a leader in its use of performance marketing to drive customer acquisition and its adoption of a subscription-based customer repeat model, which massively boosts lifetime value. Finally, it offers a great example of leading with higher values and creating a passionate brand community. In summary, it is a role model for brands and store groups looking to participate in the Retail Revival.

CHAPTER FORTY FIVE

Rapha

Another good example of a business which has grown very rapidly, by using a lot of the techniques described in this book, is Rapha Racing – the high-end cycling clothing and accessories brand. Started in London in 2004 by Simon Mottram and Luke Scheybeler, the company name was taken from the 1960s cycling-team Rapha, which was, itself, named after the apéritif drinks company, Saint Raphaël[1].

More than apparel

Rapha's vision is more than just about selling apparel, its stated purpose is to make road cycling the most popular sport in the world. The company is very serious about this goal – they have spent a lot of time thinking out a Roadmap for the future of the sport, with 10 chapters, including such themes as repairing the reputation of the sport after the doping scandals, making it more watchable for fans and improving the profitability of professional cycling[2].

Rapha prides itself on its commitment to racing. Firstly, it sponsored the British UCI Continental team Rapha-Condor from 2005 to 2012, and then became clothing supplier to Team Sky from 2012 to 2016. Team Sky members Bradley Wiggins and Chris Froome won four Tour de France competitions during that period. The Rapha Foundation funds more than 10 organizations around the world committed to inspiring, empowering and supporting the next generation of riders and racers from under-represented communities in the sport. The organization invests $1.5 million a year[3].

All the employees are keen cyclists and every Wednesday morning, the whole team goes out riding together. The staff are encouraged to share the company's values, which are: 'Love the Sport – Make it part of your life', 'Inspire Others – Lead by example', 'Suffer – Good enough isn't' and 'Think for Yourself – Be proactive, always'. At Rapha's headquarters in London, there is an internal 'Clubhouse', where racing is shown on screens throughout the day, baristas serve free coffee and a mechanic carries out repairs in an in-house bike workshop[4].

A shared joy

Key to Rapha's success is its creation of a very strong brand community. For although Rapha stores sell cycling kit, like all cycle shops, this is not what makes the Rapha brand special. Rapha is all about the shared joy of riding – the trips, the spills, the stories. The thing that binds both staff and customers together is their passion for cycling.

To feed this enthusiasm, the company has created the Rapha Cycling Club – a global network of more than 13,000 like-minded, passionate cyclists and ride leaders connected by an easy-to-use app, which offers hundreds of rides, routes and group chats every week. At the time of writing, annual membership costs £70.00 and carries a number of benefits. It gives members access to year-round riding events with unmatched support at the world's most famous 'sportives', hosted weekends away with curated routes and social get-togethers. It also offers exclusive products, special promotions and affordable bike hire[5].

According to Caroline Crosswell, Chief Retail & Development Officer at the company, it is this emphasis on community which separates Rapha from most retailers: 'Many companies talk about balancing commerce and community, but Rapha genuinely puts community first. We ask customers about how their ride was, or what their experience was with the product. We don't try to sell them things. If you build the relationship, the sales will follow'[6].

The community also helps the company with product innovation. New ideas flow directly from solving problems experienced by the brand team and customers on their rides – for example, the 'O-ring' zip pullers, which are easy to find in the middle of a difficult climb, the pads on the back of the glove thumbs for wiping away sweat and the wearable-heating technology for cold morning starts[7].

Clubhouses

The transactional backbone of the brand is online, with two-thirds of sales being through the website, which markets the products in over 100 countries. However, from the start, founder Simon Mottram realized the potential of stores as experiential rather than transactional channels. He turned Rapha's stores into physical embodiments of the brand's devotion to cycling by designating them 'Clubhouses' – as much social gathering points for the community as conventional shops. Key to this are the in-store cafés, which dispense free coffee to members. Cycling enthusiasts naturally meet for coffee and plan trips in their local Rapha clubhouses, and while there, interact with similarly enthusiastic brand team members, getting advice on equipment and local rides. The brand has 23 of these Clubhouses around the world, plus mobile ones at major race meetings. They are shrines to the world of racing, with big screens showing live events, books on leading teams and antique clothing from the famous winners of the past[8].

Crosswell underlines the critical role of physical stores in the Rapha brand universe: 'When I first joined, I questioned the fact that the café took up 50 per cent of the space in the stores, but generated less than 10 per cent of the revenues.' Then she saw a group of 40 riders pile in for coffee on a Wednesday morning: 'It was chaos – the café was absolutely rammed, with everyone talking loudly and helmets everywhere, but suddenly I had a lightbulb moment – that this was Rapha at its best. The Clubhouse was the glue which was holding together the community.

Without community – without that emotional connection – retailing just becomes a question of how much discount you are offering'[9].

The company does not look at store sales alone when considering the viability of a location. Instead they view each store as the 'hub' for a region and look at the value of all the relationships they have in that region, whether through the store itself or via the website. Even if the store itself is only performing marginally well, so long as the overall value of these regional relationships is positive, then the company is happy[10].

Cycling has been growing in popularity over the past two decades – in the UK it has gone from being outside the top 10 of most popular participation sports in 1998 to being number four in 2019, with over 6 million people biking on a regular basis. Powered by its winning strategy, Rapha has ridden the wave of this boom, with revenues growing rapidly from £2 million in 2010 to £67 million in 2016/17, and net profits of £4.5 million in the latter year. In August 2017, the brand was acquired by RZC, an investment fund set up by Steuart and Tom Walton, grandsons of the founder of the Walmart supermarket chain, for £200 million[11].

Riding through the pandemic

When the COVID-19 outbreak came along in 2020, the company was initially concerned, but in the event, it came through the crisis well, mainly due to the loyalty of its community, which stuck with the brand even during the closure of its stores. Rapha tried to keep the relationship going during lockdown with a click & collect service, virtual yoga sessions, Zoom socials and online treasure hunts (whereby ride-leaders hid prizes in empty water bottles at various locations and provided a trail of clues to help the community's riders find them)[12].

There was also an explosion of interest in cycling during lockdown and Rapha's new customer numbers increased by 50 per cent, mainly through its online channel. The influx of a new audience, many of whom were new to the sport, meant that the company had to modify its approach, holding online sessions on basics like how to change an inner tube. At the time, they wondered whether the interest would be temporary, but since the start of the lockdowns, they have seen their relationship deepening with these new customers. Many of them have evolved from buying basic kit to wanting more technical products. The net result has been that online sales have doubled since the start of COVID-19, helping the brand through the crisis[13].

The company is currently integrating its online database with its store point-of-sale system, which is enabling it to get a full view of the customer relationship. According to Caroline Crosswell, this is revealing some very interesting individual relationships. For example, there was a customer in Washington State, who used to visit his local Rapha Clubhouse every day for a coffee, but never appeared to buy anything. Once the data systems were put together, he turned out to be the brand's top customer in the area, but with all of his purchases online. This shows the importance of having a complete view of each customer's individual brand journey[14].

The success of Rapha shows the power of a brand having a vision which transcends the purely transactional. It also illustrates how such a vision can unite the brand team and customers in a passionate community, and how physical spaces can be used to gather and motivate such a community. Finally, as with other cases we have looked at, it shows how this daily interaction between the team and customers can generate a high level of innovation. It is the adoption of strategies like these that will help the brand/retail industry to find a new direction in the post-Covid world and contribute to the coming Retail Recovery.

CHAPTER FORTY SIX

Southern Co-op

The co-operative movement was set up in the UK in the nineteenth century to try and mitigate some of the exploitation that accompanied the Industrial Revolution. Groups of local people came together to set up their own businesses in order to ensure fair deals for their members.

Southern Co-op (originally Portsea Island Mutual Co-operative Society) was formed by dockyard workers who had transferred from Woolwich docks in south-east London to the Portsmouth dockyard. In December 1872, 30 people attended a public meeting and each agreed to pay a shilling (5p) towards the establishment of a local co-operative. After five months of hard work and detailed planning, the first shop was opened in Charles Street, Portsmouth, on 9 May 1873. From these humble beginnings, Southern Co-op grew until, in 2020, it had 202 food stores (plus an additional 39 franchised food stores operating under the Welcome brand). It also owned 58 funeral homes, two crematoria, a natural burial ground and 28 Starbucks franchise coffee shops[1].

Collective ownership

Southern Co-op has more than 140,000 members, who collectively own the business, with customers only having to pay £1.00 to sign up for membership. It differs from a corporation, in that all its members have an equal say at the Annual General Meeting (AGM), rather than (as is typical of Public Limited Companies) being powerless in the face of major shareholders. It also has no debt, which frees it from the potential pressure of large creditors[2].

At each AGM, the management shares with the members how much the business made during the year, the amount proposed for re-investment and what is available for distribution in the form of dividends. Members approve the plan and receive dividends in proportion to their level of spending with the business and its affinity partners[3].

What is interesting about the Co-op is that it has been beating the prevailing downward trend in retail. For example, its last set of results prior to the COVID-19 crisis – those for 2019–20 – showed a like-for-like growth of 3.5 per cent in sales[4].

Purpose beyond profit

When one digs behind these numbers, one sees some substantial differences from most retail organizations – differences that might be instructive for other shop owners. The key point is that Southern Co-op believes in what it calls 'Purpose beyond profit' – a vision of sustainable business practice and of making a difference for its members, partners and the places/communities where it operates[5].

As befits an organization set up to support its members, it strives to have a particularly close relationship with local communities. It has a program called 'Love Your Neighbourhood', which encourages each store to get involved with local groups and it contributed £1.4 million to its communities in 2019–20. It is this very localism which differentiates the Co-op's work from many corporate 'Giving Back' programs. Rather than donate large sums to high-profile national charities in order to garner positive PR, the Co-op's work is less glamorous, but more effective, because of the direct involvement of its people on a local level. It is not just about the money given, but also the way in which local Co-op teams contribute their time and skills[6].

These skills, such as product development, marketing, financial analysis and even architectural services, have been used to benefit local entrepreneurs and charities. As Gemma Lacey, Director of

Sustainability and Communications at Southern Co-op, puts it: 'We are all about the value that we drive for our community and our members, using all the tools that we have available, whether it's the funds that we distribute, the fund-raising that we leverage, the time that we volunteer or the skills that we can contribute'[7].

The organization is using the UN's Sustainable Development Goals as a strategic roadmap for its business planning and has identified a number of areas where it believes it can have the greatest impact, such as Sustainable Communities, Responsible Consumption and Production and Climate Action. It is helping by taking initiatives on sustainable buying, packaging changes and local sourcing. It has also established a new carbon target, which is aligned to the latest climate science[8].

Think local

Southern Co-op is heavily engaged in trying to encourage local food production. For example, it has a program called 'Local Flavours', which supports growers by selling their products in selected stores throughout its network and also works with Natural Partnerships to sponsor the 'Food Producers' category of the Sussex Food & Drink Awards. These prizes encourage local entrepreneurs to develop new products and Southern Co-op also gives them advice on how to make them 'retail-ready'[9].

Additionally, the organization is a major supporter of food banks in 69 of its stores. For example, the store in Freshwater, Isle of Wight, partners with the Real Junk Food Project, while in Portsmouth, three stores contribute to the Portsmouth Food Cycle, an organization which cooks free meals for those in need. It also helps local community groups in other ways. Rather than treat retail crime as purely a policing issue, it tries to address the deeper issues causing people to turn to crime. It donated £100,000 to create a 'Safer Neighbourhoods' fund, which supports local charities dedicated to helping people turn away from crime by developing employment skills or overcoming personal barriers. Linked to this, it won a prize at the Business Charity Awards in 2020 for its partnership with the Society of St James, a charity with a focus on tackling local crime, drug/alcohol addiction and homelessness. Southern Co-op worked with the charity's 'Café in the Park' project in Portsmouth, which provides opportunities for vulnerable adults. Part of this work involved launching an initiative called 'Pay It Forward', which enabled local people to help the homeless through a voucher scheme[10].

A lifeline in the pandemic

The arrival of COVID-19 made Southern Co-op's support even more crucial because it exposed the cracks in local community facilities. Services like food banks became vital lifelines to many vulnerable people during the crisis. Most charities saw a plunge in their funding and came to depend more and more on help from business organizations. Because of its outreach programs, the Co-op was well positioned to respond and its many acts of kindness have been much appreciated by local people.

Mark Ralf, Chair of Southern Co-op, summarizes the unique contribution of the organization to its local communities: 'It's a great power, when it's working well. We are important in the lives of so many of our customers. Our customers enjoy engaging with our colleagues'[11].

'For some of our customers it's the only social contact that they get, particularly among the elderly,' adds Gemma Lacey. 'A lot of our store colleagues will know them on first name terms and will have the kind of relationship where they will look out for them. If they haven't seen somebody for a period of time, they will raise questions and find out if that person is OK'[12].

The organization also pays great attention to the welfare of its workers. For example, it paid extra bonuses during the first lockdown, to thank them for their courage in serving customers at their own risk.

It has also invested £1 million in a range of measures aimed at creating a safer environment for both colleagues and customers[13].

The Co-op talks to potential recruits about its values during the recruitment process and believes that this attracts a different sort of person – people interested in having a higher purpose than just earning a wage. As we have seen in Chapter 12 (*see also* pages 79–81), consumers are moving away from rampant individualism and superficial brand image towards transparency, contribution and community. The Southern Co-op's unique approach, with its member-ownership and concentration on serving its communities, seems to chime in well with this new zeitgeist. As Mark Ralf says: 'People in our heartlands do not see us as a "corporation" – we are part of the local community'[14].

It appears that the loyalty that the group displays towards its local communities has been rewarded by their loyalty towards it as a retailer. This is borne out by the company's continued good performance even during the COVID-19 crisis. Its financial update in June 2020 indicates that it was ahead of its plan for the year – a remarkable achievement under the circumstances. Despite the challenges of the post-Covid economy, the organization remains confident that its values will help sustain it in the future[15].

The Southern Co-op is a role model for businesses looking to find a way forward in the very challenging post-Covid era. With people short of cash, and working from home in their local communities, there is an opportunity to return to the more traditional, connected world that existed before the growth of huge malls and out-of-town superstores. A world where personal relationships and mutual support were more important than having the biggest discounts.

CHAPTER FORTY SEVEN

Bonobos

One of the most innovative companies of the last 15 years is a premium menswear brand called Bonobos, which was started by Stanford Business School students, Andy Dunn and Brian Spaly, in 2007. We have already mentioned the brand in Chapters 18 and 32 in reference to its innovative stores and customer service strategies (*see also* pages 103–111 and 186–191)[1].

While still at college, Brian Spaly invented a new type of trouser, with a curved waistband, medium rise and tailored thighs. Andy Dunn tried it and after falling in love with the fit, decided to help promote it. It became so popular among their fellow students that they were trying the trousers on behind trees on the campus and handing Dunn and Spaly dollar notes in payment. Such was the demand that, after graduation, the pair took the risky decision to invest their careers in expanding Bonobos. Looking back, Andy Dunn underlines the importance of having an exceptional product to start off with: 'Consumers don't need many things from your company – they just need one thing. Make one thing great. Get one thing right.' The pair got financial support from angel investors Andy Rachleff (Chief Executive Officer of Wealthfront) and Joel Peterson (Chairman of JetBlue), both of whom had lectured Dunn at Stanford[2].

An outsider's perspective

Dunn came at the question of how to design the perfect menswear brand with an outsider's perspective: 'I'm kind of the least likely person that you could imagine to be a CEO of a fashion company – when I'm in a retail store, I feel like my soul is getting sucked out of me'[3].

Thus, when it came to scaling Bonobos, he decided to take the direct-to-consumer route, despite the then-prevailing view that it was difficult to sell clothing online. He had a feeling that this was about to change – he knew that men like him, who did not particularly enjoy shopping in stores, would appreciate the opportunity to buy online. He also saw the potential of the newly launched social media sites, like Facebook and Twitter, for spreading the word about Bonobos and creating a new type of interactive relationship with customers, based around data and personalization. Thus, as he expanded the product line into other menswear categories, he sought feedback from customers about new product designs[4].

Cult-like enthusiasm

Dunn's actions created a powerful sense of brand community. Many early customers developed an almost cult-like enthusiasm for the brand. For example, as described in a *Time* magazine article in 2010, one such customer was a man called Troy Hooper, a Minneapolis-based financial analyst and proud owner of 19 pairs of Bonobos pants. He told the magazine that he emailed or tweeted with people at the company several times a week: 'It's almost like they are my friends. These guys, they make me feel like I am part of the company even though I am just a customer'[5].

In addition to creating this strong community, Bonobos leveraged the power of the Web as a low-cost medium to sell luxury products at more accessible prices. Without all the retail mark-ups, the brand was able to sell its luxury chinos from around $90.00 a pair, as opposed to the $170.00-plus charged by brands like Ralph Lauren[6].

Bonobos also deployed a new sensibility through its advertising. For example, its 2018 campaign '#evolvethedefinition' encouraged men to move beyond the outdated notion of masculinity as being all about strength and aggression. As Joseph Saroufim, Creative Director at advertising agency, Observatory, put it: 'When we saw the limited and toxic definition of "masculine", we recognized it as a problem antithetical to our client's brand proposition – fit for every man'[7].

Customers adopted Bonobos with great enthusiasm, causing a viral spread of its online community. The brand offered its clients credits of $50.00 for introducing their friends, and referrals became over 50 per cent of the business. Troy Hooper, alone, introduced eight of his friends to the brand[8].

A breakthrough idea

After five years of growing the online business, Andy Dunn hit on a breakthrough idea – to open stores. This seemed like a kind of heresy at the time among committed direct-to-consumer aficionados: 'I really thought stores were going away at that time,' he said. But he changed his mind after the company had customers come in to try on samples. They were working on developing a new line of dress shirts and got hundreds of clients to visit Bonobos' offices to do the fittings. While there, they wanted to try on other products too, and started 'buying like crazy', according to Dunn[9].

He felt that the face-to-face contact was very important, just as it had been in the early days of the brand. However, his concept of a store was quite revolutionary: it was not going to offer stock for sale, instead it would focus on introducing the brand to customers in the right way.

In 2012, he opened a showroom in New York – a 'Guideshop' – which was not a transactional point of sale, but as the name suggests, a place where potential customers would be given a 'guided tour' of the brand. We have already seen in Chapter 18 (pages 103–111) how the Guideshops operated. High-level personal shoppers – known as 'Ninjas' – would make hour-long appointments with customers, starting with a glass of coffee or wine and followed by an exploration of the customer's needs and tastes in terms of clothing. Comfortable seating areas and fitting rooms added to the experience. If the customer wanted to buy at the end of the process then this was fine – they would be signed up to the website, and after checkout, would receive the goods directly at their homes within a couple of days. However, it was not considered essential – the key thing was that the customer should have a great first experience of the brand[10].

In taking the time to learn about the customers' preferences, and fitting them with different clothing options, Bonobos was collecting a wealth of information, which could be used to guide their future online marketing relationship with this individual. The hope was that having invested in establishing the correct fit, the brand would have gained a loyal customer who would largely transact online in the future, with fewer returns arising from incorrect sizing.

The stockless concept also worked well for the store team. Liberating them from the thankless tasks of unpacking boxes, tagging product and counting inventory changed the nature of the work and made it far more enjoyable. This, along with the high-end remuneration and share options given to the 'Ninjas', enabled Bonobos to recruit fairly sophisticated people to work in its stores.

The Guideshop concept proved very successful and the company rolled it out rapidly, such that by 2020, there were 62 showrooms in fashionable areas across the United States. Bonobos as a whole also grew fast, from initial sales of $100,000 in 2007 to over $69 million in 2013[11].

Growth and acquisition

The brand went through several successful rounds of funding between 2008 and 2014, and raised a total of $128 million from investors like Accel Partners, Lightspeed Venture Partners, Forerunner Ventures, Glynn Capital, Mousse Partners and department store group, Nordstrom. The business continued to expand rapidly and in 2015, celebrated the sale of its millionth pair of chinos. By 2016, it was generating sales in excess of $100 million and Dunn was approached by Marc Lore, President and Chief Executive officer of Walmart's e-commerce operations, with a view to acquiring the brand[12].

As we have seen, Walmart was investing heavily in growing its online business, acquiring Jet.com (along with its founder, Lore) in 2016, and, later on, direct-to-consumer womenswear brand ModCloth in March 2017. Bonobos fitted perfectly into this strategy, bringing valuable insights that the larger group could leverage. The acquisition took place in June 2016, with Walmart paying $310 million in cash[13].

The story of Bonobos' success illustrates many of the strategies covered in this book, including product innovation, selling luxury-for-less online, using personalized marketing and leveraging social media to create a strong brand community. In addition, Andy Dunn was almost certainly the first person from the digitally native world to see the potential of experiential retail as an adjunct to a strong online business. His 'Guideshops' are, in a very real sense, a guide to the future of retailing as and when it emerges from the shadow of Coronavirus.

CHAPTER FORTY EIGHT

Nike

Nike is a brand which is best known for its famous slogan 'Just do it'. The tagline is intended as a bold rallying cry for its followers to stop making excuses, get out there and take action. At no time was this sense of boldness more evident than on 15 June 2017, when the then Chief Executive Officer of Nike, Mark Parker, made a surprising announcement. He outlined a radical new strategy for the brand, which was titled the 'Consumer Direct Offense'. This was nothing less than a declaration of intent for Nike to transform itself over a five-year period from being a wholesale brand to a direct-to-consumer brand. The plan targeted the growth of Nike's e-commerce business from 15 per cent of the total in 2017 to 30 per cent by 2022. This was ambitious, but not, in itself, that radical[1].

Biting the bullet

What was radical was Parker's declaration that Nike would 'strategically withdraw' from its 30,000 retail partners to focus on the top 40 retailers worldwide that offered 'Superior customer experiences, quality service and storytelling that differentiates the brand'. This was the first example of a major brand biting the bullet by taking the decision to get out in front of the decline in the retail industry[2].

It was rumoured that while leading retailers like Foot Locker, Dick's Sporting Goods, Finish Line, JD Sports and Nordstrom had made the cut, as well as major online players like Tmall and Zalando, the vast majority had not. The shift was intended to happen over a five-year period, with some of the smaller customers expected to go out of business. As the Brand President of Nike, Trevor Edwards, put it, 'Undifferentiated, mediocre retail won't survive.'[3]

The remorseless logic of this strategy shocked many people in the sports industry, particularly among the ranks of Nike's smaller retail customers, who had relied upon the brand to drive sales through their stores. Nike was betting that its grip on the consumer's mind was stronger than that of its retail partners. To reinforce this grip, it doubled down on some of the key strategies that had built the brand – product innovation, cutting-edge marketing and relationships with celebrity athletes.

Triple Double

Nike's new 'Triple Double Strategy' targeted a doubling of the 'cadence and impact of innovation', a doubling of its 'speed to market' and a doubling of its 'direct connections with consumers'. The core of this strategy was the 'Nike Consumer Experience' (NCX), which included the organization's own direct-to-consumer network, as well as the vastly streamlined slate of wholesale distribution partners[4].

The technology at the heart of the NCX was to be the Nike app, which enhanced shopper experiences and gave access to the NikePlus rewards plan. The loyalty program offered members exclusive products, access to Nike experts, personalized workouts, priority access to VIP events, free shipping and 30-day wear tests[5].

By the end of 2018, Nike had over 100 million NikePlus members and aimed to triple that number by 2023. Part of the condition for being included in the top 40 partnership program was that the retailer should promote use of the Nike app[6].

NikePlus gave the brand substantial amounts of customer data, which allowed the company to drill down on their shopping habits and product preferences in order to personalize their future engagements with the brand. One of the other conditions for being on the Nike partnership list was that the retailer/e-tailer share the customer data with Nike[7].

The company also announced a 'Key Cities' program, which targeted 12 major centres – New York, London, Shanghai, Beijing, Los Angeles, Tokyo, Paris, Berlin, Mexico City, Barcelona, Seoul and Milan – for 80 per cent of its sales growth. The logic for this was that Nike's core customer demographic – the so-called 'HENRY's (High-Earners-Not-Rich-Yet), who could afford top-end trainers – lived in these cities and acted as opinion formers for everyone else. By using these locations as incubators for new products and technologies, Nike could get them to market faster and then gauge whether it was worth rolling them out to the rest of the market[8].

House of Innovation 002

The company focused on having the best physical presentation of the brand in these centres by ramping up the theatre and technology in its 1,000-plus company stores, including flagships like Nike New York, opened in 2018, or Paris, opened in July 2020. The Paris store is a 26,000 square-foot colossus on the Avenue des Champs-Élysées named 'Nike Paris – House of Innovation 002' which aimed to create a digitally powered end-to-end consumer experience. For example, it featured a 'mission control' area near the entrance with a wall of screens connecting consumers to 'Nike Experiences', such as sport across the city, in-store workshops and events hosted by Nike athletes and influencers. It also linked to the Nike app to unlock a range of member-only benefits in-store, such as the Nike Fit service, whereby members could get their feet scanned and alert staff to arrange the correct sizes to be placed in fitting rooms. Sizes were subsequently stored in the Nike members' profiles[9].

The app also offered services like 'Scan to Learn' (which listed more information about products), 'Shop The Look' (enabling members to scan a display and learn what sizes are available in all the items on the fixture) and instant on-app checkout[10].

Membership gave access to kids' pods that allowed for interactive gaming to keep children entertained while their parents shopped, and personalized products available through 'Maker Studios'. The key thing is that all the 'Member Unlock' features were used in order to emphasize the benefits of belonging to the elite brand community[11].

Finally, the store represented a breakthrough in sustainable technology as part of Nike's 'Move to Zero' program, with 85,000 kilos of sustainable material woven into the fabric of the environment in the store – from regrind in the floor and the walls, to sustainable hangers, to all the operational energy requirements being met through renewable sources[12].

Other flagship stores featured basketball courts, soccer-trial areas and treadmills with giant screens and cameras to analyse the runner's gait. They also made available dedicated sports coaches to offer advice[13].

Fortune favours the bold

Nike's investment in this bold Consumer Direct Offense strategy appears to be paying off. In its 2019–20 annual results, the company said that digital sales had increased by 47 per cent and 30 per cent of all sales were now online – two years ahead of its target[14].

The company has started the process of withdrawing from non-strategic retail partners, reportedly cutting ties with companies like Zappos, Belk and Boscov's. Even through the COVID-19 period, results continued to be robust, helped by the accompanying fitness boom. In the quarter ending November 2020, the company beat expectations as overall revenue grew by 9 per cent, with digital revenue growing by

84 per cent. Its valuation in November 2020 was $155 billion, versus Adidas at $95 billion and Under Armour at only $6 billion[15].

Nike's courageous and far-sighted move has thus reinforced its leadership position in its industry. The combination of a powerful online direct channel and a theatrical store channel supported by modern technology, innovative product development and data-driven marketing has proved to be unbeatable in creating a seemingly unassailable position in the fast-growing sportswear market.

Conclusion

And so we come to the end of our analysis of the key trends shaping the brand/retail industry in the post-Covid environment and the case studies of the companies who are innovating in line with these trends. Their success, despite all the turbulence created by the global pandemic, represents the first shoots of the Retail Recovery. If brands and retailers can learn from these lessons, they can guarantee themselves a bright future as the world emerges from the crisis.

Let us recap the main trends driving this recovery. The first is that the store lockdowns and the accompanying growth in e-commerce have acted as a wake-up call to the brand/retail industry. In consequence, we can see that brands and retailers are accelerating their investment in multi-channel retailing and finally seeing clearly the relative strengths of each channel. They are starting to understand that e-commerce is the superior channel for the transactional side of the business because it is lower-cost, more stock-efficient, more accessible and more convenient, and it also offers more choice. On the other hand, physical stores are better for delivering the experiential side of the business because they are three-dimensional 'live' spaces, which are perfect for brand theatre, community building, education and customer service.

As markets have been flooded with competing products, brands and retailers have also been compelled to change their vision of what they are offering consumers away from commodity goods and towards value-added services, such as solving their problems and enhancing their lives. They have stopped thinking about shifting boxes and started thinking about making things better for people. They are also realizing that an important part of this added value comes from creating a sense of shared purpose, which goes beyond the purely transactional and unifies brand, staff and customers in a single community.

In addition, at a more practical level, the industry is facing up to the reality that the twin revolutions in e-commerce and communications are effectively collapsing traditional brand/retail supply chains by making it possible for factories to trade directly with consumers. With prices and margins falling, brands and retailers are urgently seeking to disintermediate each other – brands by going direct-to-consumer and retailers by developing their own-label offerings. This radical change can feel uncomfortable, but the success of Nike on the brand side and Target on the stores side shows that it is possible.

They are also waking up to the fact that their traditional marketing models, based on using mass advertising to 'push' products at passive consumers, are no longer working and that personalized performance marketing is more effective in engaging the consumer in a two-way dialogue with the brand and measuring the precise impact of marketing initiatives on individual clients.

Linked to this, traditional brands and retailers are also appreciating the need to collect and integrate customer data across their various channels so as to create a unified vision of individual customers and their lifetime relationship with the company. Again, new technology is helping them do this by enabling them to track individual customer behaviour. Thus, we see incumbent brands and retailers investing in technology, logistics and online marketing to grow their e-commerce channels and to integrate them more closely with their stores.

They are also learning to use the 'endless aisle' of the Web to increase their ranges, turning themselves into marketplaces and leveraging their audiences to sell more products, including third-party brands. As they build their ranges online, the absurdity of stocking them all within the 'four walls' of their stores is becoming increasingly apparent. They are learning that not all products have to be held as inventory in their stores – they can focus on best sellers and sell the rest via in-store screens, with shipment direct to the home. They are increasingly coming to see digital as the main transactional channel and shifting an increasing proportion of their stock sales and shipments from being store-based to online.

The stores are increasingly seen as gateways into the brand, with the ongoing relationship management and repeat business being handled online. In addition, the shift away from the stock-intensive store model is also enabling retailers to reduce the size of their shops, thus helping them decrease costs. It is also liberating store space to be used for value-added activities which cannot be carried out online. The most important of these is to create live experiences which give people a reason for visiting the store.

Stores can be theatres for brand spectacles, using modern technology to bring the company story alive. They can be places of education, where people learn about what makes the brand special. They can be meeting places for the customer community and they can be places where skilled specialists help clients on a one-to-one basis. What they can no longer be is spaces filled with serried ranks of shelves, with boxes on them. Because you can get that more cheaply on the Web.

The changing nature of the store is also redefining what it means to work in retail. Although there are fewer roles needed in the industry, those that remain are becoming more interesting – less store-stackers than actors, stylists and community-organizers. The retail job can go back to what it used to be – a high-status, expert role, which people want to do for life and raise a family on.

The changes to brands and retailers are being accompanied by a shift in the commercial property market, with landlords offering more flexible leases and modular 'plug and play' spaces, pre-equipped with technology. A new breed of landlord is also providing Retail as a Service to online brands looking to move into stores retailing.

The combination of all these reforms represents the biggest change to the retail industry in the last 200 years. Its effects may not be immediately visible as we navigate the ongoing pandemic and its aftermath, but over time, they are going to drive a massive Retail Revival across the world. The mind-numbing uniformity of the past – with high streets and malls filled with the same tired old formats – will give way to a vibrant cacophony of ever-changing brands, offering innovative products, entertaining experiences and a sense of community. If this Retail Recovery leads to a wave of innovation, individuality and entrepreneurial passion being present in our high streets and malls, then this will ultimately represent a positive outcome from all the chaos and heartbreak of the recent past.

Notes

Introduction

1 'Next Annual Report 2020' – nextplc.co.uk – 20 January 2020.
2 'Primark furloughs 68,000 staff as sales plunge from £650 million a month to zero amid coronavirus lockdown' – itv.com – 21 April 2020.
3 'Brits spend £12.3 billion on online groceries in 2018' – mintel.com – 12 April 2019; 'Internet sales as a percentage of total retail sales' – ons.gov.uk – 2018.
4 'Covid-19: Online grocery sales grow by 92% despite easing of lockdown' – essentialretail.com – 21 July 2020; 'COVID-19 crisis sparks "inflection point" for online grocery – and huge revenue for Amazon' – geekwire.com – 7 April 2020.
5 'Internet sales as a proportion of all retailing: textiles, clothing, and footwear in the United Kingdom (UK) from January 2016 to May 2020' – statista.com – 2020.
6 'Retail sales pounds data' – ons.gov.uk – 20 November 2020; 'Internet sales as a percentage of total retail sales' – ons.gov.uk – 20 November 2020.
7 'Retail sales pounds data' – ons.gov.uk – 20 November 2020.
8 'Monthly Retail Trade' – census.gov – October 2020.
9 'Retail sales, Great Britain: October 2020' – ons.gov.uk – November 2020.
10 'List of shops that have collapsed into administration in 2020 as UK lockdown hits high street' – business-live.co.uk – 1 December 2020.
11 'The running list of 2020 retail bankruptcies' – retaildive.com – 25 November 2020.
12 'Philip Green's Arcadia on brink of collapse, putting 13,000 jobs at risk' – theguardian.com – 27 November 2020; 'Shares of parent of Victoria's Secret crater after effort to sell itself falls through' – cnbc.com – 4 May 2020; 'John Lewis may not reopen certain stores post lockdown' – retailgazette.co.uk – 7 December 2020.
13 'Surviving the cash crunch. The impact of Covid-19 on major UK retailers' – alvarezandmarsal.com – 6 April 2020.
14 'Shopping centre owner Intu collapses into administration' – theguardian.com – 26 June 2020; 'Mall operator CBL files for Chapter 11 bankruptcy protection' – ukreuters.com – 2 November 2020; 'Simon Property Group Inc' – googlefinance – 7 December 2020; 'Seritage Growth Properties Class A' – googlefinance – 7 December 2020.
15 'Unemployment' – ons.co.uk – 10 November 2020; 'HMRC coronavirus (COVID-19) statistics' – gov.uk – November 2020.
16 'The unemployment situation' – bls.gov – November 2020.
17 'IMF says decline in global growth worse than forecast' – bbc.co.uk – 24 June 2020.
18 'EMP13: Employment by industry' – ons.gov.uk – 10 November 2020.
19 'Retail Jobs – Retail supports 1 in 4 American jobs' – nrf.com – 2020.

Chapter 1: The Crisis Brews Up – The Long-term Causes

1 'Debenhams announces CVA plan to restructure store portfolio' – ir.debenhams. com – 26 April 2019; 'House of Fraser to shut more than half its stores under CVA' – fashionunited.uk – 7 June 2018; 'Mothercare creditors approve CVA plans' – retailgazette.co.uk – 1 June 2018; 'BHS chief asks public for second chance as retailer wins crucial vote' – theguardian.com – 23 March 2016; 'Sears files for Chapter 11 bankruptcy protection, to close 142 more stores' – eu.usatoday.com – 15 October 2018; 'Toys "R" Us files for Chapter 11 bankruptcy protection' – cnbc.com – 19 September 2017; 'Barneys New York files for bankruptcy' – theguardian.com – 6 August 2019; 'Claire's files for bankruptcy' – money.cnn.com – 19 March 2018; 'Aeropostale files for Chapter 11 bankruptcy protection' – uk.reuters.com – 4 May 2016.

2 'How Many Products Does Amazon Carry?' – retailtouchpoints.com – 9 December 2020; 'Macys.com Delivers Department Store Experience via the web' – public.dhe. ibm.com – September 1999.

3 '2017 Ecommerce Round-up: 16 Percent Growth; "Retail Apocalypse"?' – practicalecommerce.com – 11 January 2018.

4 'Median house prices for administrative geographies' – ons.gov.uk – 20 June 2018; 'All Employees – ASHE: Table 1' – ons.gov.uk – 2018.

5 'Total household wealth and its components by age band, Great Britain July 2006 to June 2016' – ons.gov.uk – 13 June 2018; 'Distribution of wealth in US by age' – freeby50.com – 6 September 2012.

6 'The boomerang generation – Feeling ok about living with mom and dad' – pewsocialtrends.org – 15 March 2012.

7 'Average weekly household expenditure on clothing and footwear in the United Kingdom (UK) in 2017, by age of household reference person' – statista.com – 2017; 'Consumer expenditures vary by age' – bls.gov – December 2015.

8 '900,000 UK retail jobs could be lost by 2025, warns BRC' – bbc.co.uk – 29 February 2016; 'Pound plunges after Leave vote' – bbc.co.uk – 24 June 2016.

9 'Immigration to America is down. Wages are up' – economist.com – 13 February 2020; 'U.S. retailers blast new China tariffs, say move will raise prices further, hurt jobs' – uk.reuters.com – 1 August 2019; 'Shop online? Internet retailers have a tax advantage Congress must end' – thehill.com – 9 September 2017.

10 'Private equity has killed 600,000 retail jobs, study says' – latimes.com – 24 July 2019.

11 'Internet sales as a percentage of total retail sales' – ons.gov.uk – 20 November 2020; The share of online in the US is based on Census Bureau data adjusted to remove Motor Vehicle/Parts and Gasoline sales, both of which are typically excluded from International measures of online sales. See 'QUARTERLY RETAIL E-COMMERCE SALES' – census. gov, for the base data, and 'ttps://www.census.gov/retail/mrts/www/explanatory_material.pdf – for the adjustment factor, based on the latest available breakdown in 2017.

Chapter 2: The Spectre Haunting the Land – The Coronavirus Pandemic

1 'The doctor who discovered the coronavirus: Wuhan medic raised the alarm to authorities in December after noticing mysterious pneumonia; that could spread between people' – dailymail.co.uk – 29 April 2020.

2 'First death from China mystery illness outbreak' – theguardian.com – 11 January 2020.

3 'Coronavirus was widespread across the UK earlier than previously thought' - metro. co.uk – 13 August 2020.

4   'Prime Minister statement on coronavirus (COVID-19): 23 March 2020' – gov.uk –
    23 March 2020.
5   'Boris Johnson admitted to hospital with coronavirus' – theguardian.com – 5 April
    2020.
6   'Coronavirus: How US went from one infection to one million' – independent.
    co.uk – 28 April 2020.
7   'About COVID-19 restrictions' – covid19.ca.gov – 19 March 2020.
8   'NRF Forecasts 3.5% To 4.1% Sales Growth For 2020 Despite Coronavirus, Election
    Uncertainties' – newsbreak.com – 26 February 2020; 'Macy's is planning for a coronavirus
    hit, but it's "nothing to be concerned about yet"' – cnbc.com – 25 February 2020.
9   'Macy's is planning for a coronavirus hit, but it's "nothing to be concerned about
    yet"' – cnbc.com – 25 February 2020.
10 'Coronavirus: Non-essential UK shops to re-open from 15 June' – bbc.co.uk – 25
    May 2020.
11 'UK Government announces employee "furlough" scheme' – mayerbrown.com – 23
    March 2020
12 'Furlough scheme changes – important dates and tapering of grant to 31 October
    2020' – bto.co.uk – 1 June 2020; 'More than one in four UK workers now furloughed' –
    bbc.co.uk – 9 June 2020.
13 'Coronavirus: Business rates holiday granted for all retail and leisure firms' – cityam.
    com – 17 March 2020; 'UK to allow firms to defer £30 billion of tax payments' –
    reuters.com – 20 March 2020; 'Whatever it takes: UK pledges almost $400 billion to
    help businesses through coronavirus' – cnbc.com – 17 March 2020.
14 'The CARES Act Has Passed: Here Are The Highlights' – forbes.com – 29 March 2020.
15 'Paycheck Protection Program Loans – How It Works' – sba.com – 2020.
16 'CARES Act Provides Tax Deferral and Refund Opportunities' – pillsburylaw.com –
    26 March 2020; 'Congress passes plan to send taxpayers $1,200 checks in coronavirus
    aid. How to get yours' – cnbc.com – 25 March 2020.
17 'Retailers commend U.S. House for swift approval of CARES Act' – nrf.com – 27
    March 2020.
18 'US retailers teeter on the brink as 630,000 outlets close' – ft.com – 30 March 2020.
19 'The BRC heavyweight fighting retail's corner' – drapersonline.com – 14 May 2020.
20 'Covid-19: Primark reveals 75% drop in sales due to lockdown' – essentialretail.
    com – 2 July 2020.
21 'Internet sales as a percentage of total retail sales' – ons.gov.uk – 20 November 2020.
22 'Savvy retailers will adapt and thrive in post coronavirus world' – retailtechinno-
    vationhub.com – 24 June 2020.
23 'US E-Commerce Grew 44% in the Second Quarter' – marketplacepulse.com – 18
    August 2020; 'QUARTERLY RETAIL ECOMMERCE SALES' – census.gov; for
    adjusted sales see Chapter 1, Footnote 11.
24 'Amazon to hire 75,000 more workers as demand rises due to coronavirus' – cnbc.
    com – 13 April 2020.
25 'Hospitality industry facing ruin as leaders demand help' – itv.com – 17 March 2020.
26 'Primark and Matalan among retailers allegedly cancelling £2.4bn orders in
    "catastrophic" move for Bangladesh' – theguardian.com – 2 April 2020.
27 Ibid.
28 'Under Armour sales plummet 23% as coronavirus stalls turnaround plans' – cnbc.
    com – 11 May 2020; 'Under Armour to lay off 600 employees globally' – cnbc.com –
    8 September 2020.
29 'Revlon Reports First Quarter 2020 Results' – businesswire.com – 11 May 2020.
30 'JD Sports stops paying rent to landlords' – theguardian.com – 31 March 2020.

31 'Shopping centre owner Hammerson says rent takings down two-thirds' – theguardian.com – 30 March 2020.

32 'Shopping centre owner Intu collapses into administration' – theguardian.com – 26 June 2020.

33 'Landlords and tenants feel the pain as coronavirus hits rents' – ft.com – 2 April 2020.

34 Ibid.

35 '1 Struggling Mall REIT Is Running Out of Time' – fool.com – 3 June 2020; 'Mall Giant CBL Just Filed for Bankruptcy' – footwearnews.com – 2 November 2020.

36 '1 Struggling Mall REIT Is Running Out of Time' – fool.com – 3 June 2020.

37 'Covid-19: PM announces four-week England lockdown' – bbc.co.uk – 31 October 2020.

38 'Covid: Donald Trump and Melania test positive' – bbc.co.uk – 2 October 2020.

39 'Businesses facing bleak midwinter; and must be handed more support, CBI boss warns' – thisismoney.co.uk – 1 November 2020.

40 'Covid vaccine: First milestone; vaccine offers 90% protection' – bbc.co.uk – 9 November 2020.

Chapter 3: We're Gonna Party Like It's 1929

1 'Dow Tops 30,000 For First Time Ever' – Investopedia.com – 24 November 2020.

2 '"Devastation": how aviation industry's Covid crisis is hitting towns across UK' – theguardian.com – 24 August 2020; 'The end of tourism?' – theguardian.com – 18 June 2020.

3 'The employment situation – January 2021' – bls.gov – January 2021.

4 'How does the size of the UK's fiscal response to coronavirus compare with other countries?' – ifs.org.uk – 14 May 2020.

5 'Tax receipts have fallen off a cliff amid lockdown' – ft.com – 26 May 2020.

6 'Government borrowing hits record £62bn in April over coronavirus measures' – cityam.com – 22 May 2020.

7 'UK public debt exceeds 100% of GDP for first time since 1963' – ft.com – 19 June 2020.

8 'What The $2 Trillion Coronavirus Aid, Relief, And Economic Security (CARES) Act Does For American Workers' – forbes.com – 10 April 2020; 'A Breakdown of the CARES Act' – jpmorgan.com – 14 April 2020.

9 'NYC mayor seeks federal aid as coronavirus costs New York $7.4 billion in lost tax revenue' – cnbc.com – 16 April 2020.

10 'Now Everything Depends on US Stimulus, from Billionaires to China's Manufacturers, as US National Debt Blows Out' – wolfestreet.com – 7 October 2020.

11 'Global economic outlook: Is the glass half full or half empty?' – economics.rabobank. com – 19 March 2019.

12 'Why the Next Recession Is Likely to Happen in 2020, and What It Will Mean for Housing' – finance.yahoo.com – 25 July 2019.

13 'Coronavirus a devastating blow for world economy' – bbc.co.uk – 7 June 2020.

14 'World Economic Outlook' – imf.org – April 2021.

15 'GDP monthly estimate, UK: December 2020' – ons.gov.uk – 12 February 2021; 'Gross Domestic Product, 4th Quarter and Year 2020 (Advance Estimate)' – bea.gov – 28 January 2021.

Chapter 4: Last Man Standing – The Impact on Retail

1   'Who's Gone Bust in Retail?' – retailresearch.org – 30 November 2020; 'Clarks' CVA gets green light amid landlord fury over rent write-offs' – shoeintelligence.com – 23 November 2020; '200 job cuts as Jigsaw creditors approve CVA' – retailgazette.co.uk – 4 September 2020; 'Virgin Media to disappear from UK high street' – theguardian.com – 28 May 2020; 'Women's Apparel Retailer Long Tall Sally To Cease Operations After 44 Years' –retailtouchpoints.com – 17 June 2020; 'Moss Bros gets green light for CVA proposal' – standard.co.uk – 15 December 2020.

2   'Primark sales fall from £650m a month to zero and Cath Kidston permanently closes all stores' – independent.co.uk – 22 April 2020; 'Covid-19: Next predicts up to £1bn loss of sales' – essentialretail.com – 19 March 2020.

3   'Dixons Carphone profits slump following Covid store closures'; 'Office set to close up to half its 100 UK stores' – cityam.com – 9 August 2020.

4   'Ted Baker losses widen as it reveals 950 job cuts since June' – retailgazette.co.uk – 7 December 2020.

5   'Boohoo, Debenhams and the changing face of UK retail' – retailgazette.co.uk – 26 January 2021.

6   'ASOS buys Topshop and Miss Selfridge brands for £330m' – theguardian.com – 1 February 2021; 'Boohoo acquires Arcadia brands Burton, Dorothy Perkins and Burton' – fashionunited.uk – 8 February 2021; 'Arcadia brand Evans acquired by City Chic in £23m deal' – retail-week.com – 20 December 2020; 'Topshop owner Arcadia goes into administration' – bbc.co.uk – 30 November 2020.

7   'John Lewis Partnership swings to £635m half-year loss & axes bonus' – retailgazette. co.uk – 17 September 2020.

8   'Sainsbury's to cut 3,500 jobs and close 420 Argos stores' – bbc.co.uk – 5 November 2020.

9   '14,000 shops have shut down so far in 2020, a 25% increase on 2019' – retailgazette. co.uk – 28 September 2020; 'More than 20,000 shops may never reopen after coronavirus lockdown, says report' – insider.co.uk – 25 March 2020.

10   'All the retailers that have made job cuts amid Covid-19' – retailgazette.co.uk – 25 August 2020; 'Sainsbury's to cut 3,500 jobs and close 420 Argos stores' – bbc.co.uk – 5 November 2020; 'Poundstretcher considering closing over 250 UK stores' – business-sale.com – 17 June 2020; 'Boots store closures right thing to do' – bbc.co.uk – 28 June 2020; '163 jobs at risk as Oak Furnitureland proposes 27 store closures' – retailgazette. co.uk – 27 July 2020; 'Marks and Spencer to axe 7,000 jobs over next three months' – ft. com – 20 May 2020; 'Philip Green's Arcadia on brink of collapse, putting 13,000 jobs at risk' – theguardian.com – 27 November 2020; 'Go Outdoors' future uncertain as JD Sports files for court protection' – retailgazette.co.uk – 22 June 2020; 'Halfords plans to close up to 60 stores even after huge rise in bike sales' – cyclingweekly.com – 14 July 2020; 'Oddbins closure likely unless sale completes within weeks' – thedrinksbusiness. com – 9 March 2020; 'Virgin Media is closing 53 stores permanently after lockdown restrictions are lifted with 300 shop staff offered alternative roles' – dailymail. co.uk – 31 May 2020; 'Edinburgh Woollen Mill planning to close at least 50 stores' – thebusinessdesk.com – 16 October 2020; 'Shoe retailer Office to close half its stores, reports claim' – business-live.co.uk – 9 August 2020; '25,000 jobs at risk as Debenhams closure follows Topshop collapse' – edition.cnn.com – 1 December 2020; 'Beales department store goes into administration closing 22 branches and putting more than 1,000 jobs at risk' – dailymail.co.uk – 20 January 2020; 'Fashion chain Jigsaw is shutting more stores and axing staff' – bbc.co.uk – 4 September 2020.

11 'All the retailers that have made job cuts amid Covid-19' – retailgazette.co.uk – 25 August 2020; 'Sainsbury's to cut 3,500 jobs and close 420 Argos stores' – bbc.co.uk – 5 November 2020; 'Poundstretcher considering closing over 250 UK stores' – business-sale.com – 17 June 2020; 'Boots store closures right thing to do' – bbc.co.uk – 28 June 2020; '163 jobs at risk as Oak Furnitureland proposes 27 store closures' – retailgazette.co.uk – 27 July 2020; 'Marks and Spencer to axe 7,000 jobs over next three months' – ft.com – 20 May 2020; 'Philip Green's Arcadia on brink of collapse, putting 13,000 jobs at risk' – theguardian.com – 27 November 2020; 'Go Outdoors' future uncertain as JD Sports files for court protection' – retailgazette.co.uk – 22 June 2020; 'Halfords plans to close up to 60 stores even after huge rise in bike sales' – cyclingweekly.com – 14 July 2020; 'Oddbins closure likely unless sale completes within weeks' – thedrinksbusiness.com – 9 March 2020; 'Virgin Media is closing 53 stores permanently after lockdown restrictions are lifted with 300 shop staff offered alternative roles' – dailymail.co.uk – 31 May 2020; 'Edinburgh Woollen Mill planning to close at least 50 stores' – thebusinessdesk.com – 16 October 2020; 'Shoe retailer Office to close half its stores, reports claim' – business-live.co.uk – 9 August 2020; '25,000 jobs at risk as Debenhams closure follows Topshop collapse' – edition.cnn.com – 1 December 2020; 'Beales department store goes into administration closing 22 branches and putting more than 1,000 jobs at risk' – dailymail.co.uk – 20 January 2020; 'Fashion chain Jigsaw is shutting more stores and axing staff' – bbc.co.uk – 4 September 2020; 'Hays Travel cutting up to 878 jobs out of total workforce of 4,500' – thisismoney.co.uk – 3 August 2020; 'Ted Baker to cut 500 jobs as pandemic losses add to financial woe' – theguardian.com – 19 July 2020; 'White Stuff cuts almost 400 jobs as it responds to a faster than ever shift online' – internetretailing.net – 16 July 2020; 'Over 175,000 UK retail jobs lost in 2020' – fashionunited.uk – 4 January 2021.

12 'Burberry to cut 500 jobs as luxury demand faces slow recovery' – reuters.com – 15 July 2020; 'Luxury department store Harrods to cut nearly 700 jobs' – reuters.com – 1 July 2020; 'Diane von Furstenberg's Brand Is Left Exposed by the Pandemic' – nytimes.com – 8 January 2021; 'Aspinal of London CVA to mean store closures' – uk.fashionnetwork.com – 18 September 2020.

13 'UK restaurant chains to go into administration, close branches and cut jobs in 2020' – business-live.co.uk – 7 August 2020; 'Le Pain Quotidien to close 10 UK locations in pre-pack administration' – business-sale.com – 12 June 2020; 'Bella Italia, Cafe Rouge and Las Iguanas face collapse with 6,000 jobs at risk' – mirror.co.uk – 18 May 2020; 'Chiquito falls into administration as "majority" of its restaurants permanently close' – manchestereveningnews.co.uk; 'Famous Brand's UK burger chain GBK sold in pre-pack deal to Boparan' – reuters.com – 14 August 2020.

14 'Coronavirus: Upper Crust owner SSP to cut up to 5,000 UK jobs' – bbc.com – 1 July 2020; 'Upper Crust owner SSP slumps to huge annual loss' – standard.co.uk – 17 December 2020.

15 'Pret A Manger to cut 3,000 jobs in the UK' – bbc.com – 27 August 2020.

16 'One in four pubs may never reopen after lockdown is lifted' – telegraph.co.uk – 1 November 2020.

17 'Revolution Bars set for radical restructuring' – telegraph.co.uk – 25 September 2020; 'Hospitality businesses in last ditch plea as layoffs begin' – thisismoney.co.uk – 26 September 2020; 'Premier Inn owner Whitbread to cut 6,000 jobs amid Covid crisis' – theguardian.com – 22 September 2020.

18 'AMC Theatres escapes bankruptcy thanks to $917M cash infusion from investors' – cbsnews.com – 25 January 2021; 'Cineworld considering temporary closure of all its UK and US venues' – theguardian.com – 4 October 2020; 'Vue to shut a quarter of UK cinemas three days a week' – theguardian.com – 11 October 2020.

19 'Countrywide Interim Results for the six months ended 30 June 2020' – countrywide. co.uk – 22 October 2020; 'Countrywide accepts Connells' £130m takeover offer' – theguardian.com – 31 December 2020; 'Foxtons revenue dips despite pent-up lockdown demand' – cityam.com – 29 October 2020.

20 'More than a third of UK bank branches have closed since 2015' – theguardian.com – 24 September 2019; 'Natwest to cut 550 jobs in branches and close one office' – bbc. com – 12 August 2020; 'TSB announces 164 more branch closures' – choose.co.uk – 2 October 2020; 'Lloyds to close 56 branches' – finextra.com – 18 November 2020; 'Full list of 52 Virgin Money, Yorkshire and Clydesdale bank branches closing in 2020' – mirror.co.uk – 27 February 2020.

21 'U.S. 2021 Retail Vacancy Rate May Rise To 7-Year High After Record Store Closings' – forbes.com – 13 January 2021.

22 'These 38 retailers and restaurant companies have filed for bankruptcy or liquidation in 2020' – businessinsider.com – 23 November 2020; 'G-Star Raw files for bankruptcy protection in US' – just-style.com – 6 July 2020.

23 'Dick's Sporting Goods Takes 29% Sales Hit' – cfo.com – 2 June 2020; 'Barnes & Noble Lays Off Some Employees at New York Head Office' – wsj.com – 24 June 2020; 'Barnes & Noble will shutter NYC bookstore, downsize headquarters' – retaildive. com – 26 June 2020; 'Nordstrom Reports Second Quarter 2020 Earnings' – press. nordstrom.com – 25 August 2020; 'Macy's posts $431 million loss as sales drop 36%' – apnews.com – 2 September 2020; 'American Eagle Outfitters Loses $257 Million During Coronavirus Shutdown' – wwd.com – 3 June 2020.

24 'Retail workforce could face permanent decline as companies take blow from pandemic, lockdowns' – cnbc.com – 22 July 2020.

25 'Ralph Lauren to lay off thousands as pandemic dulls luxury fashion' – reuters.com – 22 September 2020; 'LVMH Pulls Out of Tiffany Takeover' – wsj.com – 9 September 2020.

26 'The Greatest Wealth Transfer in the History of Retail' – ihlservices.com – 10 June 2020.

27 'List Of Retail Companies On Bankruptcy Watch Is Growing Fast Amid Coronavirus Crisis' – forbes.com – 3 April 2020; 'Moody's downgrades L Brands on failed Victoria's Secret sale' – spglobal.com – 8 May 2020.

28 'The Greatest Wealth Transfer in the History of Retail' – ihlservices.com – 10 June 2020.

29 'COVID crash: Companies that have filed for bankruptcy' – cbsnews.com – 15 December 2020; 'Starbucks lost half of its traffic last quarter' – restaurantbusinessonline. com – 28 July 2020.

30 '24 Hour Fitness files for bankruptcy and closes over 130 gym locations across the US' – businessinsider.com – 15 June 2020.

31 'The Running List Of Retail Store Closures And Bankruptcies In 2020' – styledemocracy.com – 17 November 2020.

Chapter 5: Rocking all over the world

1 'Iconic Dutch Retailer Hema Files for Chapter 15 Bankruptcy' – bloombergquint. com – 20 August 2020; 'Hudson's Bye: Canadian group's Dutch adventure ends in bankruptcy' – dutchnews.nl – 2 January 2020.

2 'Swedish fashion retailer MQ files for bankruptcy' – reuters.com – 16 April 2020; 'Holland & Barrett pulls plug on Swedish operation, closes all 21 stores' – naturalproductsglobal.com – 1 April 2020; 'H&M will close 250 stores next year to

focus on online sales as profits fall' – businessinsider.com – 1 October 2020; 'Virus resurgence hits H&M sales, cuts promising recovery' – m.economictimes.com – 15 December 2020; 'Ikea announces first big UK store closure' – bbc.com – 4 February 2020.

3   'German department store Galeria files for creditor protection' – reuters.com – 1 April 2020; 'German restaurant chain Vapiano files for insolvency' – reuters.com – 2 April 2020; 'Pandemic blamed as Poggenpohl files for bankruptcy' – kbbreview. com – 28 April 2020; 'Esprit to layoff 1200 employees, close 50 stores in Germany as part of restructuring' – fashionunited.uk – 1 July 2020; 'Coronavirus: 50,000 German retailers could go bust' – dw.com – 28 April 2020.

4   'Europe Confronts Reality That Many Companies Won't Survive Virus' – Bloomberg. com – 22 April 2020.

5   'Orchestra-Prémaman receives protection against creditors' – retaildetail.eu – 2 April 2020; 'Overwhelmed by the crisis, Camaïeu forced to file for bankruptcy' – world-today-news.com – 26 May 2020; 'André, Naf Naf, La Halle: quels repreneurs après les faillites?' – challenges.fr – 26 June 2020; 'Bankruptcy of Alinéa: the Mulliez family takes the opportunity to save their furniture' – world-today-news.com – 7 August 2020; 'Conforama obtains state guarantee for 300 million euros in loans' – web24.news – 9 July 2020.

6   'Galeries Lafayette's Champs Elysees store struggles as group faces $1 billion hit: CEO' – reuters.com – 8 June 2020.

7   'Rinascente Joins the Omnichannel Arena' – wwd.com – 10 June 2020; 'Geox announces first half results' – worldfootwear.com – 1 September 2020.

8   'World's largest fashion group, Inditex, reports first loss despite jump in online sales' – cnbc.com – 20 March 2020.

9   'El Corte Inglés pierde 510 millones entre marzo y mayo por la pandemia' – elpais. com – 18 September 2020; 'Fitch Places El Corte Ingles on Rating Watch Negative' – fitchratings.com – 26 March 2020.

10   'Covid-19 throws Europe's tourism industry into chaos' – theguardian.com – 1 July 2020.

11   'Japanese apparel retail sales fall 40% in 2020; monthly rebound can be seen post-pandemic' – apparelresources.com – 14 August 2020.

12   'Japan's big four department stores hit hard by virus from March to May' – phuketnews.easybranches.com – 18 July 2020.

13   'Hong Kong retail sales fall again in October' – insideretail.asia – 1 December 2020.

14   'Hong Kong Forecast To Lose 5,200 Shops; 10,400 Retail Jobs By June' – wwd.com – 16 April 2020; 'Jeweller Folli Follie becomes latest victim of coronavirus, protests, shuts all shops and lets go of 60 employees in Hong Kong' – scmp.com – 9 June 2020.

15   'MTI Forecasts GDP Growth of "-6.5 to -6.0 Per Cent" in 2020 and "+4.0 to +6.0 Per Cent" in 2021' – mti.gov.sg – 23 November 2020; 'Singapore Retail Sales YoY' – tradingeconomics.com – November 2020; 'Singapore's Robinsons department store to shut down after 162 years' – insideretail.asia – 30 October 2020; 'Topshop closing last physical store here after two decades' – straitstimes.com – 12 September 2020; 'Clothes retailer Esprit to close 56 stores in Asia outside China, including Singapore' – straitstimes.com – 28 April 2020; 'Home-grown sports retailer Sportslink goes out of business' – straitstimes.com – 8 July 2020; 'Retail business closures in Singapore hit 10-month high in September' – straitstimes.com – 1 November 2020; 'Singapore retail sales fall by sharper 10.8% in September' – straitstimes.com – 5 November 2020.

16   'South Korea Retail Sales YoY' – tradingeconomics.com – November 2020; 'South Korea Unemployment Rate' – tradingeconomics.com – November 2020;

'Golden goose is tarnished as Shinsegae's duty free business drags on group results' –moodiedavittreport.com – 13 May 2020; 'Lotte Duty Free and Shilla close Jeju downtown stores from June' - moodiedavittreport.com – 28 May 2020.

17 'Australia Retail Sales MoM' – tradingeconomics.com – November 2020; 'Australian Retailing: Who's Gone Bust or Retrenched? A Catch-up on Events End-2019 to 2020' retailresearch.org – 12 September 2020; 'David Jones boss admits it has "too many stores" as losses deepen' – smh.au – 17 September 2020; 'Fashion retailer Colette saved from collapse, but more than 100 stores to close' – smh.au – 9 September 2020; 'Target to close up to 75 stores across Australia, costing more than one thousand jobs' – theguardian.com – 22 May 2020; 'Mosaic Brands which owns Noni B, Katies, Millers and Rivers announces it WILL close 250 stores' – dailymail.co.uk – 28 October 2020.

18 'South Africa Retail Sales YoY' – tradingeconomics.com – January 2021; 'South Africa Unemployment Rate' - tradingeconomics.com – January 2021; 'South Africa GDP' – tradingeconomics.com – January 2021.

19 'Edcon files for bankruptcy protection' – news24.com – 29 April 2020; 'Woolworths faces possible further S&P downgrade' – businesslive.co.za – 26 September 2020; 'Woolworths Group profit plunges despite panic buying at supermarkets' – 9news. com.au – 27 August 2020; 'South Africa's Truworths sees annual profit drop 28% on lockdown impact' – reuters.com – 4 September 2020; 'Massmart loss widens to $65m due to Covid-19' – iol.co.za – 27 August 2020; 'Steinhoff's first-half loss more than doubles to $1.7 bln' – reuters.com – 30 July 2020.

20 'Coronavirus Update' – Worldometers.info – 12 January 2021; 'Brazil government keeps 2020 GDP forecast at a record 4.7% fall' – reuters.com – 15 September 2020.

21 'COVID-19 Seen Wiping Out 50 Percent of Brazil's Fashion Sales' – wwd.com – 27 April 2020; 'Brazil fashion retailer Restoque to restructure debt with financial creditors' – reuters.com – 5 June 2020.

22 'COVID-19 CORONAVIRUS PANDEMIC' – worldometers.info – 12 January 2021; 'Russia is the world's biggest loser from oil's crash, and that's reason to worry' – marketwatch.com – 26 April 2020.

23 'Russia Retail Sales YoY' – tradingeconomics.com – January 2020; 'Russia Unemployment' – tradingeconomics.com – January 2020; 'Losses in Russian non-food retail in 2020 may be 6.08 trillion rubles' – smenews.org – 12 October 2020; 'Russian small businesses reopen to uncertain future' – france24.com – 31 May 2020.

24 'COVID-19 CORONAVIRUS PANDEMIC' – worldometers.info – 12 January 2021.

25 'World Bank estimates India's GDP to plunge 9.6% in 2020-21' – cnbctv18.com – 6 January 2021; '"On ventilator mode": 20 per cent of traders may shut shop permanently, warns CAIT' – thehindubusinessline.com – 5 May 2020; 'Aditya Birla Fashion and Retail Q2 results: Net loss widens to Rs 188.25 cr' – retail.economictimes.indiatimes.com – 7 April 2020; 'Reliance Retail profit hit by coronavirus, EBITDA nearly halves to Rs 1,083 crore' – businesstoday.in – 12 September 2020; 'Reliance Buys Future Assets for $3.4 Billion; Bonds Jump' – Bloomberg.com – 29 August 2020; 'Future Retail Q1 results: Reports net loss of Rs 562 crore' – retail.economictimes.indiatimes.com – 15 September 2020; 'Avenue Supermarts Q2 results: Profit drops 38% to Rs 199 crore, margin contracts 240 bps to 6.2%' – retail.economictimes.indiatimes.com – 17 October 2020.

26 'China Retail Sales YoY' – tradingeconomics.com – January 2020.

27 'China Exports Sales' – tradingeconomics.com – January 2020; 'Beijing issues $1.7 bln in vouchers to boost virus-hit consumption' – cgtn.com – 7 June 2020.

28 'China's Structural Shift Towards Online Retail' – fitchratings.com – 21 June 2020; 'How Is JD's 618 Grand Promotion Faring?' – jingdaily.com – 11 June 2020.

29 'GCC e-commerce unleashed: a path to retail revival or a fleeting mirage?' – middleeast. kearney.com – 2020; 'Gulf mall operators rein in expansion as retailers reel from COVID-19' – reuters.com – 8 June 2020; '70% of Dubai companies expect to go out of business within six months due to coronavirus pandemic, survey says' – cnbc.com – 21 May 2020.

30 'Coronavirus: Alshaya Group revenues plummet 95% amid store closures' – arabianbusiness.com – 1 April 2020.

31 'Gulf mall operators rein in expansion as retailers reel from COVID-19' – reuters. com – 8 June 2020.

32 'RETAIL FUTURE: WHAT NEXT FOR DUBAI'S SHOPPING MALLS?' – ice.it – 13 May 2020.

33 'Dubai-headquartered The Toy Store owner ceases operations' – gulfbusiness. com – 11 January 2020; 'UAE group Gulf Marketing buys Royal Sporting House' – insideretail.asia – 17 December 2020.

34 'The global Travel retail market size is expected to reach $153.7 billion by 2025' – finance.yahoo.com – 14 November 2019; 'Duty Free and Travel Retail Industry – Statistics & Facts' – statista.com – 20 March 2020.

35 'Heathrow loses its status as Europe's busiest airport and suffers £1.5BILLION loss in 2020' – dailymail.co.uk; '"A ghost town": retail business in Australian airports in lockdown limbo' – theguardian.com – 6 June 2020.

Chapter 6: Where Has All the Business Gone? The Effect on Brands

1 'HanesBrands Reports First-Quarter 2020 Financial Results' – businesswire.com – 30 April 2020.

2 'Wolford revises outlook on coronavirus as Italian sales plunge' – fashionnetwork. com – 12 March 2020.

3 'VF Corp Posts 1st Quarterly Results Amid Coronavirus Pandemic' – board-sportssource.com – 18 May 2020.

4 'UNDER ARMOUR FIRST QUARTER 2020 RESULTS' – underarmour.com – 11 May 2020.

5 'PVH Corp. Reports 2020 First Quarter Results and Provides Business Update Relating to COVID-19 Pandemic' – businesswire.com – 11 June 2020.

6 'Mattel stock tanks after company reports lower Q1 sales; Uno, Pictionary sales rise' – marketwatch.com – 5 May 2020.

7 'Hasbro Reports First Quarter 2020 Financial Results' – businesswire.com – 29 April 2020.

8 'Revlon to Avoid Bankruptcy Filing Upon Completing Debt Deal' – bloomberg. com – 12 November 2020; 'Revlon Q3 2020 Results Show 20% Net Sales Decline' – gcimagazine.com – 13 November 2020; 'Revlon Inc' – google.com – 13 January 2021.

9 'Moody's downgrade Coty's CFR to Caa1; outlook negative' – moodys.com – 9 April 2020; 'Coty Sells Off Its Wella Beauty and Hair Care Brands for Over $4 Billion' – fool.com – 12 May 2020; 'Coty Inc. Reports Fiscal 2020 Fourth Quarter and Full Year Results' – finance.yahoo.com – 27 August 2020; 'Coty Inc. Reports Fiscal 2020 Fourth Quarter and Full Year Results' – coty.com – 27 August 2020.

10 'L'Oréal Q3 9 Month 2020 Results – Global Cosmetic Industry' – gcimagazine.com – 23 October 2020; '"Growing two times faster than the rest of the market" – Inside L'Oreal's e-commerce playbook' – digiday.com – 6 November 2020.

11 '2020 Annual Report' – elccompanies.com – June 2020; 'Estée Lauder will cut jobs and close stores as it embraces online sales' – bizjournals.com – 24 August 2020.

12   'UNILEVER TRADING STATEMENT THIRD QUARTER 2020' – unilever.com –
      22 October 2020.
13   'Kraft Heinz Co share price' – google.com – 13 January 2021; 'Kraft Heinz Is Still
      a Mess' – fool.com – 14 February 2020; 'Kraft Heinz Reports Third Quarter 2020
      Results' – ir.kraftheinzcompany.com – 29 October 2020.
14   'Coca-Cola Co share price' – google.com – 13 January 2021; 'Coca-Cola earnings
      fall 33%, but company sees improving demand as lockdowns ease' – cnbc.com –
      21 July 2020; 'Highlights of the severance package Coca-Cola is offering its 4,000
      employees' – bizjournals.com – 2 September 2020.
15   'Tyson Foods chairman warns "the food supply chain is breaking"' – nbcnews.
      com – 27 April 2020; 'Tyson Foods will use an algorithm to track Covid-19 cases' –
      thecounter.org – 17 November 2020.
16   'BAT warns of sales hit from lockdowns' – ft.com – 9 June 2020; 'Philip Morris
      International Inc. Reports 2020 First-Quarter Reported Diluted EPS of $1.17 Versus
      $0.87 in 2019' – Bloomberg.com – 21 April 2020; 'Philip Morris International Inc.
      Reports 2020 Second-Quarter Reported Diluted EPS of $1.25 Versus $1.49 in 2019,
      Reflecting Currency-Neutral Adjusted Diluted EPS Decline of 7.5%' – businesswire.
      com – 21 July 2020.
17   'Q3 2020 sales – Danone' – danone.com – 19 October 2020.
18   'AB InBev sees worse ahead, but some light in China' – reuters.com – 7 May 2020.
19   'Nike Inc share price' – google.com – 13 January 2020; 'Nike's digital sales spike
      36%' – digitalcommerce360.com – 26 March 2020; 'NIKE, INC. REPORTS FISCAL
      2021 SECOND QUARTER RESULTS' – investors.nike.com – 18 December 2020.
20   'Hanes Brands Inc Annual Report 2019' – ir.hanesbrands.com – December 2019.
21   'Canada Goose, Under Armour, Yeti and Groupon report 2018 online sales' –
      digitalcommerce360.com – 15 February 2019.
22   'Revlon 2019 Annual Report' – investors.revlon.com – 2019.
23   'PVH Annual Report 2019' – pvh.com – 2019; 'Mattel Annual Report' – investors.
      mattel.com – 2019; 'Hasbro Annual Report' – investor.hasbro.com – 2019; 'Coty Inc.
      Reports Fiscal 2020 Fourth Quarter and Full Year Results' – coty.com 27 August 2020.
24   'PepsiCo's online business grows to $1 billion' – digitalcommerce360.com – 14
      February 2018.
25   'Coca-Cola Annual Report 2019 – investors.coca-colacompany.com – 2019; 'Coca-
      Cola: We're going to embrace some seismic consumer behavior shifts, especially in
      e-commerce' – beveragedaily.com – 30 April 2020.
26   'Unilever grows ecommerce by 30%' – digitalcommerce360.com – 28 July 2020.
27   'E-commerce sales as a share of Nestlé's group sales worldwide 2012–2019' – statista.
      com – 30 November 2020.
28   'Mondelez International Inc Annual Report 2019' – mondelezinternational.com –
      2019; 'Annual Report 2019 Danone' – danone.com – 2019.
29   'ABInBev 2019 Annual Report' – ab-inbev.com – 27 February 2020; 'BAT Annual
      Report 2019' – bat.com – 2019; 'Philip Morris International Annual Report' – pmi.
      com – 2019.

Chapter 7: Mall Cried Out

1   'The Biggest Problem for Department Store Stocks' – fool.com – 30 September
     2019; 'US Department Store Sales' – ycharts.com – 2020; 'With Department Stores
     Disappearing, Malls Could Be Next' – nytimes.com – 5 July 2020; 'Dead Malls' –
     deadmalls.com – January 2021; 'A Haunting Look Inside America's Creepiest
     Abandoned Malls' – sephlawless.com – January 2021.

2   'Investors jump ship as American Dream collides with coronavirus' – bondbuyer.
     com – 11 June 2020; 'Can the American Dream mall survive the pandemic?' –
     therealdeal.com – 30 November 2020; 'American Dream owners defaulted' – cnbc.
     com – 30 March 2021.
3   'Horror on the Hudson: New York's $25bn architectural fiasco' – theguardian.com –
     9 April 2019; 'How Will Hudson Yards Survive the Pandemic?' – nytimes.com – 19
     June 2020.
4   'The next big problem for the economy: Businesses can't pay their rent' –
     washingtonpost.com – 4 June 2020; 'National Chains Paid 86% of September 2020
     Rent' – therealdeal.com – 8 October 2020; 'Nordstrom Notifies Landlords That It
     Will Pay Only Half of Its rent' – footwearnews.com – 6 July 2020; 'List of Retail
     Tenants Not Paying Rent' – therealdeal.com – 22 April 2020; 'Mall Landlord Simon
     Property Suing Retailer Gap Over Missed Rent' – wsj.com – 4 June 2020.
5   'The future of UK high streets' – abcfinance.co.uk – 22 May 2020; 'More than 200 UK
     shopping centres "in crisis"' – bbc.com – 1 November 2018.
6   'Spotlight: Shopping Centre and High Street – Q2 2020' – savills.com – 6 August 2020.
7   'Why the great malls of China are starting to crumble' – cbsnews.com – 28 June 2018;
     'Chinese "ghost mall" back from the dead?' – edition.cnn.com – 24 June 2015; 'Can
     "smart malls" save China's failing shopping centres from collapse?' – theguardian.
     com – 17 September 2015.

Chapter 8: Dislocation, Dislocation, Dislocation

1   'Sorry, we're closed. The decline of established American retailing threatens jobs' –
     economist.com – 13 May 2017.
2   'Dow Jones U.S. Retail REIT Index' – marketwatch.com – 13 January 2020.
3   'Mall operator CBL files for Chapter 11 bankruptcy protection' – reuters.com – 2
     November 2020.
4   'Mall owner PREIT files for Chapter 11 petition to implement restructuring plan' –
     reuters.com – 2 November 2020.
5   'Washington Prime Group: How High Can A Dead Cat Bounce?' – seekingalpha.
     com – 2 June 2020; 'S&P Downgrades Washington Prime to Junk Territory' – wsj.
     com – 25 February 2019.
6   'Simon Property Group to Acquire Taubman Centers, Inc.' – investors.simon.com –
     10 February 2020.
7   'Simon Property (SPG) Finally Concludes Taubman Centers Buyout' – finance.
     yahoo.com – 30 December 2020.
8   'CMBS Delinquencies Decline As Forbearance Increases: Trepp' – cpexecutive.
     com – 4 November 2020.
9   '"Higher Than We Ever Saw in the 2008 Crisis": Why the Coming COVID-19
     Mortgage Crisis May Be Worse Than the Last One' – vanityfair.com – 10 April 2020.
10   'Shopping centre owner Intu collapses into administration' – theguardian.com – 26
     June 2020.
11   'Hammerson plc share price' – google.com – 14 January 2021; 'Fitch Revises Outlook
     on Hammerson to Negative' – fitchratings.com – 15 May 2020; 'Hammerson Capital
     Reorganisation Done, Rights Issue' – Morningstar.co.uk – 2 September 2020.
12   'Unibail-Rodamco-Westfield CDI share price' – google.com – 14 January 2021;
     'Moody's cuts Unibail-Rodamco-Westfield ratings' – spglobal.com – 13 November
     2020; 'British Land Company PLC share price' – google.com – 14 January 2021;
     'British Land suffers £1bn hit from retail tumult' – ft.com – 27 May 2020.

13   'Park Hotels & Resorts Inc share price' – google.com – 14 January 2021; 'Pebblebrook
      Hotel Trust share price' – google.com – 14 January 2020; 'DiamondRock Hospitality
      Company share price' – google.com – 14 January 2020.
14   'Office REITs: Coronavirus Killed Corporate Culture' – seekingalpha.com – 21 May
      2020; 'Facebook Tells Employees To Work From Home Up Until 2021' – forbes.
      com – 7 August 2020; 'Twitter tells employees they can work from home "forever"' –
      cnbc.com – 12 May 2020.
15   'WeWork To Cut More Staff Through May' – therealdeal.com – 1 May 2020; 'Cash-
      strapped WeWork dumps about fifth of Hong Kong coworking space' – scmp.
      com – 5 June 2020; 'Rating Agency Thinks WeWork's Survival is "Questionable"' –
      commercialobserver.com – 9 June 2020; 'WeWork valuation has fallen from $47
      billion last year to $2.9 billion' – businessinsider.com – 18 May 2020; 'WeWork
      co-founder Adam Neumann is suing SoftBank over failed $3 billion stock deal' –
      theverge.com – 5 May 2020.
16   'Boston Properties Inc share price' – google.com – 14 January 2020; 'Vornado Realty
      Trust share price' – google.com – 14 January 2021; 'Equity Commonwealth share
      price' – google.com – 14 January 2021; 'Empire State Realty Trust Inc share price' –
      google.com – 14 January 2021; 'Empire State Realty Trust Announces the Departure
      of President and COO John B. Kessler' – businesswire.com – 16 June 2020; 'A third
      of Empire State Realty Trust tenants sought rent relief' – therealdeal.com – 23 April
      2020; 'U.S. construction value of new private office buildings 2000–2019' – statista.
      com – 19 November 2020.
17   'Commercial property investment – Investors' love affair with commercial property
      is being tested' – economist.com – 27 June 2020.

Chapter 9: To the Victor the Spoils – The Triumph of the Dot-coms

1   'Internet sales as a percentage of total retail sales' – ons.gov.uk – 18 December 2020.
2   'Retail sales, Great Britain: May 2020' – ons.gov.uk – May 2020; 'QUARTERLY RETAIL
     ECOMMERCE SALES' – census.gov; for adjusted sales see Chapter 1, Footnote 11.
3   'Amazon.com Announces Financial Results and CEO Transition' – ir.aboutamazon.
     com – 2 February 2021; 'Amazon to hire 100,000 more workers in its latest job spree
     this year' – cnbc.com – 14 September 2020; 'Amazon.com, Inc Mkt cap' – google.
     com – 14 January 2020.
4   'Alibaba's quarterly consolidated revenue Q3 2014-Q3 2020' – statista.com – 23
     November 2020; 'JD.com Announces 2020 Second Quarter and Interim results' –
     globalnewswire.com – 28 August 2020; 'JD.com Announces 2020 Third Quarter
     Results' – globalnewswire.com – 16 November 2020.
5   'Boohoo share price set to rise on raised revenue guidance' – cmcmarkets.com – 14
     January 2021; 'Boohoo swoops again to snap up Oasis and Warehouse brands' –
     bbc.co.uk – 17 June 2020; 'Boohoo acquires Karen Millen and Coast out of
     administration' – internetretailing.net – 6 August 2019.
6   'ASOS final year results cement strong 2020 with 329% climb in profits' – verdict.
     co.uk – 14 October 2020; 'Trading Statement for the four months to 31 December
     2020' – asosplc.com – 14 January 2021; 'Zalando Records Exceptionally Strong and
     Profitable Growth in Third Quarter' – corporate.zalando.com – 4 November 2020.
7   'Retail sales, Great Britain: December 2019' – ons.gov.uk – December 2019; 'Retail
     sales, Great Britain: May 2020' – ons.gov.uk – May 2020; 'UK online grocery growth
     clicks up as lockdown trends continue' – kantar.com – 23 June 2020.

8   'Ocado expected to impose rationing on more products' – theguardian.com – 19 March 2020.
9   'Ocado plans to raise £1bn as online deliveries boom in the UK' – theguardian.com – 10 June 2020.
10 'Amazon Fresh is now free for Prime members' – theverge.com – 29 October 2019.
11 'Huel Launches Ground-breaking New Products, As Sales Surge' – welltodoglobal.com – 14 September 2020; 'Chicago startup Equilibria grows as women flock to its CBD products' – bizjournals.com – 11 September 2020; 'BarkBox Has More Than a Million Subscribers. Now It's Going Public Via a SPAC' – barrons.com – 17 December 2020.
12 '6 Ways Peloton Will Get to 100 Million Subscribers' – fool.com – 17 September 2020; '1.1 million users, 97% satisfaction, and $607 million in revenue: How Peloton mastered user engagement to become the Apple of fitness' – businessinsider.com – 6 December 2020.
13 'Breakingviews – Deliveroo's IPO is a dish best served soon' – reuters.com – 7 October 2020; 'Just Eat Takeaway delivers big orders rise' – thetimes.co.uk – 14 January 2021; 'Grubhub sales beat estimates with more Covid takeaway diners' – businesstimes.com – 29 October 2020.

Chapter 10: Together Alone

1   'Twitter tells employees they can work from home "forever"' – cnbc.com – 12 May 2020; 'Mark Zuckerberg on taking his massive workforce remote' – thevirge.com.
2   'Canada's Shopify CEO says era of "office centricity is over"' – reuters.com – 21 May 2020.
3   'Here Are The Companies Leading The Work-From-Home revolution' – forbes.com – 24 May 2020.
4   'Groupe PSA presents its new principles of working methods' – businesswire.com – 6 May 2020.
5   'Reviewing Remote Work in the U.S. Under COVID-19' – news.gallup.com – 22 May 2020.
6   'Zuckerberg: 50% of Facebook employees could be working remotely' – cnbc.com – 21 May 2020; 'Work-at-Home After Covid-19—Our Forecast' – global-workplaceanalytics.com – 24 May 2020.
7   'Manhattan new rentals plunge 71% as coronavirus freezes the market' – cnbc.com – 15 May 2020; 'Why high earners in finance and tech left New York City' – cnbc.com – 31 October 2020.
8   'Rents see biggest drop on record as seven in 10 tenants opt to renew rather than move while the coronavirus lockdown continues' – thisismoney.co.uk – 30 April 2020.
9   'Capital & Counties Properties PLC share price' – google.com – 14 January 2021; 'Land Securities Group plc share price' – google.com – 14 January 2021; 'Fitch Downgrades Land Securities Capital Markets Plc' – fitchratings.com – 6 April 2020.
10 'Daily Economic Impact of Coronavirus On Real Estate Sectors' – irwinmitchell.com – 11 May 2020; 'Ghost Town London's £5.7BILLION black hole: Taxpayers face huge bill as lost fares leave TfL £3.5bn short – and the capital's economy bleeds £575m a DAY putting GLA and councils £2bn in the red' – dailymail.com – 19 August 2020.
11 '"We're at War": New York City Faces a Financial Abyss' – nytimes.com – 29 September 2020; 'Violence Surged in N.Y.C. in 2020' – nytimes.com – 29 December 2020.

Chapter 11: Generation 'C'

1 'How COVID-19 Will Shape the Class of 2020 For the Rest of Their Lives' – time. com – 21 May 2020.
2 'Spring 2020 Harvard Youth Poll' – iop.harvard.edu – 23 April 2020.
3 'Transcript of October 2020 World Economic Outlook Press Briefing' – imf.org – 14 October 2020.
4 'UK schools to be closed indefinitely and exams cancelled' – theguardian.com – 18 March 2020.
5 '29 states announce school closures amid coronavirus' – cnn.com – 15 March 2020.
6 'How COVID-19 Will Shape the Class of 2020 For the Rest of Their Lives' – time. com – 21 May 2020.
7 'How COVID-19 Will Shape the Class of 2020 For the Rest of Their Lives' – time. com – 21 May 2020.
8 'Young and minorities hardest hit after UK job support schemes end' – ft.com – 28 October 2020.
9 '"Recruitment is on hold": the students graduating into the Covid-19 recession' – theguardian.com – 10 April 2020.
10 'Coronavirus: "My graduate jobs were suddenly all taken away"' – bbc.com – 2 May 2020.
11 'Coronavirus: Graduates struggling for job leads amid COVID-19 lockdown emergency' – euronews.com – 29 April 2020.
12 'These industries suffered the biggest job losses in April 2020' – cnbc.com – 8 May 2020.

Chapter 12: Fish Swimming in the Venice Canals

1 'Carbon emissions are falling sharply due to coronavirus' – nationalgeographic. com – 3 April 2020.
2 '"Nature is taking back Venice": wildlife returns to tourist-free city' – theguardian. com – 20 March 2020; 'As coronavirus restrictions empty streets around the world, wildlife roam further into cities' – cnbc.com – 10 April 2020; 'Climate crisis: in coronavirus lockdown, nature bounces back – but for how long?' – theguardian. com – 9 April 2020; 'Air pollution impacts fall as a result of Corona-related measures' – airclim.org – 2 May 2020.
3 'Climate crisis: in coronavirus lockdown, nature bounces back – but for how long?' – theguardian.com – 9 April 2020.
4 'Coronavirus: Why the fashion industry faces an "existential crisis"' – bbc.com – 29 April 2020.
5 'ONLINE RESALE APPEARS TO BE PANDEMIC-PROOF' – fashionista.com – 23 June 2020; 'ThredUp chases sizzling demand for used clothing in $1.3 billion IPO' – forbes.com – 26 March 2021; 'Resale growth during Covid-19: sellers engage in "quarantine clean out frenzies"' – fashionunited.uk – 8 June 2020; 'StockX Sees Accelerated Growth Amid Pandemic' – sgbonline.com – 16 July 2020.
6 'Professor Thomai Serdari discusses how the COVID-19 pandemic has upended the luxury retail space' – stern.nyu.edu – 1 July 2020.
7 'We've hit peak home furnishings, says Ikea boss' – theguardian.com – 18 January 2016.

Chapter 13: Summary – A 'Reset' Moment for Retail

Chapter 14: Embracing the Omniverse

Chapter 15: Push Me, Pull You

Chapter 16: Beyond the Transaction

1   'Buy a Pair, Give a Pair' – warbyparker.com – January 2021; 'Our Sustainability' – allbirds.com – January 2021; 'MAKING A DIFFERENCE' – sfbaycoffee.com – January 2021.

Chapter 17: 'Servicizing' a Goods Business

1   'CVS Health shows off new HealthHUB store design' – cnbc.com – 13 February 2019.
2   'CVS Wants to Make Your Drugstore Your Doctor' – fortune.com – 17 May 2019.
3   'CVS Health to expand HealthHub format nationwide' – drugstorenews.com – 4 June 2019.
4   'CVS is opening 1,500 HealthHUBs. What's their endgame?' – advisory.com – 19 July 2019; 'CVS Health Reports Third Quarter Results With Diversified Assets Delivering Strong Enterprise Performance' – prnewswire.com – 6 November 2020.
5   'Fnac Darty propose un nouveau Contrat de confiance' – ecommercemag.fr – 15 October 2019; 'Fnac Darty: Strong revenue growth of +7.3% in the third quarter of 2020' – globenewswire.com – 21 October 2020.

Chapter 18: Feelings

1   'Nordstrom customer service tales not just legend' – bizjournals.com – 7 September 2012.
2   'Building a Customer Service Culture: The Case of Nordstrom' – courses.lumenlearning.com – 14 January 2021.
3   'Nordstrom Armani Tuxedo: The Most Influential Storytelling' – couture.agency – January 2021.
4   'Trust Your Employees, Not Your Rule Book' – hbr.org – 20 April 2017.
5   'Nordstrom Reports Fourth Quarter and Fiscal 2019 Earnings' – investor.nordstrom.com – March 2020; 'J. C. Penney Company, Inc. Reports Fourth Quarter and Full Year' – ir.jcpenney.com – 27 February 2020; 'Neiman Marcus Group LTD LLC Reports Third Quarter Results' – businesswire.com – 11 June 2019. 'Nordstrom Reports Third Quarter 2020 Earnings' – press.nordstrom.com – 24 November 2020.
6   'Bonobos is opening retail stores – but you can't actually take any of the clothes home' – businessinsider.com – 16 July 2015.
7   'Let's get to know each other offline' – modaoperandi.com – January 2021; 'Lauren Santo Domingo's Incredible New Showroom Is Reinventing Retail' – architecturaldigest.com – 2 November 2016.
8   '5 Ways Fashion Retailer Everlane Earned Insane Word-of-Mouth' – referralcandy.com.

9   'How to Use A Kickstarter Campaign to Launch Your Brand' – business2community. com – 18 April 2018.

10 '3 Super-Engaging UGC Campaigns (and How to Do It Yourself)' – squareup.com – 16 April 2018.

11 'American Eagle Outfitters Reports Third Quarter Results' – businesswire.com – 24 November 2020; 'Analyst: American Eagle's Aerie Could Be a $3 Billion Business' – fool.com – 12 August 2020; 'Victoria's Secret rebound lifts L Brands as Q3 profits soar' – retaildive.com – 19 November 2020; 'Sycamore tries to back away from Victoria's Secret deal' – ft.com – 22 April 2020.

12 'Lululemon's New Experimental Store Hints at the Future of Retailing' – fool.com – 23 July 2019; 'Lululemon Unveils "Power of Three" Strategic Plan to Accelerate Growth' – businesswire.com – 24 April 2019; 'Lululemon unveils extensive line-up of SeaWheeze 2020 events and apparel' – dailyhive.com – 7 August 2020; 'Lululemon earnings, sales top estimates on strong demand for workout gear' – cnbc.com – 10 December 2020.

13 'Rapha on riding the trend for community retail' – retailconnections.co.uk – 18 February 2020.

14 'GYMSHARK'S BIGGEST EVENT EVER | THE BIRMINGHAM POP UP' – youtube.com – 21 June 2018; 'How Gymshark Became A $1.3 Billion Brand, And What We Can Learn' – forbes.com – 17 August 2020.

Chapter 19: 'Congratulations on your happy news!'

1   'How Target Figured Out A Teen Girl Was Pregnant Before Her Father Did' – forbes. com – 16 February 2012.

2   'boltdigital.media'; 'propeller.co.uk'; 'frac.tl'; 'markitors.com'; 'webfx.com'; 'ignitevisibility.com'.

3   'Traditional media suffer as digital ad spend grows in 2020' – searchengineland. com – 2 September 2020; 'Performance branding and how it is reinventing marketing ROI' – mckinsey.com – 15 June 2020.

4   'On Target: Rethinking The Retail Website' – forbes.com – 4 December 2018; 'Demand for data scientists is booming and will only increase' – searchbusinessanalytics. techtarget.com – 31 January 2019.

Chapter 20: Purpose-built

1   'Buy a Pair, Give a Pair' – warbyparker.com – January 2021; 'Our Sustainability' – allbirds.com – January 2021; 'MAKING A DIFFERENCE' – sfbaycoffee.com – January 2021.

2   '5 "Ridiculous" Ways Patagonia Has Built a Culture That Does Well and Does Good' – business.linkedin.com – 27 December 2019; 'Patagonia's Unapologetically Political Strategy and the Massive Business It Has Built' – inc.com – 30 November 2018.

3   'The Body Shop's campaign offers reality, not miracles' – nytimes.com – 26 August 1997.

4   'EU Set to Ban Animal Testing for Cosmetics Forever' – prnewswire.com – 30 January 2013.

5   'L'Oréal Is Paying $1.1 Billion for Body Shop' – nytimes.com – 18 March 2006; ' The Body Shop founder says being good is good for business' – bizjournals.com – 10 March 2003.

6 'Unilever Sustainable Living Plan' – theguardian.com – 5 October 2011; 'Unilever's purpose-led brands outperform' – unilever.com – 11 June 2019; 'Unilever first half H1 financial results see net earnings rise 10%' – cosmeticsdesign-europe.com – 23 July 2020; 'unilever plc share price' – google.com – January 2021.
7 'Former Best Buy CEO Hubert Joly defied expectations at Best Buy' – cnbc.com – 19 June 2019; 'Best Buy Assured Living Lets Aging Parents Stay at Home' – corporate. bestbuy.com – 4 October 2017.

Chapter 21: Hot Data

1 'TOYS "R" US, INC 10-K' – sec.gov – 2016.
2 Ibid; 'Nike to add perks to super-successful customer loyalty program' – nypost. com – 3 April 2019.
3 Ibid.
4 '31,000 Toys "R" Us employees: No job and no severance' – money.cnn.com – 16 March 2018.
5 'M&S Sparks Relaunching as digital first loyalty scheme' – corporate. marksandspencer.com – 2 July 2020.
6 'Marks & Spencer relaunches Sparks loyalty programme' – retail-week.com – 2 July 2020.
7 'Macy's Launches Next Phase Of Loyalty Program' – macys.com – 10 February 2020; 'Nordstrom expands rewards to non-card holders' – retailwire.com – 23 May 2016; 'J. Crew bets on brand loyalty with new membership program' – retaildive.com – 6 August 2018.
8 'Walmart to revamp 1K stores with digital in mind' – retaildive.com – 1 October 2020.
9 'Urban Outfitters bolsters foot traffic, marketing opportunities via in-store phone chargers' – retaildive.com.
10 'Shopify launches all-new POS globally to help merchants adapt for the future of retail' – news.shopify.com – 4 May 2020.

Chapter 22: Digital Converter – Making Online the Backbone of the Business

1 'The Zara retail empire is spending $3 billion on its post-pandemic future' – edition. cnn.com – 10 June 2020.
2 'H&M unveils digitalisation plans after fall in sales during pandemic' – essentialretail. com – 26 June 2020; 'H&M to close 250 stores next year' – retaildive.com – 1 October 2020.
3 'H&M unveils digitalisation plans after fall in sales during pandemic' – essentialretail. com – 26 June 2020.
4 'Gap shares up 11% store closure plans, shifts focus to e-commerce and off-mall retail' – cnbc.com – 22 October 2020.
5 'A Smaller Nordstrom Footprint' – therobinreport.com – 2 December 2020; 'The pandemic has forced Nordstrom to invest more in its off-price e-commerce business' – modernretail.co – 1 June 2020.
6 'Covid-19: JD Sports to focus on eCommerce following pandemic' – essentialretail. com – 7 July 2020.

7   'Next Annual Report' – nextplc.co.uk – January 2020; 'Next upgrades profit forecasts as third quarter sales come in better than expected' – proactiveinvestors.co.uk – 28 October 2020.

8   'Bed Bath & Beyond (BBBY) reports fiscal Q2 2020 earnings beat' – cnbc.com – 1 October 2020; 'Bed Bath & Beyond targets "stable" sales growth in 2021, low-to-mid single-digit gains by 2023' – cnbc.com – 28 October 2020.

9   'Kingfisher profit jumps as online sales rise during lockdown' – cityam.com – 22 September 2020; 'Kingfisher ecommerce sales soar as Garnier praises "resilient" results' – retail-week.com – 22 September 2020.

10 'Lockdown prompts Dixons Carphone's online sales to surge 124%' – retailgazette. co.uk – 10 September 2020.

11 'Ralph Lauren to Cut Jobs Amid Accelerated E-Commerce Push' – businessoffashion. com – 22 September 2020.

12 'Armani and Yoox Net-a-Porter launch new tie-up' – drapersonline.com – 22 July 2020.

13 'HUGO BOSS takes its online business to the next level' – group.hugoboss.com – 1 July 2020.

14 'Marketplace Is Driving Walmart's Online Progress' – marketplacepulse.com – 14 November 2019; 'Confirmed: Walmart buys Jet.com for $3B in cash to fight Amazon' – techcrunch.com – 8 August 2016.

15 'Walmart earnings top expectations as customers' new shopping habits send e-commerce sales soaring 79%' – cnbc.com – 17 November 2020; 'Walmart is hiring 20,000 seasonal workers' – marketwatch.com – 29 September 2020; 'Walmart looking at up to $25 billion investment in Tata' – ca.mobile.reuters.com – 28 September 2020.

16 'Tesco to create 16,000 more permanent jobs in online boom' – reuters.com – 24 August 2020; '3Q and Christmas Trading Statement 2020/21' – tescoplc.com – 14 January 2021.

17 'Third Quarter Trading Statement for the 15 weeks to 2 January 2021' about. sainsburys.co.uk – 7 January 2021; 'The online shopping shift is a habit that will be hard to give up post-COVID-19 – the last word from Sainsbury's outgoing digital champion CEO Mike Coupe' – diginomica.com – 4 May 2020.

18 'M&S agrees £750m food delivery deal with Ocado' – theguardian.com – 27 February 2019; 'Ocado shows the M&S effect on its business – with fourth-quarter sales up by 35%' – internetretailing.net – 10 December 2020.

19 'Ocado's market value closes in on Tesco's as online grocer hails M&S switch' – theguardian.com – 15 September 2020; 'M&S to "turbo-charge" ecommerce with third-party brands' – drapersonline.com – 21 May 2020.

20 'Lidl owner acquires marketplace to bolster online presence' – internetretailing.net – 23 June 2020.

21 'Covid-19: Aldi UK starts selling groceries online' – essentialretail.com – 17 April 2020; 'Aldi trials click & collect in UK for first time' – essentialretail.com – 14 September 2020.

22 'Aldi and Lidl to continue push into online delivery' – chargedretail.co.uk – 19 June 2020.

23 '85,000 online businesses launched during lockdown' – uktechnews – 3 July 2020; 'Five ways coronavirus will change British retail' – ft.com – 1 May 2020; 'Ecommerce is the future: helping independent retailers' – brevity.marketing – 2 October 2020.

24 'Ecommerce is the future: helping independent retailers' – brevity.marketing – 2 October 2020.

25 'How Local Stores Are Moving to Selling Online' – uschamber.com – 23 April 2020.

26 'Simon launches an online marketplace for its brands' – digitalcommerce360.com – 8 April 2019.

Chapter 23: Back from the Dead

1   'Forever 21 Returns To The U.K. Market Online' – forbes.com – 17 July 2020; 'British Home Stores' – en.wikipedia.org – January 2021; 'American Apparel returns – with a focus on empowerment' – theguardian.com – 20 April 2018.

2   'Thomas Cook relaunches as online travel agent' – theguardian.com – 16 September 2020; 'Toys "R" Us relaunches its website' – techcrunch.com – 9 October 2019.

3   'Maplin's head of IT on relaunching the business as online-only' – essentialretail.com – 15 May 2019.

4   'What Is the Direct-to-Consumer Sales Model and Why Should You Care?' – racked.com – 11 August 2016.

5   'Mothercare shares jump as FY'20 adjusted loss narrows' – spglobal.com – 25 September 2020; 'City snapshot: Mothercare to relaunch in the UK with Boots' – thegrocer.co.uk – 20 August 2020.

6   'These E-Comm Investors Are Bringing Back Dressbarn & Pier 1 — Now They're Poised to Buy IP Assets of Bankrupt Modell's' – finance.yahoo.com – 10 August 2020.

7   'Boohoo swoops again to snap up Oasis and Warehouse brands' – bbc.com – 17 June 2020; 'New Raydiant Report Shows How Brick and Mortar Retailers are preparing to re-open' – prnewswire.com – 18 June 2020.

8   'From Barneys To Topshop, Authentic Brands Looks To Build Retail Empire' – forbes.com – 15 December 2020; 'JD Sports "links with" Authentic Brands on Topshop bid' – fashionnetwork.com – 12 January 2021; 'Authentic Brands Group' – authenticbrandsgroup.com – January 2021.

9   'Online business of TM Lewin acquired but shops closing' – insidermedia.com – 1 July 2020; 'James Cox – Founding Partner Stonebridge' – uk.linkedin.com – January 2020.

Chapter 24: Have You Seen the Middleman?

1   'D2C Direct To Consumer Brands Directory' – channelape.com – January 2021.

2   'The Warby Parker Marketing Strategy Decoded' – tapjoy.com – 19 September 2019.

3   'Dollar Shave Club Sells to Unilever for $1 Billion' – nytimes.com – 20 July 2016; 'How Dollar Shave Club Rode a Viral Video to Sales Success' – inc.com – January 2021.

4   'Next wave: digital-first challenger brands are nailing customer data and experience and most are going in-house' – mi-3.com.au – 17 May 2019.

5   'Warby Parker now valued at $3 billion' – axios.com – 27 August 2020.

6   'Dollar Shave Club Debuts New Look with New Omnichannel Model' – wwd.com – 18 September 2020; 'What happens when a business built on simplicity gets complicated? Dollar Shave Club's founder Michael Dubin found out' – cnbc.com – 24 March 2019.

7   'Huel Launches Groundbreaking New Products, As Sales Surge' – welltodoglobal.com – 14 September 2020; 'Startup Huel has focused on talent recruitment' – businessinsider.com – 8 January 2020.

8   'Glossier: How this 33-year-old turned her beauty blog to a $1 billion brand' – cnbc.com – 20 March 2019; 'Glossier on the IPO Path' – wwd.com – 1 March 2018.

9   'ThirdLove, the direct-to-consumer lingerie startup, gets a $55M boost' – techcrunch.com – 26 February 2019; 'Next Billion-Dollar Startup: Entrepreneurs Create $750M Bra Business By Exposing Victoria's Weakness' – forbes.com – 18 October 2018.

10 'Boohoo Group plc: Interim Results' – investigate.co.uk – 30 September 2020.
11 'Nike's Consumer Direct Offense Is Paying Off' – fool.com – 22 December 2019.
12 'Procter & Gamble is looking to add more direct-to-consumer brands' – digiday. com – 1 May 2019.
13 'P&G paying $100 million for deodorant startup' – axios.com – 15 November 2017; 'P&G acquires competitor Snowberry New Zealand' – bizjournals.com – 6 February 2018; 'P&G Acquires First Aid Beauty' – wwd.com – 17 July 2018.
14 'Procter & Gamble has acquired the startup aiming to build the Procter & Gamble for people of color' – vox.com – 12 December 2018; 'P&G Acquires This is L. for $100M' – bizjournals.com – 7 February 2019.
15 'M13 and P&G to Partner on Consumer Innovation Incubator' – prnewswire. com – 21 February 2019; 'P&G launches Kindra brand for women coping with menopause' – bizjournals.com – 15 November 2019.
16 'Procter & Gamble is looking to add more direct-to-consumer brands' – digiday. com – 1 May 2019.
17 'Exclusive: Unilever Invests In Meal-Kit Startup Sun Basket' – fortune.com – 11 May 2017; 'Unilever acquires Graze' – unilever.com – 5 February 2019; 'Unilever's Ice Cream Shift Shows Anything Can Be Sold Online' – bloombergquint.com – 23 July 2020; 'Unilever rides DTC wave from razors to mustard' – warc.com – 26 April 2019.
18 'Unilever plots to cut out the supermarkets and target online' – thisismoney.co.uk – 19 July 2018.
19 'L'Oréal boosts digital's share of marketing spend from 50% to 70%' – campaignlive. co.uk – 16 June 2020; '"Growing two times faster than the rest of the market": Inside L'Oréal's e-commerce playbook' – digiday.com – 6 November 2020; 'L'Oréal launches direct to consumer hair dye brand Color&Co' – thedrum.com – 9 May 2019.
20 'Kraft Heinz to acquire Primal Kitchen for $200m' – foodnavigator-usa.com – 11 December 2018; 'Heinz Launches Direct-to-Consumer "Bundle" Delivery Service' – stylus.com – 23 April 2020.
21 'PepsiCo to buy SodaStream for $3.2 billion' – cnbc.com – 20 August 2018; 'PepsiCo Launches New Direct-to-Consumer Efforts' – foodprocessing.com – 11 May 2020.
22 'Nestlé Waters North America Expands ReadyRefresh' – prnewswire.com – 10 January 2020; 'Nespresso website' – buynespresso.com – January 2020.

Chapter 25: Going Private

1 'Regional value share for private label grows to highest levels at 39.4%' – iriworldwide. com – 2018; 'Private Label Brands Roar At Retail' – forbes.com – 2 May 2019.
2 'Store-brand sales surge in Q1 from COVID-19 stock-up' – supermarketnews.com – 27 April 2020.
3 'Why Target is one of Fast Company's Most Innovative Companies' – fastcompany. com – 19 February 2019.
4 'Costco's Kirkland brand drives growth' – businessinsider.com – 22 March 2019.
5 'How Kohl's figured out the Amazon era' – edition.cnn.com – 30 October 2018.
6 'Bed Bath Surges as New CEO Could Crib From Target's Playbook' – bloomberg. com – 10 October 2019.
7 'In-depth: Seasoned industry vets build BB&B's private label approach' – storebrands. com – 10 November 2020; 'Bed Bath & Beyond Inc. share price' – google.com – 17 January 2021.

8   'How Best Buy is winning against all odds' – retaildive.com – 13 December 2017.

9   'Walmart and the Power of Private Labels' – scrapehero.com – 12 June 2019; 'Walmart's Great Value brand earns more than $27 billion' – storebrands.com – 18 February 2020.

10 '"They're all scared half to death": Retailers accelerate private-label push' – digiday. com – 18 March 2019; 'Walmart's Sub-$100 Tablets Are About The Future Of Retail' – forbes.com – 22 May 2019.

11 'The Simple Truth: Private Selection, other Kroger brands drive sales' – cinncinnati.com – 26 July 2017; 'Kroger unveils Simple Truth plant-based food line' – supermarketnews. com – 5 September 2019; 'Kroger Co share price' – google.com – January 2021.

12 'Whole Foods is updating its 365 private label branding' – grocerydive.com – 16 January 2020; 'Trader Joe's Strategy: 12 Keys to its Success' – indigo9digital.com – 2 July 2020; 'Why Southeastern People Love Shopping at Publix So Much' – envzone. com – 29 July 2020; 'What grocery retailers can learn from the Wegmans store model' – grocerydive.com – 10 February 2017; 'How Walgreens Is Innovating Through Private Label' – cspdailynews.com – 20 May 2019; 'As Power Of Name Brands Wanes, CVS Is Betting On Private Label' – forbes.com – 12 October 2017; 'Rite Aid includes private label growth in "Store of the Future" push' – storebrands. com – 18 March 2020.

13 'Macy's Inc Form 10K' – macysinc.com – 2018; 'Macy's Inc share price' – google. com – January 2021.

14 'How it all went wrong at JCPenney' – edition.cnn.com – 27 September 2018.

15 'Dick's Sporting Goods launching new private-label brand' – chainstoreage.com – 1 August 2019.

16 'Dick's Sporting Goods launches new private label collection' – fashionunited.uk – 2 August 2019.

17 'Dick's Sporting Goods is strengthening its private-label' – digiday.com – 13 March 2019; 'Dick's Sporting Goods 2019 Annual Report'.

18 'Can Dick's big private label push save it from Amazon' – econsultancy.com – 15 March 2019.

19 'Dick's SG Sees Opportunities To Build On Momentum Amid Pandemic' – sgbonline. com – 9 September 2020.

20 'Quintessentially British Brands: Not Just Branding, Marks And Spencer Branding' – fabrikbrands.com; 'New John Lewis strategy sees massive focus on own-brand fashion' – uk.fashionnetwork.com – 27 June 2018.

21 'Amazon triples its private-label product offerings in 2 years' – digitalecommerce360. com – 20 May 2020.

22 'With Taobao Xinxuan, Alibaba enters into private-label goods' – techinasia.com – 5 July 2018.

23 'Online retailer JD.com follows Amazon's footsteps with own label' – scmp.com – 16 January 2018.

24 'How Yanxuan became popular in China' – businessinsider.com – 18 October 2017; 'Flipkart aims to expand into new categories via SmartBuy' – livemint.com – 8 August 2018.

25 'Yoox launches its own fashion label "8 by Yoox"' – cpp-luxury.com – 6 November 2018; 'Moda Operandi Launches The Platform' – businessoffashion.com – 30 October 2017.

26 'Moda Operandi Launches The Platform' – businessoffashion.com – 30 October 2017.

Chapter 26: The Endless Aisle

1   'Amazon Marketplace a Winner for Customers, Sellers' – press.aboutamazon.com – 19 March 2001.
2   '10 Fascinating Amazon Statistics Sellers Need To Know in 2020' – bigcommerce. com – January 2021; 'List of Top 65 Marketplaces Across the Globe' – vinculumgroup. com – January 2021.
3   'Analysis: Why 44% of retailers are launching marketplaces' – retail-week.com – 16 April 2018.
4   'Walmart.com Adds Nearly One Million New Items' – corporate.walmart.com – 31 August 2009; 'Marketplace Is Driving Walmart's Online Progress' – marketplacepulse. com – 14 November 2019.
5   'H&M tests selling external brands' – ecommercenews.eu – 20 September 2019.
6   'Myer unveils online marketplace in last-ditch effort to fend off Amazon' – smartcompany.com.au – 2 November 2017; 'M&S to "turbo-charge" ecommerce with third-party brands' – drapersonline.com – 20 May 2020; 'Business model – Next Plc' – nextplc.co.uk – January 2021; 'Best Buy Canada Evolved Its Business Model and Became a Marketplace Leader' – blog.miraki.com – 19 November 2019; 'Sell on OfficeDepot. com' – acenda.com – January 2021; 'Kroger launches a web marketplace to compete with Amazon' – digitalcommerce360.com – 11 August 2020; 'French supermarket chain Auchan to launch new online marketplace' – ecommercenews.eu – 24 September 2015; 'Marketplace Darty : encore plus de choix!' – darty.com – 28 February 2020.
7   emcosmetics.com; hudabeauty.com; kyliecosmetics.com.
8   'How the pandemic is accelerating e-commerce's shift to the marketplace model' – glossy.co – 31 July 2020.
9   Ibid.
10 Ibid.
11 Marketplacer.com; Code-Brew.com; Arcadia.com; Wordpress.org; Mirakl.com; Luminoslabs.com; 'How the pandemic is accelerating e-commerce's shift to the marketplace model' – glossy.co – 31 July 2020.
12 'How the pandemic is accelerating e-commerce's shift to the marketplace model' – glossy.co – 31 July 2020.

Chapter 27: Whither the Store?

1   'Amazon opens its first full-size cashierless grocery store' – cnbc.com – 25 February 2020; 'Inside Hema, Alibaba's new kind of superstore' – cnbc.com – 30 August 2018; 'Tencent opens first cashierless pop-up store' – europe.chinadaily.com – 2 February 2018; 'First Warby Parker Brought Glasses to Your Laptop. Now It's Opening Stores' – inc.com; 'Bonobos And Dollar Shave Club: Online-Only Brands Get Physical' – forbes.com – 27 July 2018; 'Everlane to open first physical stores' – retaildive.com – 29 February 2017.

Chapter 28: Showrooming

1   'Showrooming' – wikipedia.com
2   'Something Special About Sonos' New Experiential Store' – futurestores.wbresearch. com.

3   'How Zero-Inventory Stores Like Bonobos Supercharge Customers And Make Retailers More Productive' – forbes.com – 29 September 2019.

4   'Why retailers are trying on showrooms' – retaildive.com – 20 April 2017.

5   'Canadian Optical Brand "Clearly" Relaunches Brick-and-Mortar Store' – retail-insider.com – 22 December 2020.

6   'Retail Focus: Made.com moves into physical retail' – designcurial.com – 6 April 2020.

7   'Glossier's London Pop-Up Will Stay For The Rest Of The Year' – forbes.com – 31 January 2020.

8   '"A big touchpoint for acquisition": Brands are opening service-based stores to attract new customers' – glossy.com – 5 September 2019.

9   'Well.ca opens virtual store in Toronto' – marketingmag.ca – 2 April 2012.

10   'Amazon to double down on expansion of Amazon 4-star stores' – chainstoreage.com – 31 January 2020.

11   'AliExpress Paris pop-up store' – altavia-shoppermind.com – 13 October 2020; '35 Statistics about AliExpress Market Share and Global Reach' – techjury.net – 25 July 2020.

12   'Inside Hema, Alibaba's new kind of superstore' – cnbc.com – 30 April 2018; 'Alibaba rolling out 2000 Hema supermarkets' – insideretail.asia – 8 December 2017.

13   'The Nike Live Secret to Retail Success: The Human Touch' – rga.com – 4 November 2019; 'Nike plans up to 200 small-format stores' – retaildive.com – 26 June 2020; 'Nike's First Concept Store Ever: Nike by Melrose' – youtube.com.

14   'Store Concept of the Year: Nordstrom Local' – retaildive.com – 9 December 2019; 'Nordstrom to open boutique-y Nordstrom Local Shops' – youtube.com.

15   'Ikea is opening a small-format store in New York' – cnbc.com – 10 April 2019; 'You can't take anything home from Ikea's new store' – fastcompany.com – 10 April 2019; 'Ikea opens first Manhattan store. Take a look inside' – youtube.com.

16   'Macy's plans rollout of smaller stores away from malls' – cnbc.com – 2 September 2020; 'Macy's Concept Store Opens In Southlake' – youtube.com.

17   'Apple is expanding its new "Express" stores for the iPhone 12 launch and holiday shopping — see what's it's like to shop at one' – businessinsider.com – 24 October 2020.

18   'Kohl's pilot program shrinks stores by leasing space to Aldi' – marketwatch.com – 4 March 2018; 'Kohl's shrinks stores, leases space to Planet Fitness gyms' – edition.cnn.com – 5 March 2019.

19   'Dixons Carphone rapidly switches on omni-channel as online sales surge 114%' – internetretailing.net – 16 December 2020; 'Dixons Carphone PLC: Interim Results 2020/21' – investigate.co.uk – 16 December 2020.

Chapter 29: Spectacle Frame

1   '9 Case Studies That Prove Experiential Retail Is The Future' – thestorefront.com.

2   'Museum of ice cream' – museumoficecream.com; 'Museum of ice cream' – Wikipedia.org.

3   'Rose Mansion Home' – rosemansion.com; 'I Went to The Rosé Mansion. Here's What It Looks Like Inside' – foodandwine.com – 11 July 2018.

4   'Confectionery Wonderland Candytopia Celebrates the Success of Newest Location with 500,000th "Sugar Rush" Photo' – prweb.com – 28 April 2019; 'Inside the candy theme park Gwyneth Paltrow and Drew Barrymore are obsessed with' – marketwatch.com – 14 August 2018.

5   'Tokyo's fanciest purikura at Moreru Mignon' – tokyocreative.com.

6   'TeamLab Borderless Tokyo Official Site' – borderless.teamlab.art; 'TeamLab Borderless in Tokyo: TOP 10 Rooms' – youtube.com.
7   'The Most Interesting Store In The World Pops Up In New York City' – forbes.com – 16 December 2018.
8   'Shopping, Seduction and Mr. Selfridge' – cannonballread.com.
9   '11 secrets of Selfridges' – londonist.com – 19 October 2016; 'Selfridges in bloom' – selfridges.com.
10 'Selfridges opens UK's only free wooden indoor skate bowl' – retailgazette.co.uk – 29 October 2018; 'Selfridges opens rooftop to reveal lake and cocktail bar' – dailymail. com – 22 July 2011; 'Selfridges is filled with a sense of Wonder' – theguardian.com – 21 November 2007.
11 '10 Corso Como' – wikipedia.org.
12 'Virtual Reality Flavor Journeys : Boursin' – trendhunter.com – 18 August 2015.
13 'Nestlé rolls-out its chocolatory personalised KitKat web store' – confectioneryproduction.com – 12 March 2020; 'Fancy a cheese flavour KitKat? How about green tea, chilli or purple potato? Boutique dedicated to cult chocolate bar opens in Japan... where it's considered a lucky charm' – dailymail.com – 21 January 2014.
14 'House of Vans' – houseofvanslondon.com; 'House of Vans' – vans.com.
15 'Avengers S.T.A.T.I.O.N. Newest Attraction on the Las Vegas Strip' – youtube.com; 'What Marvel Taught Us About Targeted Creative Technology' – brightlineinteractive. com.
16 'Sephora tests new "phygital" store concept in France' – fashionnetwork.com – 5 April 2017; 'Specsavers' virtual eye glasses try-on tool' – retailinnovation.com – 11 November 2019.

Chapter 30: Edutainment

1   'Timberland stages "flex in the city" activity' – campaignlive.co.uk – 11 May 2017.
2   'Today at Apple' – macrumors.com.
3   'How DTC brands see the purpose of stores' – retaildive.com – 6 February 2019; 'Mattress startup Casper has a space in New York City where you can pay $25 to take a nap. Here's what it's like to visit' – businessinsider.com – 23 January 2019; 'The Dreamery By Casper' – timeout.com – 10 July 2018.
4   'How DTC brands see the purpose of stores' – retaildive.com – 6 February 2019.
5   'littleBits Announces the littleBits Store' – busineswire.com – 16 July 2015; 'Ayah Bdeir introduces the littleBits store' – youtube.com.
6   'Educational Beer Shops: bottle shop' – trendhunter.com – 13 November 2015.
7   'Interactive Whiskey Architecture' – trendhunter.com – 3 September 2015.

Chapter 31: Clubhouses

1   'Social Media and Mental Health' – helpguide.org.
2   'Maslow's hierarchy of needs' – simplypsychology.org – 29 December 2020; 'Coronavirus and depression in adults, Great Britain: June 2020' – ons.gov.uk – June 2020.
3   'Clubhouses' – raphe.cc.
4   'About Us' – eu.lululemon.com; 'A look inside Lululemon's massive new store in Chicago' – cnbc.com – 11 July 2020; 'Inside: Lululemon flagship store in Chicago – a

customer experience brief' – youtube.com; 'Lululemon (LULU) reports Q3 2020 earnings, sales beat' – cnbc.com – 10 December 2020; 'Lululemon Athletica Inc Share Price' – google.com – January 2021.

5   'Lomography Gallery/Store comes to Los Angeles' – youtube.com; 'An old-fashioned start-up' – ft.com – 24 June 2012.

6   'Gymshark confirms opening date of first high street store in London' – retailgazette. co.uk – 20 February 2020.

7   'How Peloton exercise bikes and streaming gained a cult following' – cnbc.com – 12 February 2019; 'Peloton share price' – google.com – September 2020.

8   'Our Story – About Kelly, Brian and Itzy Ritzy' – itzyritzy.com.

9   'Supporting Our Communities – Southern Co-op' – thesouthernco-operative.co.uk.

10   'Evolution of the outdoorseiten.net community and brand' researchgate.com.

Chapter 32: 'A good stylist is cheaper than a good therapist'

1   'Retail: How Stores Are Changing the Way You Shop' – money.com – 20 November 2017.

2   '9 Stats About the Retail Customer Journey' – salesforce.com – 9 April 2019.

3   'Retail: How Stores Are Changing the Way You Shop' – money.com – 10 November 2017.

4   'How REI's Co-op Retail Model Helps Its Bottom Line' – 21 March 2017.

5   'How to Greet Customers in Retail' – vendhq.com – 2 March 2018.

6   'The Untold Truth Of Publix' – mashed.com; 'Publix' – wikipedia.com; 'Publix Reports Third Quarter 2020 Results' – finance.yahoo.com – 2 November 2020.

7   'Retail: How Stores Are Changing the Way You Shop' – money.com – 10 November 2020; 'How Walmart Has Changed in the Last 5 Years' – fool.com – 29 January 2018.

Chapter 33: Phigital

1   'In Stores, Secret Surveillance Tracks Your Every Move' – nytimes.com – 14 June 2019.

2   'The All-Seeing Ceiling. How retailers are embracing cameras' – medium.com.

3   'Macy's hit with consumer privacy suit over facial recognition' – retailcustom-erexperience.com – 10 August 2020.

4   '"Retail without technology is not going to work": Ruti is using facial recognition technology in stores to boost sales' – glossy.co – 23 September 2019.

5   'Farfetch Announces Store of The Future Augmented Retail' – vogue.com – 12 April 2017.

6   'Showfields: the most interesting store in the world'?' – retail-week.com – 15 January 2019; 'Neighborhood Goods: Making retail relevant' – thecurrentdaily.com – 29 November 2019; 'Is B8ta Reimagining the Retail Store Model?' – martechvibe.com.

Chapter 34: Techs and the City

1   '"Just walk out": Amazon debuts its first supermarket' – theguardian.com – 26 February 2020.

2   'RFID (Radio Frequency Identification)' – Wikipedia.com; 'Amazon offers retailers access to the tech behind Amazon Go' – zdnet.com – 9 March 2020.

3   '"Grab-and-go" – why autonomous retail is ready for a breakout' – diginomica – 21 October 2020.

4   'AiFi emerges from stealth with its own take on cashier-free retail' – techcrunch. com – 27 February 2018.

5   '7-Eleven Taiwan opens first unmanned "X-Store"' – taiwannews.com.tw – 3-January 2018; 'Checkout-free and unmanned stores' – mag.euroshop.de – 31 July 2020; 'Pandemic Gives China's Unmanned Shops New Lease on Life' – sixthtone.com – 12 March 2020.

6   'Schnuck Markets Deploys Tally Robot to More Than Half of Stores' – businesswire.com – 30 September 2020.

7   'Grocery stores turn to robots during the coronavirus' – fox5vegas.com – 7 April 2020; 'Asda becomes first UK supermarket to roll out automated cleaning robots' – chargedretail.co.uk – 16 July 2020.

8   'Lowe's introduces LoweBot, a new autonomous in-store robot' – cnbc.com – 30 August 2016; 'Pepper in retail' – softbankrobotics.com – 23 July 2020.

9   'Smart shopping carts at 7Fresh' – retail-innovation.com – 11 November 2019; 'Walmart Announces FAST Unloaders from CASI' – youtube.com – 8 May 2019.

10 'Robots at Work: Robots dish out the food at a Dutch restaurant' – youtube.com – 7 June 2020.

11 'Cashless payment is booming, thanks to coronavirus' – theconversation.com – 9 September 2020.

12 'Safe Queue: enhanced social distancing with app' – developer.ibm.com – 6 May 2020.

13 'Inside Nike's New Futuristic Store – Fast Company' – youtube.com – 21 November 2018.

14 '20 QR Code Tools and Uses' – practicalecommerce.co – 16 June 2011.

15 'Kroger's smart shelves ditch the paper, drop the lights' – news.microsoft.com – 25 June 2018.

16 'The future of work in retail automation' - mckinsey.com – 23 May 2019.

Chapter 35: Please Re-lease Me

1   'The retail apocalypse has officially descended on America' – businessinsider.com – 21 March 2017.

2   'Report: Retailers must reduce US brick-and-mortar footprint' – retaildive.com – 24 January 2017.

3   'Extent of Britain's high street decline laid bare in official data' – theguardian.com – 10 August 2020.

4   'When the mall owns the retailer' – retaildive.com – 17 August 2020; 'America's biggest mall operator gets go-ahead for $1.75bn JCPenney deal' – ft.com – 10 November 2020; 'Forever 21 reaches $81 million deal to sell its retail business' – cnbc.com – 3 February 2020.

5   'Why More Online Retailers Are Opening Brick-And-Mortar Locations' – npr.org – 26 September 2019; 'Landlords Predict More Flexible Retail Leases' – therealdeal.com – 6 May 2020.

Chapter 36: Retail as a Service

1   'How Retail-As-A-Service is making us feel again' – valtech.com – 24 January 2020.

2   'Neighborhood Goods Proves Its New Department Store Model ' – forbes.com – 5 July 2020; 'Neighborhood Goods launches dashboard' – modernretail.com – 13 March 2020.

3   'Prim and Proper' – primandproper.com.
4   'Brands / Neighborhood Goods' – neighbourhoodgoods.com.
5   'Retail-as-a-service companies go digital to stay afloat' – glossy.com – 17 April 2020.
6   'The Most Interesting Store In The World – SHOWFIELDS' – showfields.com.
7   'Feminist start-up Bulletin is reinventing brick and mortar retail' – fastcompany.com – 6 August 2018.
8   'b8ta: Retail store designed for trying & buying new technology' – b8ta.com; 'What b8ta has figured out about retail' – retaildive.com – 28 June 2018.
9   'As the Classic Department Store Falters, These 4 Challengers Want to Upend the Retail Model' – tefter.io.
10   'Toys "R" Us, Macy's store tests use sensors, data in B8ta' – businessinsider.com – 12 February 2020.
11   'Leap Inc – The retail platform for growing brands' – leapinc.com; 'Retail-as-a-service provider Leap raises $3M' – techcrunch.com – 1 November 2018.
12   'Brandbox' – brandbox.com; 'Mall Owner Macerich Is Making It Easier For Online Brands' – forbes.com – 13 November 2018.
13   'The Edit @ Roosevelt Field. A Simon Mall' – simon.com; 'Simon bridges online and brick-and-mortar with "The Edit"' – retaildive.com – 30 November 2017.
14   'Empowering Brands at Lightning Speed, Simon Launches The Edit' – prnewswire.com – 13 October 2017.
15   'Mall operator gives online retailers a spot with "In Real Life" shop' – retaildive.com – 8 August 2017; 'A reimagined shopping destination in the heart of Silicon Valley' – urw.com.

Chapter 37: Target

1   'Target Corporation – Wikipedia.org; "Is Target Losing Its Cool?"' – theatlantic.com – 1 March 2017; 'Stock's one-day percentage decline is biggest since December 2008' – marketwatch.com – 1 March 2017.
2   'Target to acquire same-day delivery company Grand Junction' – retaildive.com – 14 August 2017; 'Why Target bought delivery startup Shipt' – digitalecommerce360.com – 20 March 2018.
3   'Target is cutting costs by 90% thanks to its same-day delivery' – cnbc.com – 23 May 2019; 'Target stores' Drive Up brings your order to your car' – twincities.com – 3 October 2017.
4   'With Shares Up 93%, Target's Turnaround Suggests Powerful Investment Strategy' – forbes.com – 18 October 2019.
5   'Target will spend $3 billion a year to remodel stores' – finance.yahoo.com – 9 December 2019; 'Target opens 100 mini stores, remodels 500 bigger ones' – cnbc.com – 23 August 2019.
6   'How Target is using small-format stores to score with younger shoppers' – retaildive.com – 24 August 2017.
7   '8 Target private label brands that launched this year' – retaildive.com – 20 November 2018.
8   'Why Target is one of Fast Company's Most Innovative' – fastcompany.com – 19 February 2019.
9   'Target Corporation Reports Third Quarter Earnings' – investors.target.com – 18 November 2020; 'Target Inc stock price' – google.com – February 2021.

Chapter 38: Best Buy

1   'Best Buy' – en.wikipedia.com.
2   'Why Best Buy is Going out of Business…Gradually' – forbes.com – 2 January 2012; 'People thought Amazon was going to kill us' – adnews.com.au – 28 March 2019.
3   'How Best Buy shifted from being retail-led to customer-led' – cmo.com.au – 27 March 2019; 'Renew Blue: Best Buy's Turnaround' – tjwaldorf.com.
4   'How Best Buy shifted from being retail-led to customer-led' – cmo.com.au – 27 March 2019.
5   'Best Buy CEO talks melding digital with physical for a winning strategy' – retailcustomerexperience.com – 29 March 2019.
6   'How Best Buy shifted from being retail-led to customer-led' – cmo.com.au – 27 March 2019.
7   'How Best Buy reinvented its CX strategy to counter Amazon' – marketing-interactive.com – 27 March 2019.
8   'How Best Buy shifted from being retail-led to customer relationship led' – cmo.com. au – 27 March 2019.
9   'Ibid'.
10 'Ibid'.
11 'Ibid'.
12 'Ibid'.
13 'Best Buy Co Inc share price' – 21 January 2021.

Chapter 39: Aerie

1   'American Eagle's Aerie Can Adopt Competitor Victoria's Secret's Ways' – forbes.com – 24 March 2014; 'Intimates Line aerie Gets Real' – prnewswire.com – 17 January 2014.
2   'How Aerie Gains Market Share With the Mirror Strategy' – medium.com – 7 July 2020; 'Aerie rapidly gaining market share off social media' – cnbc.com – 22 June 2018.
3   '#AerieREAL Life' – ae.com; 'American Eagle claims nearly 2B impressions on TikTok campaign for Aerie' – marketingdive.com – 5 June 2020.
4   'Meet your 2020 #AerieREAL Role Models': 'Meet the 2020 #AerieREAL Changemakers'; 'Are You Our Next #AerieREAL Ambassador?' – ae.com.
5   'ae.com/aerie-real-life/better-world#x2019;.
6   'Aerie rapidly gaining market share off social media' – cnbc.com – 22 June 2018; 'EATING DISORDERS GROUP PARTNERS WITH AERIE' – associationsnow. com – 16 August 2018. 'How Aerie Built a Great Brand, its Strategy for Success' – indigo9digital.com – 6 October 2020.
7   'Can Aerie Continue To Lead Revenue Growth?' – forbes.com – 1 November 2019; 'Aerie leads sales growth at American Eagle' – fashionnetwork.com – 5 March 2020; 'L Brands Annual Report' – 2015 and 2019; 'Aerie Surpass $1 Billion in Revenues' – wwd.com – 21 January 2021.

Chapter 40: Gymshark

1   'How Gymshark Became A $1.3 Billion Brand, And What We Can Learn' – forbes. com – 17 August 2020.

2   'How I Started The UK's Fastest Growing Company: My Gymshark Story' – youtube. com – 26 February 2017; 'The 20 Best Butt-Lifting Leggings For Every Budget' – womenshealthmag.com – 11 June 2020..

3   'How Influencer Marketing Made Gymshark a Million Dollar Brand' – influencermatchmaker.co.uk – 18 January 2021.

4   'HOW TO CHANGE YOUR LIFE IN 66 DAYS | Gymshark66' – youtube.com – 8 December 2020; 'Case Study: Gymshark Influencers Synchronize in TikTok Duets' – mediakix.com.

5   'How Gymshark Built a Thriving Fitness Brand Through Influencer Marketing' – webhub.hi2y.com.

6   'GYMSHARK'S BIGGEST EVENT EVER | THE BIRMINGHAM POP UP' – youtube. com – 21 June 2018; 'Gymshark opens doors on first pop-up store' – essentialretail. com – 2 March 2020.

7   'Why Gymshark is the UK's Fastest Growing Company' – manyofmany.com – 24 April 2018; 'Ben Francis' – en.wikipedia.com; 'Gymshark Has Officially Gone from Instagram-Favorite to Celeb-Favorite Brand' – shape.com – 16 October 2020.

8   'Ben Francis' – en.wikipedia.com; 'Gymshark: Ex-pizza delivery boy's sportswear firm' – bbc.com – 14 August 2020.

9   'General Atlantic Invests in $1.3 Billion Gymshark Brand' – 14 August 2020; 'Gymshark: Ex-pizza delivery boy's sportswear firm' – bbc.com – 14 August 2020.

Chapter 41: Rosé Mansion

1   'Rosé Mansion – rosewinemansion.com.

2   'Morgan First maps a career out of entrepreneurship' – bostonherald.com – 1 June 2008; 'Interview with author' – August 2020.

3   'The Second Glass Wine Riot' – vimeo.com – 8 February 2010; 'Interview with author' – August 2020.

4   'Interview with author' – August 2020.

5   'The Rose Wine Mansion Opens In New York Summer 2018' – refinery29.com – 5 June 2018; 'Featured Artists – Rosé Mansion' – rosewinemansion.com.

6   'Rosé Mansion in NYC lets you drink wine picture-perfect paradise' – youtube. com – 23 August 2018; 'I Went to The Rosé Mansion. Here's What It Looks Like Inside' – foodandwine.com – 11 June 2018; 'Interview with author' – August 2020.

7   'Interview with author' – August 2020.

Chapter 42: Walmart

1   'Walmart' – en.wikipedia.com; 'Wal-Mart's E-Stumble With Amazon' – wsj.com – 19 June 2013; 'How Walmart Has Changed in the Last 5 Years' – fool.com – 29 January 2018; 'Amazon to take 50% of US e-commerce share by 2023' – retaildive.com – 12 September 2018; 'Walmart vs Amazon online sales' – businessinsider.com – 9 November 2015.

2   'Walmart Completes Acquisition of Jet.com, Inc.' – corporate.walmart.com – 19 September 2016; 'Marc Lore' – en.wikipedia.com; 'How Much In Online Revenue Can Walmart Generate In 2020?' – forbes.com – 2 March 2020; 'Walmart E-Commerce Boss Marc Lore to Leave' – wsj.com – 15 January 2021.

3   'Why Wal-Mart is betting big on e-commerce acquisitions' – retaildive.com – 21 May 2017; 'How Walmart Is Leading The Omnichannel Strategy Charge' – insights. digitalmediasolutions.com – 5 October 2020.

4 'Walmart to launch its Walmart+ membership service' – retaildive.com – 1 September 2020; 'As Walmart grows in e-commerce, investors look for a plan' – cnbc.com – 14 February 2020.
5 'Walmart's "Last Ten Miles" - Quicker and Cheaper Than Amazon' – therobinreport. com – 21 February 2018; 'Map of Amazon warehouses' – cnbc.com – 19 January 2020; 'Walmart is spending $11 billion to improve stores' – digiday.com – 15 April 2019.
6 'Walmart Reports Strong Earnings' – forbes.com – 18 November 2020.

Chapter 43: Showfields

1 'The Most Interesting Store In The World' – showfields.com.
2 'Ibid'.
3 'Author interview' – 30 September 2020.
4 'Showfields debuts brick-and-mortar space' – retaildive.com – 15 March 2019.
5 'Author interview' – 30 September 2020.
6 'Bright Ideas: Showfields' – youtube.com – 29 March 2019; 'Are new brick and mortar solutions the key to digital brand growth?' – retailwire.com – 29 January 2019.
7 'Author interview' – 30 September 2020.
8 'Ibid'.
9 'Ibid'.
10 'New invite-only retail concept makes it a breeze for digital brands' – businessofhome. com – 6 March 2019.
11 'Author interview' – 30 September 2020.
12 'Ibid'.
13 'The Loft at SHOWFIELDS' – eventup.com.
14 'Author interview' – 30 September 2020.
15 'Ibid'.
16 'Showfields raises $9M for a more flexible approach to brick-and-mortar' – techcrunch.com – 22 February 2019; 'Author interview' – 30 September 2020.
17 'Ibid'.
18 'Ibid'.
19 'This automated checkout app tries to make shopping feel safe' – fastcompany. com – 9 July 2020; 'Inside a NoHo Department Store's Quick Pivot' – psfk.com – 1 September 2020.
20 'Author interview' – 30 September 2020.
21 'Ibid'; 'Showfields, the "Most Interesting Store in the World," Opens on Lincoln Road' – miaminewtimes.com – 21 December 2020.
22 'Author interview' – 30 September 2020.

Chapter 44: Huel

1 'Huel | Complete Food' – huel.com.
2 'Ibid'.
3 'Huel Shakes Up Meal Replacement Market With $100 Million Revenue Run-Rate Claim' – forbes.com – 25 February 2020; 'Fighting The War On Delicious Food With Huel' – pymnts.com – 20 March 2019; '"Why overcomplicate nutrition?" Huel co-founder and CEO' – nutritioninsight.com; 'Author interview' – 16 December 2020.
4 'Huel Powdered Food – Fast food, not junk food' – huel.com.
5 'Ibid'.

6   'Number Of Vegans In Britain Skyrocketed In 2020' – plantbasednews.org – 8 January 2021; '"Flexitarian" diets key to cutting climate change, new study claims' – standard.co.uk – 11 October 2018.

7   'Huel Launches Its First Nutritionally Complete Hot Meal' – vegworldmag.com – 8 September 2020; 'How This Vegan Powdered Food Brand Is Set To Hit £45M' – forbes.com – 20 July 2018.

8   'How Huel Uses Social Media to Reach an Audience of 400,000' – buffer.com – 11 August 2020; 'Huel sets bold example with socially-distanced pop-up launch' – eventindustrynews.com – 10 September 2020.

9   'Julian Hearn is putting an end to unhealthy eating with Huel' – elitebusinessmagazine.com – 10 April 2019.

10   'Huel – Business of Purpose' – businessofpurpose.com – 15 October 2019.

11   '50 million meals sold in 80+ countries' – huel.com; 'Power powder Huel gets £20m fuel boost to keep up growth' – cityam.com – 4 October 2018.

12   'How Huel keeps on growing – despite its questionable taste' – wired.co.uk – 17 July 2019; 'Huel Shakes Up Meal Replacement Market With $100 Million Revenue Run-Rate Claim' – forbes.com – 25 February 2020; 'Huel' – en.wikipedia.org.

13   'Huel Launches Groundbreaking New Products, As Sales Surge' – welltodoglobal.com – 14 September 2020.

Chapter 45: Rapha

1   'Rapha' – rapha.cc; 'Gamechangers: Rapha Cycle Club Case Study' – youtube.com.

2   'An Open Road' – rapha.cc.

3   'Rapha to give $1.5m to grassroots with new charity foundation' – cyclist.co.uk.

4   'People and culture' – rapha.cc.

5   'Rapha Cycling Club' – rapha.cc.

6   'Author interview' – 18 November 2020.

7   'Ibid'.

8   'Ibid'; 'Why Rapha is the new Harley-Davidson' – research.people-and.com – 12 October 2017; 'Rapha is not a brand, it's brand community management at its best' – brand-experts.com – 18 April 2019.

9   'Author interview' – 18 November 2020.

10   'Ibid'.

11   'Growing popularity of cycling led by increase in female riders, according to Sport England survey' – bikeradar.com – 22 October 2019; 'Rapha – More than clothing, more than a store, more than a sport' – thegeniusworks.com; 'With New Investment, Cycling Apparel Maker Rapha Hopes to Break Away' – wsj.com – 14 August 2017.

12   'Author Interview' – 18 November 2020; 'How Rapha is building its online community post lockdown' – essentialretail.com – 5 June 2020.

13   'Author interview' – 18 November 2020.

14   'Ibid'.

Chapter 46: Southern Co-op

1   'Southern Co-operative' – en.wikipedia.org; 'About Southern Co-op' – thesouthernco-operative.co.uk.

2   'Author interview' – 17 September 2020; 'Southern Co-operative' – en.wikipedia.org.

3   'Author interview' – 17 September 2020.

4 'The Southern Co-operative Limited' – thesouthernco-operative.co.uk – 27 January 2019; 'Southern Co-operative' – en.wikipedia.org.

5 'Southern Co-op Home' - thesouthernco-operative.co.uk.

6 'Love your Neighbourhood' – thesouthernco-operative.co.uk; 'Author interview' – 17 September 2020.

7 'Author interview' – 17 September 2020.

8 'Our plan' – thesouthernco-operative.co.uk.

9 'Southern Co-op celebrates 10 years of Local Flavours' – thenews.coop – 3 August 2017; 'Sussex Food and Drink Awards' – thesouthernco-operative.co.uk.

10 'Author interview' – 17 September 2020; 'Making a difference' - thesouthernco-operative.co.uk.

11 'Author interview' – 17 September 2020.

12 'Ibid'.

13 'Our Plan' – thesouthernco-operative.co.uk.

14 'Author interview' – 17 September 2020.

15 'Ibid'.

Chapter 47: Bonobos

1 'Bonobos (apparel)' – en.wikipedia.org; 'Andy Dunn of Bonobos on Founding and Selling a Successful Company' – youtube.com – 14 June 2018.

2 'The Universe Conspires' – linkedin.com – 7 May 2019; 'Get One Thing Right' – dunn.medium.com.

3 'Bonobos CEO: "I'm the Least Likely Person That You Could Imagine to be the ceo of a fashion company"' – inc.com – 17 April 2017.

4 'Ibid'.

5 'Zappos-inspired Startup Is All About Men's Pants' – cbsnews.com – 9 October 2009.

6 'Bonobos Chinos' – bonobos.com.

7 'Marketing Archives – Page 423 of 637 – Bristol Marketing Agency – thepixelworks.uk'; '#EvolveTheDefinition' – youtube.com – 18 July 2018.

8 'We Analyzed 22 Of The Biggest Direct-To-Consumer Success Stories To Figure Out The Secrets To Their Growth — Here's What We Learned' – cbinsights.com 8 December 2020.

9 'Bonobos CEO says "guideshop" model is working' – chicagotribune.com – 25 April 2016.

10 'What are Bonobos Guideshops? Look inside this innovative menswear retailer's clothing showrooms' – youtube.com – 2 January 2020; 'Andy Dunn of Bonobos on Founding and Selling a Successful Company' – youtube.com – 14 June 2018.

11 'Bonobos – number of locations' – bonobos.com – May 2019; 'Bonobos: A Better Fitting Model for a Better Fitting Pant' – digital.hbs.edu – 2 December 2015.

12 'How The Bonobos Founder Went from "Insufficient ATM Funds" to Over $100 Million in Revenue' – thehustle.co – 25 January 2016.

13 'Walmart to Buy Bonobos, Men's Wear Company, for $310 million' – nytimes.com – 16 June 2017.

Chapter 48: Nike

1 'About Nike' – nike.com; 'Nike, Inc.' – en.wikipedia.org; 'NIKE, Inc. Announces New Consumer Direct Offense: A Faster Pipeline to Serve Consumers Personally, At Scale' – news.nike.com – 15 June 2017.

2   'Nike to Drastically Cut Number of Retail Partners' – mytotalretail.com – 27 October 2017.

3   '"Undifferentiated, Mediocre Retail Won't Survive": Nike Rolls Out Retail Revamp' – investors.com – 25 October 2017.

4   'Nike's New Consumer Experience Distribution Strategy Hits The Ground Running' – forbes.com – 1 December 2018.

5   'How Nike is Using Mobile Apps to Significantly Increase Sales' – indigo9digital. com – 14 January 2020.

6   'Here's how NikePlus has spawned more customer loyalty' – bizjournals.com – 6 February 2018.

7   'Nike's New Consumer Experience Distribution Strategy Hits The Ground Running' – forbes.com – 1 December 2018.

8   'Nike To Stay Out In Front With Biggest Data Of All: Demographics' – forbes.com – 19 June 2017.

9   'Why Nike Opened a Sprawling Paris Flagship in the Middle of a Pandemic' – footwearnews.com – 29 July 2020; 'Inside Nike NYC House of Innovation' – youtube. com – 12 February 2020.

10 'Nike Opens Nike NYC House of Innovation: The Most Personal and Responsive Sport Retail Experience' – businesswire.com – 14 November 2018; 'How Do I Use the Nike App in a Nike Store?' – nike.com.

11 'Introducing NikePlus Unlocks' – youtube.com – 25 November 2017; 'Nike's By You Studio Is a Glimpse at the Future of Retail' – highsnobiety.com.

12 'NIKE weaves 85,000 kilos of sustainable material into new store' – designboom. com – 31 July 2020.

13 'Nike's new store in New York has a basketball court' – qz.com – 14 November 2016.

14 'Nike Annual Report 2020' – investors.nike.com.

15 'Nike cuts ties with Zappos, Belk, Dillards, and others' – businessinsider.com – 25 August 2020; 'NIKE, Inc. Reports Fiscal 2021 Second Quarter Results' – news.nike. com – 18 December 2020; 'Nike share price' – google.com – November 2020; 'Adidas share price' – google.com – November 2020; 'Under Armour share price' – google. com – November 2020.

Index